Dora L. Fl___

Hibiscus

NATIVE ▶▶▶▶▶
STRANGER

A Black American's Journey
into the Heart of Africa

▶▶▶▶ EDDY L. HARRIS

SIMON & SCHUSTER
NEW YORK • LONDON
TORONTO • SYDNEY
TOKYO • SINGAPORE

SIMON & SCHUSTER
Simon & Schuster Building
Rockefeller Center
1230 Avenue of the Americas
New York, New York 10020

10 9 8 7 6 5 4 3 2 1

Library of Congress Cataloging-in-Publication Data
Harris, Eddy L.
    Native stranger : a Black American's journey into the heart of
Africa / Eddy L. Harris.
      p.   cm.
      1. Africa—Description and travel—1977–   2. Harris, Eddy L.—
Journeys—Africa. I. Title.
    DT12.25.H37   1992
    916'.0432—dc20   91-40579
                                                                   CIP

ISBN 0-671-74897-1

My thanks to the many strangers who have become new friends, new friends who have become old friends, old friends who remain forever like family: Sheilagh, Jan, Marion, Nat and Pam, Mbaye, Abdullah, Gabuh Briébia, João, Mark, Harry, Brian, and my dear Aunt Can. They have opened their doors and their hearts to me. They have shown by their goodness, and taught by their generosity. They have helped me to endure. But this book is dedicated to those who have not endured:

To Tim McDonnell
To Matthew Barry
To Richard Holloman

Contents

8 CONTENTS

Il faut, d'abord, durer.

—ERNEST HEMINGWAY,
from a letter to F. Scott Fitzgerald

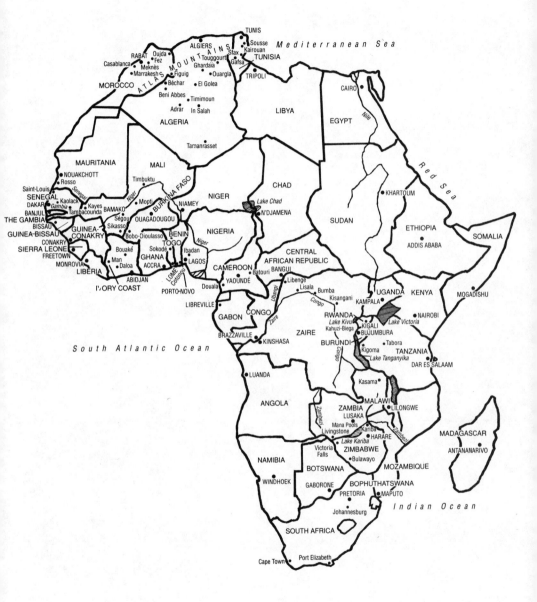

ONE

INTO AFRICA
THROUGH THE BACK DOOR ▶▶

Paris

Because my skin is black you will say I traveled Africa to find the roots of my race. I did not—unless that race is the human race, for except in the color of my skin, I am not African. If I didn't know it then, I know it now. I am a product of the culture that raised me. And yet Africa was suddenly like a magnet drawing me close, important in ways that I cannot explain, rising in my subconscious and inviting me. It was time I went, and when an acquaintance asked what I planned to do next, where I planned to go, it was as if some invisible hand moved me to go there. I answered without missing a beat. Africa!

In the mind and perhaps dreams of every person with black skin, the specter of Africa looms like the shadow of a genie, dormant but not altogether harmless, always there, heard about since childhood as some magnificent faraway world, a place of magic and wonder. Africa as motherland. Africa as a source of black pride, a place of black dignity. Africa as explanation for the ways of black men and women, their way of walking and their passion, their joys and their sorrows. Africa as some germ in the genes that determines more than skin and hair. Although I am not African, there is a line that connects that place with this one, the place we come from and the place we find ourselves, those lives and our lives. And I longed to follow that line. But what if those old promises of Africa were only lies? What if I hated the place? Only in traveling there could I discover the truth.

Long before I ever went there Africa was alive in my imagination, crowding the dark corners of my dreams, stirring my fears. Now that I have been there, Africa lives in my memory like a gigantic vessel bearing all that I am and all that I will ever be, for Africa has opened my eyes and awakened my fears, brought them to life and kindled my compassion.

Shortly before the trip to Africa I suffered the suicide of a friend; shortly after, the death of another. Between the two sadnesses of their surrender, Africa showed me what some men suffer, and that all men must endure. Africa has taught me that men can.

I eased into Africa through the back door, beginning my journey in Paris, and there I met a lonely man from Senegal. His name is Mbaye and he spends his days walking the streets of Paris, walking, lingering, looking for someone to pass the long days with, someone to talk to. He is thin, near emaciation. In his eyes there is a tiredness so heavy it is like sadness. The whites of his eyes have yellowed and are bloodshot. He has no money, very few friends, and no job. But he has a wife, a French woman who fell in love with him while visiting Dakar. He moved to Paris and they married. They have two daughters.

In Senegal, Mbaye's father was the chief of some little village. The family was well-off. But well-off in Senegal and well-off in Paris are not quite the same thing.

"In my head for a long time," he said, "was the desire to find work in Paris. From the time many of us are young, we see France as a second home, and getting married was my excuse to come. Now that I am here, I am lost. We live on the money my wife makes sewing clothes."

Paris is the back door into Africa. In the same sense that Latin America begins in Chicago or New York, or that India and

Pakistan begin in London, Africa's outer edges reach all the way to Paris, where you can stand like a colossus with one foot in each world, one foot among the French and one among the Africans. They are Algerians and Moroccans, Ivorians and Senegalese, Africans from the coast, from the desert, from the bush, and they live a little in both worlds—a bit in Paris, and a bit in the Africa they have brought with them. They are part of the great migration from village to city, from African city to France, and they've come to find what they cannot find at home. They come looking for decent jobs, but they end up doing what the French would prefer to avoid. They are the men who sweep trash and dog shit from the sidewalks and into the gutters of the city. Their skin is ashy, dry, and brittle; their hands are dirty. They do not often smile. They carry on with their sweeping and look away. They do not show their eyes. It doesn't matter. I have seen their shadowy eyes in black faces on the streets of New York City.

Up at Barbès-Rochechouart, not far from the Moulin Rouge and Pigalle, the afternoon sidewalks are so crowded with North Africans and black Africans that the people spill into the streets and block the traffic. The crowd moves rapidly but goes no-where. People pause to paw through the cheap clothes on the display tables outside the shops, and each seems to be carrying a pink plastic sack from Tati, the discount department store on the corner. This *quartier* is always crowded, always seems darker at night, always just a little bit hotter.

Here the Métro comes up from underground and goes overhead. The shadowy areas beneath the overpass reek of urine. The white French coming from the station and going home walk a little more quickly through this neighborhood. Women will get off the Métro a stop farther on, at Gare du Nord, and walk the long way around rather than change lines here at Barbès. They clutch at their purses and cross the street to avoid the flood of black humanity.

Up the hill near the basilica, the long rows of steps leading up to Sacré-Coeur are lined with fleet-footed Africans selling their wares displayed on sheets spread on the ground. It's all the same stuff, identical merchandise arranged in identical fashion on sheet after sheet after sheet. They sell shiny jewelry and leather bracelets and all manner of trinkets, carved plastic vases and windup plastic pigeons that fly for twelve noisy seconds before crashing. Perhaps what they do is illegal. Perhaps they are illegally in the country and cannot take any risks. When the cops come by, the Africans grab up the four corners of the sheets, sling the bundles over a shoulder, and dash to hide until the coast is clear. Then they return, content to wait all day for a sale or two, to earn a few francs and watch the tourists go by. They don't mind the waiting. It was like this on my first visit to Paris nearly twenty years ago, and scenes like this will go on as long as Paris is the end of the long African road, as long as France and Africa remain intertwined.

Most of North and West Africa was colonized by France. French is widely spoken and in much of Africa it is the official language. France and Africa have become strange bedfellows, and the destiny of one seems to revolve around the destiny of the other. That is why Mbaye dreamed so often of coming to Paris to find work, and why so many Africans see Paris as a second home.

This is not the only *quartier* where you find Africans, and these are not the only Africans in Paris. But here at Barbès, these Africans and their Arab cousins live in a world removed from Paris. Here there is enough to remind them of home. This *quartier* is crowded like home, and noisy, not the cleanest part of Paris, which is not the cleanest of cities, and walking up the boulevard Rochechouart toward Pigalle you can find couscous and merguez almost as easily as french fries.

Mbaye lives on the sixth floor of an old building not far from the place de la République. There is no elevator. The wooden steps are old, creaking eerily when trod upon. Someone has been using the stairway as a *pissoir* and the sharp stench of urine commands the second-floor landing. On the sixth-floor landing there is a toilet in a little closet opposite Mbaye's door. The toilet half hides behind a wooden gate barely hanging on its hinges. The slats are far enough apart to be seen through clearly. The smell escapes. The little closet has been recently used. The toilet was not flushed.

Mbaye's door too is like an old wooden gate hanging on rusted hinges. There is no doorknob, only the metal fixture where a padlock hangs when Mbaye is not home. The same fixture is nailed to the inside of the gate and at night Mbaye padlocks himself in his apartment.

Mbaye spends his nights as he spends his days: alone. His wife has taken the children to visit the countryside where her parents live. She has been gone for three weeks and has not written. Mbaye does not know when she will return, and he is lonely, almost lost without her.

The apartment is dimly lit. It has no heat in winter. The green paint on the walls is spotted with mildew and is peeling. The carpet is matted and torn. Mbaye and I sit on the floor, listening to Senegalese music playing on an old cassette recorder. Pigeons roost on the ledge outside the window. They peck at the chipped glass and leave droppings like polka dots along the brick shelf.

Mbaye asks if I will have a cup of coffee with him.

"I don't drink coffee, but I'll have a cup of tea."

Mbaye brightens. I don't know why. He disappears into the kitchen, where I can hear him striking matches and rattling pots. In a few minutes the faint hissing of water beginning to boil drifts to me. After a time, a strange slurping sound comes to my ear and a panic comes over me that Mbaye might be slobbering into the tea I'm about to drink. I have a neurotic phobia about germs, especially around food, and am so neurotic, in fact, that a friend at home refused to believe when I told him I was going to Africa.

"What about all those flies," he said, "and the germs they carry?" He wiggled his fingers close to my face and droned. "Swarms of flies buzzing all around the open sewers and the garbage and the human excrement, and then landing on your food. You'll go crazy."

He was teasing, of course, but what he said was true. Every word chilled me.

So I get up to check on Mbaye. He is just about to dump a fistful of sugar into the pot.

"Do you want your tea the way we drink it in Africa?"

"How do you drink it in Africa?"

"Very sweet," he says. "Very sweet."

He adds more sugar and tastes the tea, which is still not quite right. He adds a bit more sugar, slurps again, and smiles. He doesn't smile often.

"If you were not here," he says, "I would not drink it this way. The sugar is expensive. But with a guest in the house, the price of sugar means nothing."

Mbaye slurps his tea as noisily as he can, and I do as he does. But the tea is so sweet it makes me shiver.

When it is finished we sit without speaking, but the silence is not an uncomfortable one. There is just nothing I can think to say. I have asked him enough already about the weather in Senegal and the food and his family and the different tribes. And I feel like an idiot asking him once more, for want of anything else to say: "How do you say 'pigeon' (or 'pig' or 'man' or 'dog') in Wolof?" Wolof is the language of his tribe and he has already taught me a few phrases. By morning I will have forgotten them.

The pigeons roosting at the window have flown. Night has come quietly down. I get up and stretch, telling Mbaye I ought to be leaving.

"You cannot leave without eating," he says. "I cannot offer you much, but I can offer you what I have. Don't go yet." He folds his hands together prayerfully. "Do you ever eat chicken and potatoes?"

"All the time," I tell him, but the fried chicken and mashed potatoes in my mind are not what he is thinking of.

He goes back into the kitchen. The pots rattle together again, the clanging competing with the music that still comes noisily from the cassette player. A man with a woman's voice is singing in Wolof, but the music sounds a little Moroccan, a little Algerian, magically transporting me to the places I will visit. It is a little like dreaming.

The Africa in my dreams and the Africa I remember, now that I have been there, come together and diverge to form crisscrossing patterns of texture and color, light and shadow, like a haunting abstract work of art that dominates corners of the imagination, a tapestry weaving itself out of what is real and what is pure imagination, a tapestry whose colors and cultures collide and overlap, changing from country to country, religion to religion, from place to place and village to village.

Africa is a myriad of peoples and their ways. Algeria is Arab and Berber, depending on where you look, Kabyle, Chaouia and Mzabite. Senegal is Wolof and Fulani and Serer,

Moor and nomadic Bassar. Cameroon is fifty different ethnic groupings, Zaire more than two hundred. They come together on the tapestry, the peoples and their customs, habits, and practices, merging in ways that underscore what they share, what they have in common, their struggles to move forward in time without losing their links to the past; a sense of where they have come from, who they are, and how they came to be where they are; their yearning for self-determination, perhaps not as individuals but as a people; the desire for a little human dignity. It was this—these things they have in common—that I came to find, for these are burnings in the spirit of man and they are not racial or tribal, only human. They are the colors of the African tapestry and they blend in places like Paris. They are all that is right and all that is wrong with Africa, the worst of the colonial past, the best of Africa's spirit. They come together here in Mbaye's apartment where, with a guest in the house, the high price of sugar means nothing.

"You will find that generosity is common in Africa," Mbaye says. "One man's good fortune belongs to every man, just as his misery does."

Mbaye sets one plate and one spoon on the folding table he has placed near the window. He brings out a metal bowl clouded with steam and fragrant with the aroma of chicken and spices. He carries the hot bowl in his bare hands and walks quickly. The trail of mist from the bowl wafts out behind him and fills the room with its perfume. My stomach growls in anticipation. Mbaye smiles again.

"I'm hungry too," he tells me.

He places the bowl in the center of the table. He is, of course, carrying as well a crusty baguette tucked under his arm, a long thin loaf of bread. He puts that on the table too. No meal in Paris begins or ends without one.

Unlike other colonizers, France has always shown a generous and fairly liberal attitude toward the peoples it subjugated, benevolently bestowing on the colonies it raped all the windfall benefits of French culture: language and baguettes, wine and cheese, citizenship (in limited form, of course) and conscription into the French army. As a result many Africans see France as a second home, but it is not *home* home.

Mbaye is a Muslim stranded in a Catholic country, black in

a white man's world. He has few friends and his wife seems to have left him.

Have they fought? Is he jealous that she has friends who are men? Have their cultures clashed in ways they never expected?

The bowl holds pieces of stewed chicken covering a layer of potatoes and carrots and celery all swimming in a shallow pool of sauce. Mbaye breaks off a bit of bread and dips it into the sauce.

"*Fais comme chez toi,*" he says. "Be at ease, be at home." He gestures for me to dig in.

"Do you eat with your hands?" he asks.

"If you do, I do."

"I brought the spoon for you, but for us *le goût est à la main*. The taste is in your hand."

I jump up quickly to wash my hands. I hope Mbaye has already washed his.

"The right hand is for eating," he says. "With this hand"—the left—"we do other things."

Mbaye's left hand never touches the food. His right hand has the dexterity of a surgeon's. One-handed he rips a bone from the chicken in the bowl and peels the meat off. He grabs a potato, breaks it into pieces, tosses a piece into his mouth. He tears off bread, dips it in sauce, eats it.

Fais comme chez toi, he says, and yet there is an African proverb that advises: If someone sits on the floor in his own home, do not ask him for a chair. A contradiction I will never manage to escape.

I unclench my fist and reach for the meat. It is hot and moist and soft. I roll it in my fingers and let it slide across my palm. The potatoes and carrots too. I close my eyes to feel the rough ridges of carrots rinsed but not scraped clean. And the potatoes, which look so smooth, are uneven and textured.

"Eat this piece," Mbaye tells me. He peels a tender piece of chicken from the bone and drops the meat, a choice and sweet piece, into the bowl. The bone he drops onto the plate.

Mostly we eat without talking. The bones pile up on the plate, and it is easy to see which bones I have picked at and which ones Mbaye has taken care of. Little shreds of meat hang from my bones, but Mbaye has cleaned his of meat and sinew and gristle, bits I throw away when I've eaten all I think there is to eat. To *my* mind I am not wasteful, but Mbaye sees what I cannot. He follows behind and finds the morsels of meat I've missed. I have never seen chicken bones so naked of meat.

Mbaye breaks the silence of our eating to answer a question I have not yet asked, but it is one that is as much on his mind as it is on my own.

"Economically," he says, "in Africa there is zero. We have nothing but our vitality. We celebrate life every day—in our music, in our dancing, in the way we walk. It is how we know that we are alive. And so we share all that we have, even though we have nothing. It is how we know how much we have. It is, too, how we know how much we lack."

His eyes flash with a half second of memory and then dim. He quiets. His face loses all expression but weariness.

"I don't like it here," he says. "And still somehow it is better here. My children will not starve here. At least there is that."

Better to live, perhaps, in a land of plenty, even if the plenty is not yours and is not shared.

"There is always the chance for a change, the chance for a miracle," Mbaye says. "For now, we live only on the money my wife makes. But soon the government will give us some assistance." The prospect doesn't seem to cheer him. "Very soon," he says, and you can almost hear him thinking: *I hope.*

I help him wash the dirty dishes, and as we stand side by side in the bright light of the kitchen, he moves away from me. He leans back as if that will help him see better and he looks at me.

"You know," he says, "you look Senegalese. Your ancestors might have come from there. We could be brothers."

We laugh together. "You never know," I say. "You never know."

But I am not African, and the differences are more than apparent, the similarities only slight and superficial.

In the days that followed, Mbaye and I walked the streets together, up to Barbès and Montmartre, through his *quartier* and down to the place de la Bastille, spending the days as Mbaye always spends them, walking and looking, thinking and missing home. There isn't much else for him to do.

We parted company one quiet afternoon. Rain was falling softly. I was going to meet someone and Mbaye preferred not to come. He seemed to sense that we would not meet again, but there was no change in his face, no change in his voice. His French was as clear as always, heavily accented but easily understood. His last words were about his home and his people. He asked me to be kind to them.

"When you write about them, be honest," he said. "And try to do justice to them."

He slipped his bony hand into mine; his fingers were very long and very thin. They felt almost brittle.

We walked to the Métro together. He took the train toward Aubervilliers; I went to République. That was the last I ever saw of him.

Alfa, the man I was going to see, is from the Ivory Coast, and he is the antithesis of Mbaye. Alfa has plenty of friends. Time spent with him would be a far cry from an evening with Mbaye, for Alfa has made Paris his home. He has learned to adapt to the French way of doing things, and in fact he seems to prefer them.

If Mbaye is colonial Africa, slow moving and ancient in his practices, Alfa is modern Africa, looking energetically to the present. He is frenetic, absorbed in things French, and eager to turn his back on old-fashioned customs. He is just as lost as Mbaye, but in a totally different, almost spiritual, way—running without knowing where or why.

When I entered his apartment, the first thing he did was offer me a glass of wine. Although Alfa is a Muslim, he loves wine and he loves to be drunk.

Alfa is married to an Englishwoman who is about to have a baby, a big baby by the looks of her. They have one child already who is old enough to walk and talk but who still wears diapers. She stays close to her mother and silently clings to the hem of her dress. She is taking her time to develop, and, as often happens with the children of parents whose native languages are not the same, she is not quite sure who she is—African, English, or French, black or white. The child speaks neither English nor French, makes sounds rather than words, hasn't yet decided which language is the right one, which word is the proper word to use when she wants to eat. She is cross-eyed and wears very thick glasses, and her skin is a very light tan. Her hair is wiry, the color of sand.

In the dining room of their apartment a clothesline has been strung from one wall to another. It hangs just behind the table, so that when you sit there to eat, you have to lean forward to avoid the towels and the underwear and the diapers hanging on the line to dry. Empty wine bottles and beer bottles litter the floor; there are books and papers and dirty dishes everywhere.

Alfa kicks aside the clutter and invites me into the apartment. If he cares how the place looks, he doesn't show it. He merely clears a path with his feet, takes me by the hand, and leads me in to meet his wife, his two friends, and a long-legged blond in a very short leather skirt. They are about to eat a simple meal of eggs and potatoes and small pieces of chicken. They are not going to eat from the same bowl or use their fingers. There are plates, knives, and forks. But when I hold up my glass to drink the wine, the glass is spotted and a hint of someone's lipstick remains stuck to the rim. My plate is crusted with bits of last night's dinner, and my fork has dried egg on it. I would rather eat with my fingers.

Conversation is lively and loud, and Alfa dominates. He and Omar, an Algerian, are arguing the subtler points of Islam, shouting as they debate. They speak lightning fast; their French sounds backwards. I focus so intently on their words that I squint, but unless one or the other is talking directly to me and helping me with facial expressions and hand gestures, I can barely understand even half.

French is a barrier between us, one of many. Try as I might there will always be some nuance that I will misinterpret, some gesture, some meaning, some Africanism—not only in the language—that I will misunderstand.

Listening to Alfa and Omar is, in a way, a language exercise. When the French comes that fast, there is no time to translate each morsel in your head. You try at first, but eventually the brain tires and gives up the conscious struggle. It relaxes into submission. The unconscious takes over, and from the well of memory, countless French classes and drills bubble to the surface, all of them miraculously stored deep inside. At some point it clicks together like a well-blended sauce: suddenly you're speaking French. Perhaps in time an understanding of Africa will come in the same way, by surrender.

Omar shouts at Alfa. "How can you call yourself a Muslim?" he asks. "You drink, you do not pray, you do nothing the faith calls for."

"You do not have to read all that is written to know how to read. You do not have to follow all the rules of a religion to have faith. I have faith," he says emphatically, shouting just as wildly as Omar.

"Then call yourself something else," Omar orders him. "You are not a Muslim."

"I am a Muslim."

"Can a Muslim be baptized Catholic and go to mass and worship the pope? When does he cease to be a Muslim? If you do not obey the rules of the faith, you are something else, but you are not a Muslim."

It is a faith I know little about, so little in fact that I had no idea Islam was widespread in Africa and not confined to the Arabs. But the Arabs were themselves great colonizers in Africa and once a great Islamic Empire stretched into the heart of the continent. Where Islam reached into Africa, cultures and colors clashed, and the religions that emerged differed from one place to another, for each country brought to Islam memories and traditions of old. Islam in its many forms is one of the base threads in the tapestry that is Africa.

Alfa and Omar continued to argue. Alfa's wife poured more wine. The woman in the short skirt slowly crossed her legs, keeping them close together as she crossed them. Her stockings rustled in a most distracting way. I tried not to stare but I lost my concentration. My French faltered and I got left behind in the argument.

It was an argument about religion but could just as easily have been an argument about being African and adopting European ways, about defining oneself. That is the struggle, in Africa as elsewhere—each man trying to define who he is.

When I left, my head was pounding from the shouting and from the heavy concentration. I walked into the mist of a warm winter's night, and during the walk a quiet melancholy entered the fog and settled softly around me. I felt torn. I did not want to leave Paris. And yet Africa was pulling.

I thought I knew very little about Africa, no more than the clichés everyone learns, images from books I had read, little more than place-names on a map. But deep within that same well of memory out of which I'd pulled old French lessons as I listened to Alfa and Omar, there was a knowledge of Africa I never knew was there, or at least never thought about. Much of it was learned from newspapers and magazines—Africa was very much in the news lately. Much of it was residual history learned in school, not so much the history of Africa as the histories of the Roman Empire, the Catholic Church, Muslim expansion, European civilization.

But I wanted to know more than the postcard views and the clichés, the glamorous and glossy images of *National Geographic* photos, the stories and feelings other people had put in books, images of Tarzan and apes and of black men the color of night dancing with bones in their noses. I wanted to find the truths of Africa and I wanted to see them for myself. And as frightening as it was, I wanted to go alone.

That night Omar had given me the name and address of one of his friends in Algeria. Apart from that I knew no one. It was the way I wanted to travel: to go in cold, with no idea what path I would follow, to travel like a leaf on a breeze and go where wind and whim would dictate, where rumor of something strange or wonderful or merely interesting would draw me. I would stay ahead of the rains and listen to the wind to tell me when it was time to leave. It was, I think, Oliver Cromwell who said that no man ever travels so high or so far as he who does not know where he is going. And someone else once said: "When you don't know where you are going, any gust of wind will take you there."

That night I hoped hard for a sudden gust of wind. It came as I walked through the place des Vosges. The four fountains in the square were brightly lit, spraying water and mist into the air.

The days had been idyllic and made for strolling, for sitting at sidewalk cafés, for sipping wine under a canopy out of the

drizzle, reading the paper, doing a crossword, dunking a crois-
sant in a big bowl of hot chocolate. I could have lingered forever,
happily shopping the open-air markets and selecting fruit and
cheese and pâté, breathing in the smells of newly baked bread
and waiting for the lady in the checkered apron to slice a hunk
of fresh butter, then talking to the old man who makes marmalade and sells it near the place de la Bastille.

But a cold fog had formed in the night, and a wet wind
blew. It crept up the legs of my pants and down into my open
collar. When I looked up, acid rain from Paris's filthy skies
burned my eyes. It was time to go.

Africa was hot on my mind, singeing it. I couldn't sleep. Excitement, like needles of electricity, burned in my fingertips. My
mind flashed forward and backward at the same time, thoughts
and feelings swirled together like the eddies of dust that form in
desert breezes. I was afraid.

The Africa of my dreams tasted of dust and sand and sweat,
smelled of heat and dried fish, echoed jungle rhythms and roaring laughter and the sounds of children starving. Cattle rustled
in the marketplace and stirred up the dust. Women hurried
along a sunbaked road walking barefoot, baskets on their heads,
their backs noble and straight as arrows. The stew they rushed
home to cook was pungent and vaguely sweet. The meat in the
stew was rat. In the dark with my eyes closed, I could hear their
children cry.

Africa is Ethiopian babies with their bellies distended from
starvation. Africa is a massive, hundred-million-dollar Catholic
basilica carved into the jungle of the Ivory Coast and surrounded by hunger and illiteracy, Muslims and animists.

Africa is dread and terror and worse. Africa is mosquitoes.

Africa is AIDS and malaria, river blindness and something
called green monkey disease.

Africa is death and darkness and flies.

Africa was unknown and mysterious to me, inhabited by
pygmy cannibals and Watusi giants and Berber nomads on
horseback in deserts where it seems no man can survive for long.
Jungles and mountains and infinite plains. Endless miles of
nowhere. And in the middle of nowhere, strange cities with
stranger-sounding names rolling magically in the ear, firing the

imagination and conjuring up visions: Timbuktu, Malindi, and
Mombasa. Mbanza-Ngungu, Ouagadougou, and Bujumbura. I
longed to spend nights in a place called Bujumbura. The word
sounded like magic to me, the night there a velvet cloak draped
over the sky by some sorcerer and sprinkled with the stars of the
Southern Hemisphere, the Southern Cross reminding me that I
am in another world far far away.

And I longed to be in Kenya by spring—African spring. I
longed to see migrating herds of wildebeest crossing into the
Masai Mara from the Serengeti Plain in Tanzania, lion cubs
hiding in the tall grass, baby elephants learning to galumph.
Spring is the season of new life, of course, and in a place as wild
and strange as Africa, life springs forth jubilant and exotic and
abundant. Africa to me was Eden and these were the visions of
Africa in my mind.

But there was another vision of Africa that nagged at me:
the vision of Africa as homeland. A black man cannot visit Africa
without such thoughts creeping upon him and altering the pano-
rama.

I am not African, but somewhere deep in the hidden
reaches of my being, Africa beats in my blood and shows itself
in my hair, my skin, my eyes. Africa's rhythms are somehow my
rhythms, and Africa speaks to me its languages of love and
laughter.

I had some eerie feeling Africa could teach me about life
and what it means to be human, deepen my appreciation for all
that I am and all that I have, help me to find, perhaps, the face
of God, perhaps even my own face, help me to step out of my
cozy little world, out of myself so that I could see myself better
and better define myself. Even if, as Thomas Wolfe suggested,
you can't really go home again, perhaps it helps to know where
home is, to know where you have come from.

When I was six or seven my father would take me to see the
part of Saint Louis where he grew up. Streets that had once
been dirt and then cobblestones were now paved with asphalt
and concrete. Very little of his childhood remained, but the old
brick buildings were still standing and the tree he used to climb
was still there. He would point out the place where he and his
pals pulled their wagons loaded with coal, and where his father's grocery shop stood.

I liked driving through my father's old neighborhood and listening to stories of how it all used to be, stories I had heard a thousand times. They are part of the history of who I am. But I never wanted to live there. My time and place are elsewhere. I have a sense of who I am and where I belong, but I do struggle with the knowledge that I would not be who I am if all the pieces had not come into place as they did, if the slightest wind had blown vaguely off course.

Perhaps, then, by going to Africa I could see the past and then get rid of it, shed myself of this *roots* business once and for all, those invisible shackles that chain us too often to the past.

My father's old house is torn down now. My mother's family estate lost long ago. I do not want them back. It is enough that I realize what once was. It would be enough to go to Africa and smell the earth, enough to walk some of the same ground as my ancient ancestors, choke on the same dust and burn under the same searing sun.

I am American. And I am black. I live and travel with two cultural passports, the one very much stamped with European culture and sensibilities and history. The other was issued from the uniquely black experience, which is like no other, born of slavery and hardship and tied to a land we might call home but that we blacks do not know, and most have never seen—Africa.

Blackamericans are different from white Americans, different from Americans who are also Italian or French or Irish, different in our experience. Their distinctions are not racial but ethnic and regional. They share common histories and culture and color. Because they are not marked they can hide inside American society in ways we cannot. And they have access to their homelands in ways we have been denied. Proximity, money, cultural awareness. Africa is far away and expensive to reach. More than that, our education tends to be as European as the education of any white kid. We do not know about Africa, only learn about it in geography class. Place-names on a map. Climate.

So how does a Blackamerican travel to Africa? Certainly not as an African, for that I am not. Nor as a cultural European, for I am more than merely that. And more, too, than hybrid. Another race, perhaps, newborn and distinct, forged in the blast furnace of slavery, tempered and tested in the foundry of survival.

We are an African people and perhaps we see the world and react to it differently. Perhaps we have different ideas about style and love, language and religion, and about the earth.

At the same time we are an American people, products of a new culture and defined by it. And we see the world through American eyes.

I felt like Jekyll and Hyde.

France in late winter is green and wet, the Alps snow covered and forbiddingly majestic. The train passes along some mountain river and I open the window of my compartment. I lean out and look straight up and still I cannot see the top of the mountain. The air is cool and fresh like a promise unbroken, and spring, though not exactly in the air, sends signs of its arrival. Melting snow cascades in clear streams over the cliffs and down into gorges below. The hills vary in height and roundness and in shades of green.

Heading toward the Italian peninsula and down, I see the green of those hills give way to brown and gold, colors of warmth and sunshine. Alpine cottages perched high on the sides of mountains, with their bright red roofs and the delicate *snickarglädje* (carpenter's joy—overhanging eaves and exterior woodwork beautifully carved), surrender now to Mediterranean architecture: tiled roofs of burnt orange and walls the color of adobe brick. The houses become simpler, more functional and less decorative, either from the warmer climate or a poorer populace. Maybe in heat you just want shelter and you want it quickly, no time for *snickarglädje*. In colder climes you need a certain beauty to see you through the winter, to distract you from the blizzard outside and sustain you until spring. Farther south the sun saps your energy. You search for shade and you wait for rain.

Renoir's deft touch with color and light has been given a broad stroke of brightness and sepia, a peasant woman planting in the garden, a grave marker in the middle of a field of wildflowers and weeds, the farmhouse of brown stone and red tile roof up on the hill. Luigi Nono's painting of *First Rain*. Or the brown scapes of Giovanni Boldini.

The blond hair of the north becomes darker on the way south and thicker, wavier; eyes go from blue to hazel to dark brown. The influence of Africa in the blood is evident here and cannot be denied, though some will. Skin darkens and thickens, not quite white and not yet brown, no longer that pale, pasty complexion that burns rather than tans, but one that gets richer in sunlight and more golden. The bottom definitely rises, south comes north, Africa in the blood is visible and profound.

As I descend the Italian peninsula and pass through Rome, I begin to notice evidence of Italy's attempts at colonialism. The blacks are no longer Senegalese or Ivorian, but the sharp-featured, silky-haired peoples of Somalia and Ethiopia. Their activities, however, do not change. These Africans too form the dregs of their promised land. They hang around train stations and public *piazze*. They sell what they can and they beg for money. Women with babies sucking at their bared breasts approach and reach out a grubby hand and grimace toothlessly to beg a few coins. Their clothes are filthy and shabby; they sleep in train station corridors or in doorways along the *strada* or in any unoccupied spot they find. Always the women and the children; the men, too ashamed, must be hiding. And the children learn early to plead with eyes so sad, to tug on coattails and on heartstrings. They ought to be in school.

The boldest beggars walk along the station platforms and peer sadly into the open windows of waiting trains. The trains never leave on time.

From a place where I could almost set my clock by the movement of the trains, I have entered a world where trains arrive so late, I am sure I must have crossed a time zone or two and forgot to change my watch. But it is not a time zone that has been crossed; it is more like a time warp. I am in a world now where a train ride that is supposed to be only an hour long can somehow manage to be over an hour late.

Africa has come up to meet me, to prepare me for what is to come, to help ease my way down.

Hold on to your sense of humor, I tell myself, *and wait like everyone else.*

Africa may begin in Paris, but the waiting begins in Sicily. Thinking I was still in Europe, I was shocked to find there would be no ferry to Tunisia until next Thursday, no plane until Monday. It was Friday and I had missed the boat by a day. Two days to roam the twisting streets of Cefalù, an old Sicilian fishing village perched on the hills overlooking the Mediterranean. Two days for Africa to take complete control of my dreams and imagination.

Africa was a only stone's throw away now and suddenly very real, so near that it was haunting my nights, pulling at my bones. I lay in the dark and drifted in and out of sleep, half of my mind on the clock, the other half on fire.

I would have preferred to go to Tunisia by ship rather than by plane, to ease into Africa, but I didn't want to spend five days in Sicily. I wanted to be in Africa. I flew to Tunis.

I don't like to fly. There is the boredom. There is the weirdness of entering an enclosed capsule, napping, waking up suddenly in a different time and place, no sensation of getting there, only of arriving, no transition, no acclimation. And there is the creepy knowledge that planes fall out of the sky.

An Arab sits beside me on the flight to Tunis. I take the aisle seat; he sits by the window. He wears black jeans and a black leather jacket and he sweats a lot. He is more nervous even than I am, more nervous than anyone ought to be. On his lap he clutches very tightly a brown leather satchel. It could easily fit under the seat in front of him, but he won't let go of it. He looks out the window for what must be the fiftieth time before we take off. When he isn't looking out the window, he is looking around the plane, but not just glancing around; this man is nervous and looking for something, maybe the emergency exits. He is definitely in a hurry to take off. Is he a smuggler and hiding from the police and the bag stuffed with jewels and money? He certainly doesn't seem like a Tunisian businessman merely returning home from a holiday in Italy.

Then I realize. Arabs, Palestinians, they're all the same.

His hair is jet black and curly tight, stylishly coiffed close and tapering toward the back of his head. He wears a thick mustache and razor stubble covers his chin. He looks as if he hasn't slept any more than I have, and he could use a cigarette.

Of all the places to sit, why did I have to sit next to an Arab terrorist? And why did he, with all the empty seats on this flight, choose to sit next to me? To be over the wing, of course, where an exploding bomb would do the most damage. In the satchel he must be carrying a bomb.

He looks at me looking at him, and I look away. I don't want him to know that I know. Left alone, he might chicken out. Suspicion might cause him to panic right away, pull the cord, and trigger the bomb. His nerves are already shattered, and I hear him muttering to himself in Arabic: *Come on, hurry, and let's get the hell out of here.* He has his orders, his mission. He will fail if he gets caught or if he has to detonate before takeoff. Planes exploding in midair and especially out over the sea have no survivors and they are so much more dramatic.

I close my eyes and imagine this plane engulfed in a fireball after the explosion and streaking through the sky and down into the sea. I will not hear the boom and I will feel nothing. I look over and silently thank this Arab terrorist for sitting so close to me. There will be no time for pain, no time to scream or panic or even to know what's happening.

We are already taxiing. I will go to my death calmly. I will see how brave I can be with death sitting right beside me, not just death but a violent explosion, being ripped out through a gaping hole along with dozens of others, seats, baggage, shards of shattered and twisted metal and flesh, and plunging through the sky like a fallen angel.

We are in the air and already out over the Mediterranean. The stewardess passes by and gives out bottled water and midget cans of soda. She offers no food, no snacks, and no alcohol. I could use a drink. But in the strict Muslim world, no alcohol is allowed. And too, this is Ramadan, the season of fasting, the holiest time of year for Muslims. So of course there is no food. This terrorist will die martyred and he will die holy, but at least he will die hungry.

The plane takes a violent dip. The seat belt sign comes on. We are buffeted severely, knocked around in the sky. I grit my teeth, praying for a pilot who has trained with the U.S. Navy, wondering why I didn't fly to Tunisia on a real airline, like Pan Am.

I'm losing it, going crazy. I look over at my terrorist and he is going crazy too.

The stewardess comes back down the aisle. She is handing

out landing cards for passengers to fill out and give to immigration officials once we land. The Arab leans over to me.

"Can you help me, please?" he asks.

The look on my face, I wonder what it says to him.

"Do you speak French?" he asks.

I shake off my stupor and answer him. He asks me to help him fill out his landing card. He cannot read or write. He hands me his passport—written in Arabic—and what he says in French I write for him.

He had been living and working in Naples, and now he was going home to be with his family in Tunis. He hated airplanes. Flying made him nervous.

I nodded in agreement. "Me too," I said.

Tunis sprawled out below the plane and reached from the edge of the sea toward the desert, a huge city spreading endlessly, sand colored and white, reflecting sun and heat. The man beside me smiled the smile of a homecoming. To him Tunis was beauty, tradition, home. To me it was just the beginning.

I had eased into Africa all right, eased in with a jolt. The whole of Africa lay before me. And I was as racist as anyone else.

TWO

DESERT AWAKENINGS ▶▶▶▶▶▶▶

Tunisia
Algeria
Morocco

       The road lay before me like a path into an enchanted forest and fanned out like the tentacles of an octopus. I stood as if at a crossroads, as if Africa were a mystery to unravel. Only one route was the right route. Only one thread unraveling would lead into the center of the labyrinth and out again. It was a pilgrimage, a personal quest for understanding, and if I asked the right questions, I would find the right answers.

       The heat of Africa fused the elements within me and the icy disquiet of being a stranger in a strange land melted away under wave after wave of overwhelming excitement, the thrill of discovery. From the moment I stepped off the plane and passed through the crowded airport, warmth flooded over me. My eyes opened wide with wonder. I smelled the air. I was in another world, a child in a candy store of sight and sound, aroma and new sensation.

       From a distance, Africa on a map looks like a single entity and the continent lives in the imagination as if it were one place. We think of jungles and wild game and black faces, but we forget about the Sahara and the Arabs. We think of the slave trade, and lately we think of South Africa. We think of all these, if we think of Africa at all, as if Africa were homogeneous and unified, no more different from place to place than Idaho is different from New York.

But Africa is vast, a land mass not a country, and as diverse as a patchwork quilt. The road is a thread that crosses cultures and colors that are only loosely and arbitrarily connected. There is no single Africa. From top to bottom there are only Africas, and they are as distinct as the various shades of a single color.

From a distance, I might look African. My skin is dark, my hair is dense and curly. My nose is broad. In many ways the similarity ends there, for the external me and the internal do not always match. I am like Alfa's daughter. Half one thing and half another. Searching to discover who I am.

It was a voyage of discovery, to find what it is that men share, that black men share, that all of Africa shares, apart from only poverty and heat.

In a sense, all roads lead to the same place. They all lead to a better understanding of place and self. In Africa all roads lead south to the tail that wags the dog. They lead deep into a dark well of suffering and despair. They lead out again into the bright morning of hope. There is no despair as there is in Africa. There is no hope brighter than the hope of Africa. Africans have been waiting and hoping a very long time.

I wanted to be African for a while. I wanted to shed my former self as if it were a snakeskin and see life, if possible, from a new point of view. Simply that. To make their joys my joys. To make their pain my pain.

I walk through the center of Tunis and I look into the eyes of the strangers I pass. The face of Africa here has Arab eyes. All the eyes are brown, a deep rich and dark brown, eyes that speak to me but in a language I do not understand. Every woman sneaks a glance; every man stares. I am more than stranger, I am also strange.

I am tall and I am very dark. I have not shaved my beard and there is not another beard in this city. I wear clothes that set me apart and attract attention: a bright red T-shirt with long sleeves, baggy pants held up by blue suspenders, hiking boots that are heavy and durable. From a belt loop on my trousers hangs a watch I refuse to wear. My clothes are not African clothes.

I lope when I walk and swagger a little, not consciously boasting but there is a definite pride in my long stride, an arrogance that comes from nothing special, nothing of this moment. My walk is not an African walk.

By journey's end, I will not be the man I am today. Africa will have changed me in ways I cannot predict, perhaps in ways profound, perhaps only superficial. Perhaps I will lose a few pounds, perhaps the arrogance in my walk. Perhaps my walk, even my way of looking at things, will be a little more African. But for now, I am different. I am not one of these Africans. Not yet, and may not ever be. The color of my skin says that I could be Algerian or Senegalese or from Chad. But the Tunisian eyes that watch me can see that I at least am not from Tunisia. They know I am not one of them, but they do not know where I come from.

The whole of Africa lies before me and I have no plan, no itinerary. It might be better if I were searching for some three-legged zebra, for at least I would know when I found it. Without a plan, without a goal, a traveler is at the mercy of the road. Traveling overland is not like traveling on a river. The river has a beginning. It has an end. The path, though not straight, is defined. Not so traveling overland. The prospects, like the possibilities and promises of life, are endless and varied and arbitrary.

An old man asks, "Where in Tunisia do you want to go?"

I have no idea. It isn't always the getting there that is important. Sometimes it's just the going.

"Go to Sousse," he tells me. "Go to Sfax."

I have been feeling my way through town, searching the brown eyes of Arabs for some sign of recognition. Somewhere on this continent there is a man who looks like me. When I find him, our hearts will shake hands.

There is an excitement in searching. It is the excitement of travel, following hunches, getting into a crowd that looks as if it might be going where I might like to go and letting the crowd lead me there. And if the crowd is going somewhere else, then I will go where it goes. I guide myself with a mixture of instinct and common sense that keeps an eye on the sun and knows which way south is. It knows too where the train station ought to be, since there is only one place it really can be, just as the shore is always near the sea.

But I have gotten lost. I have come to the wrong train station.

This is the station commuters use going back and forth between home and work, between the city and nearby suburbs. The tracks come straight as time lines side by side all the way from the horizon to the middle of the city, where they abruptly stop. People mill about on the platform waiting for the train. They read newspapers. They buy bread. They wait. No schedule is posted and there is no information booth. The station is a tiny concrete shelter with a window where tickets are sold, but there is no one inside.

Across from the station are three little wooden stalls in a line of shade from a row of low palm trees. The merchants are selling bread for the evening meals. It is Ramadan and no one eats, no one even nibbles, and it would be an offense if I did. There are many foreign tourists who come here and ignore Ramadan. They eat like pigs all day while everyone else fasts. It is like a slap in the face.

I stop an old man on the corner to ask him where the train station is. He is short and stooped at the shoulders and he walks with a limp. His face is like old leather left out in the sun, dry and cracked, so completely lined that it is a maze of concentric circles, his nose in the middle. His lips are thin and tight; they have not seen a smile in a very long time. His eyes frown. He looks at me with a quizzical expression, as if he hasn't understood what I am asking. I try again.

He does not speak and continues to look perplexed. His face asks: Are you blind, or just stupid? He steps aside and points across the street.

"No, not that station. Aren't there trains to other parts of Tunisia?"

"Ah!" he says. The dry leather cracks into a stiff smile. "You mean *la station des grandes lignes.*"

He points out the way, directing me with broad gestures, waving his arms and telling me to pass in front of "that big hotel just there—don't you see it there?—and walk two or three more streets, and then you turn right, no, left." He's not sure. So he walks with me to show me the way.

He is an old man trying to be hospitable. He is an old man with nothing better to do than sit with his friends and talk about things. For these few moments I am his friend, and he wants to show me Tunis.

It is an ancient city, noisy and crowded and full of frenzy, abutted against the modern world and so influenced by it that old ways and customs will get diluted here first. For although many of the men on the streets wear business suits, and others wear plain trousers and simple shirts, still there are many others who wear light-colored cotton robes called *djelabahs*, their heads wrapped in white *cheche*s to protect head and face from sand and sun. Old ways get diluted, but they do not disappear, for many customs are more than tradition. They were born out of good sense. In the desert, many loose layers of clothing repel heat better than no clothes at all.

Everywhere there are signs of the Muslim faith. Slender minarets on mosques rise against the sky. They are the only beauty in the skyline, for although there are a few tall buildings, the architecture is simple and angular. The feeling here is not so much of the present and certainly not the ancient past, but of the near past, a city squirming into modernity, a city where old ways have not yet surrendered and the new ways have not yet conquered. Instead, the two have collided and they contrast and they come together. Women dress modestly, even if a few wear high heels. Many women cover their heads with *hijabs*, but not all, and only very old women wear veils that completely hide their faces. The hijab ties these women to their religion and to their culture, links them to one another and to the past.

The buses in Tunis are old and broken down, second-hand buses discarded by France and Germany. They are cheaper than buying new ones. They rattle and smoke, emitting obnoxious fumes and tremendous clouds of black, smelly exhaust. They pass with a horrible, deafening roar. No one holds his breath when the buses go by, or plugs his ears—no one but me.

The train station stands at the end of a great square that serves as the depot for buses. There is a riot of crowds and activity, men selling, people traveling, everyone in a hurry.

The inside of the station is as huge, as open, and as hollow as any train station in France. There are beggars inside and a poster of a smiling President Zine el-Abidine Ben Ali. He stands in front of a bright sunrise and seems to be urging his people to follow him.

The old man with me curls up the corners of his nose.

"That is Ben Ali," he says. "He is our president." The old man spits on the ground in disgust. "You see how he smiles, how he hangs himself all over the city so we will not be able to forget that he is the one who is president. He disgusts me." He spits on the ground again. "Habib Bourguiba was overthrown two years ago."

Habib Bourguiba was president until Ben Ali seized power in 1987, claiming that Bourguiba was too old to manage. Bourguiba was well into his eighties at the time. He was put under house arrest and remains out of the way in a well-guarded villa south of the city.

"We will have an election soon," the old man says. "But nothing will change. Ben Ali will still be there."

The old man speaks with the courage of old age, not afraid to speak unkind words about dictators. He has lost his fear because he has nothing more to lose.

"Habib was no better. He promised us a voice when he became president. Soon he proclaimed himself president for life. He took away our voice, and we still have no voice."

Habib Bourguiba was first elected in 1957, the year after independence from France. The constitution called for no more than three consecutive five-year terms. Bourguiba was still president in 1975 when he decided to claim the job for life. But in 1987 he was ousted by Ben Ali. Now Ben Ali's photographs hang where Bourguiba's used to, all over town, all over the country.

In the station there is a snack bar and a newspaper stand. Both are closed. High up one wall there is a big board with a train timetable, and on another wall hangs an enormous map with names of cities I do not recognize.

"Yes, of course," the old man says. "Go to Sousse. It is beautiful. And go to Monastir. Go to Sfax. Oh, and Gabès. It is a beautiful country."

Like all patriots, as much as he is filled with disgust for the politicians, he is filled with love for his country. He wishes me well and welcome. He points me to the information bureau.

I reach into my pocket to offer him a few coins, but he shakes his head, smiling that crusted old smile again, and refuses. He pats me on the shoulder and walks away. He is stooped and he limps, but his eyes carry the fire of an ancient pride.

Hannibal was a Carthaginian, an ancient Tunisian. During the Punic Wars with Rome, Hannibal crossed the Pyrenees Mountains and slipped into France. He had sixty thousand soldiers, six thousand horses, and a herd of elephants that he used as battle tanks to crush his enemy's positions. He crossed the Alps and invaded Italy, defeating the Romans in the Battle of the Trebbia River. At Cannae his army killed more than fifty thousand Romans in a single day, lighting the fires of that ancient pride.

In the end, the Romans conquered Carthage and buried it.

The Arabs came to win the land in A.D. 670. The European crusaders battled the Arabs and their religion throughout the Middle East to secure Jerusalem and the Holy Land in the name of Christianity, but the Eighth Crusade never made it to the East. Louis IX, king of France and future saint, died while his knights were laying siege to Tunis in 1270. Disease obliterated his army. The Arabs and Islam are still here.

The two men behind the information counter greeted me with good cheer and open arms. One of them kissed my cheek. He called me his brother. In an instant we formed a friendship not like a friendship at all, but more like dogs meeting and sniffing each other, a friendship so quickly started and so easily ended, so easy and open in its expressions of warmth and happiness. When strangers meet, the contact is small. Our lives are like two lines intersecting at a single point. They do not run parallel. They merely come together. They touch momentarily. They drift apart. At best they reach some common sentiment that binds them, something they can recognize and carry, each in his own direction.

I had come to this counter for a little tourist info. What I took away would stay with me throughout the journey, perhaps, and I hoped a lot longer.

The wife of one of the men came by to deliver an armload of bread.

"For our dinner," the man said, and my stomach growled. The men laughed.

"Hungry? Would you like a piece of bread?"

"No," I said. "I'm fasting."

One face lit up, then the other.

"You're making the fast? You're not Muslim, are you?"

"No," I said. "I do it out of solidarity. When I am in Tunisia, I do as the Tunisians."

They shouted with exhilaration. The thin man brought out a chair. The other man introduced me to his wife. His two young children came by, and after some instruction in Arabic from the father, they greeted me as if I were a long-lost cousin. The children shook hands with me. The littlest one patted my knee.

Then I got my first lesson.

When asked if I knew what Ramadan was, I answered that it was a month of fasting. I didn't know much else, and when they taught me, they taught me about more than just Ramadan.

They spoke rapidly, mixing in Arabic words with the French. I often had trouble understanding. Several times I had to ask them to repeat.

"Ramadan is the ninth month of the Islamic calendar. During the entire month, from daybreak until sunset, we fast. That means no eating, no drinking, and for the very devout, no swallowing. You will see them spitting all day so that nothing enters their bodies."

"It doesn't sound easy," I said.

"It isn't," he said. "Hunger and heat combine to fatigue men and make them crazy. They argue and fight. They spend their energy quickly and sleep all afternoon."

It was a stupid question, but I asked him why, if fasting was so hard, did they do it?

"We do it," he said, "for the same reason you do it. We go without so that we can better understand those who *must* go without. Like the *zakat*, giving to the poor, it is a way of purifying the rest of what we have and eat. It is a voluntary thing. You do what you can afford to do. If you are sick, if you are a mother nursing a baby, if you are old, you do not need to fast."

I asked him how long Ramadan lasts, and the second man answered, as if to show he knew the faith too.

"This goes on for the entire month," the other said. "It was during the month of Ramadan that the Koran was revealed to Mohammed by Jibril. You call him Gabriel."

"Gabriel?" I asked in surprise. "You mean the angel Gabriel?"

"Does it shock you that we share so much?" the second man continued. "You have your Lenten fast. We have Ramadan." He said it as if to show that he knew my faith as well as his own. It wasn't religion. It was a way of life.

"It was the same Jibril," he said, "who revealed to Mohammed and who revealed to Daniel, and the same Jibril who announced to Mary, the same angel of God who saved the neck of young Isaac, Ibrahim's son."

It was certainly something I had never learned in school.

"We have the same God," he said. "The same prophets, the same patriarchs, the same father in Ibrahim. There is only one God, and Mohammed is his prophet."

"Jews too?" I asked.

"Especially Jews," he said. "We have a common ancestor in Ibrahim and his two sons, Isaac and Ishmael. We even share the same myths. According to your Bible, God told Isaac that his descendants would inherit the earth. According to our teachings, God blessed Ishmael and promised that he and his descendants would build a great nation. That nation is Islam."

"And is that why Arabs and Jews are fighting?"

"Why do Christians hate Jews? Do you forget that Jesus was a Jew? Or that Paul, before he became a saint, was a Jew? Do not confuse religion with politics," he said. "Unlike you, we do not fight the Jews because they are Jews. We fight the *jihad*, the holy war, which is the constant struggle against corruption on the earth. It is a fight to insure good and to abolish evil. The war in Palestine is not about religion. It is not a holy crusade. It is about human rights and about human dignity. It is political. We are fighting over a piece of land. The Jews say God gave Palestine to them, but historically the land is just as much ours. Jerusalem is of course a holy city for Jew and for Christian, but for Muslim as well. We ignore what we share and instead we look for those things that separate us."

It was the way of the world, he told me, to try and cut loose those things that bind us. We concentrate instead on what makes us different.

That was why I had come to Africa, I told him: to search for those things that we share. To find some sort of common bond, some common sentiment, a simple recognition of what pulls us together. To suffer with someone, not merely for suffering's sake but to walk a mile in another's moccasins, to see what other men endure and to endure it with them. To learn what makes them endure. It is the difference, perhaps, between travel and tourism.

The two men kissed me and wished me well.

"May God go with you," they said. "May you find peace and do the will of Allah."

I took the slow train to Sousse. A breeze crept through the open window.

The terrain outside was sand and dust and an occasional cluster of palm trees. Every little oasis was a town and we stopped at each one. Except for the names painted on a placard on the side of each station, we could have been going in a circle, stopping at the same village over and over again. People climbed off the train at these little stations and rushed exuberantly into the arms of waiting family and friends they hadn't seen since yesterday.

The train sat in the station until the crowd had dispersed. Only the young children lingered. Like children everywhere they were fascinated by trains. They waved as we pulled from the station and they chased the train a short distance. When they could no longer keep up, they threw rocks.

In three hours we arrived in Sousse.

A group of German tourists got off the train. I was tempted to stay on board and avoid them, but I got down too. When they turned left to go to the tourist hotels, I turned right and followed boulevard Hassoun down to the big intersection at the end of the street.

Traffic was dense. Cars zoomed by at terrific speeds. People crossing the street could not afford to stroll, and didn't. There were no traffic signals to help them. They waited for an opening in the traffic and dashed to the other side. The cars did not slow down. They honked vigorously instead to let people know they were coming. The pedestrians took the warnings very seriously.

Out of the main flow of traffic, very old horses and very old donkeys with their heads hanging low dragged rickety wooden carts loaded with building materials, straw or sacks of cement. They moved slowly along the curbs. When they wanted to merge with the traffic and cross the street, the animals broke into short trots of great effort and much sadness. Cars swerved to avoid them but did not slow down. Horns blared, but the pandemonium stayed calm.

Men and women wore djelabahs and hijabs, little children wore T-shirts and shorts. Beside them and behind them walked tourists with cameras stuck to their faces. The tourists posed and photographed each other, and they took pictures of veiled women who quickly turned away. If one happened to get caught, she would raise an angry finger and chastise the photographer.

The tourists walked slowly, staring at everything, searching for decent places to eat.

At the far corner of the diagonal there is the *medina*, the old walled city that has been here a thousand years. Its walls are a reddish kind of gray. From its parapets at the top, ancient invaders were once repelled. From outside, you cannot see in.

The minarets of the Grande Mosque rise in the background. The quiet clopping of donkeys pulling carts ruffles the air. It is a very old scene, but right alongside is the frenzy of autos and buses and rushing people drowning out the serenity.

A little man came up to me. He was very thin and very short and a little stooped as well. He walked with a limp.

"*Mon grand,*" he said. He was exuberant. "How are you, my big man?"

I bent down to talk to him.

"I'm very well. How are you?"

"It is your first day here," he informed me. "Do you want to buy cigarettes?"

"Don't smoke."

"Do you want to buy hashish, or maybe a woman?"

"No," I said. "Just a hotel."

"A tourist hotel?" he asked, and pointed up the street. "Or perhaps an Arab hotel?"

"Which one is cheaper?"

"The Arab hotel, of course."

"Then I want the Arab hotel."

He laughed and reached for my bag, but it was too heavy for him. I lifted it and slung it over my shoulder. The little man smiled and squeezed my arm.

"You Americans," he said. "You are so big and so strong."

I asked him how he knew I was American and he smiled, saying, "It's evident."

He took me by the arm and guided me across the street to a little café where his friends were sitting, gesturing to them as we approached.

"Come see my friend," he yelled to them. "He's American." He was very proud to have found me.

We sat in the shade of the café and someone brought me a coffee that was strong and dark and gave me shivers. When I finished drinking there was a thick black sediment in the bottom of the glass. Another man offered bread. They were all eating, but I declined.

"You are making the fast?" one man asked. "That is good. You have the good fortune to choose. But we must eat when we can."

He wore the dry smile and disillusioned expression of a man who had not been treated like a man in a very long time. He threw his cigarette butt on the floor and kicked at it. He missed it. The cigarette finally extinguished itself.

He and his friends sat in the bar and drank coffee and wine and tried to turn their backs on tradition. They ignored Ramadan. They complained of no money and no food, but there was somehow enough money for wine.

The man who had been smoking lit another cigarette and dreamed through a cloud of smoke. "I would like to go to America," he said. "I would buy a car."

He dreamed like a child, without shame.

The limping little man had been ignored until now. He said with great pride, "I have been to America. I have been to Chicago." And he said something in Arabic that for the moment earned him everyone's attention, and he glowed with conceit. For him this moment was better than wine or women to make him feel like a man.

We lounged several minutes on the red vinyl benches. I drank another coffee. They spoke in Arabic unless they were talking to me.

"Our friend will show you a good hotel," said the man who wanted to buy a car. "Come back tonight. We will drink together."

I said I would.

After a very cold shower I walked alone into the medina.

The late afternoon was cooling off and I wandered through the twisting alleys and narrow corridors of the *souk*, which is the marketplace, a labyrinth of shops and stalls with awnings draped everywhere. You could find everything in this bazaar, spices and dates and figs, souvenirs for the tourists, carpets and brass and leather, shoes and tea and meat, old television sets that had been repaired. It was a very tight squeeze to get through the corridors, an amazing traffic jam of people and donkeys.

The shop owners, when they finished staring at me, invited me inside to browse and to buy. One merchant grabbed me by the arm.

"*Al-salaam alaikoum*," he said, and I said it too. He took my hand and shook it. He lifted his hand to his heart.

"*Labass?*" he said, and I just smiled.

"You don't speak Arabic?" he asked.

"I don't."

"You are not a Muslim?"

"I'm not."

"You are not from Senegal?"

I shook my head.

"Not from Niger?"

"No."

"Where do you come from?"

"From America."

His nephew inside overheard us and came out to greet me.

"Do you come from Jamaica?" he said, and when I shook my head, the guessing game went on. "From Brazil?"

Just as white Americans tend to forget that Mexicans and Colombians are Americans too, so Blackamericans forget that there are other black Americans besides those who live in the United States.

"I come from the United States," I finally told them.

The nephew raised a fist in jubilation and shook my hand again. He turned abruptly and walked proudly back into the shop.

"We have never met a Blackamerican before," the older man said. "But we don't see many white Americans either. Most of the tourists here are French, without doubt, and Germans and Scandinavians. Why did you come?"

"I am making the grand tour of Africa," I said.

"To see how your African brothers are living?"

"Yes," I said. "Something like that."

"And you don't speak Arabic?"

"Not yet," I said.

"Then I will give you your first lesson," he said. "When I say, '*Labass*,' I have asked about your health. You should say, '*Alhamdu l-illah*,' thanking God, thanking him that you are alive. Sometimes that is all we have to be thankful for."

He said it in a sad way but quickly brightened and asked me to step inside his shop.

"I can't buy anything."

"Come in all the same. Have a look," he said, "and maybe your next time in Tunisia you will remember me."

His nephew emerged again. He was carrying a brass tray and on the tray were a pot of tea and three small glasses. He told me to sit. He poured tea for us and we sat quietly drinking it. The tea was minty and very sweet.

Outside, from the minaret rising above the Grande Mosque, through a scratchy loudspeaker a voice was wailing singsongy exhortations to pray.

The sun was going down. Shops were beginning to close. Outside their shops men were washing their hands and faces and feet and unrolling their prayer mats.

Five times a day they do this, sunrise, noon, midafternoon, immediately after sunset, and at bedtime. Before they pray, they must wash. The *muezzin*, the one who calls believers to pray, chants aloud from a raised place, the minaret in a mosque. These days the chanting is likely to come over a loudspeaker. It almost sounds like an old recording.

I walked over to the mosque. Rows and rows of shoes were left neatly lined up outside the prayer room. No one ever enters with his shoes on. Inside, the men were all wearing white djela-bahs. There were no women.

The *imam* led the prayers. He stood facing Mecca, the holy city in Saudi Arabia, and the congregation behind followed him in different prayer postures called genuflection units. They did them over and over again. They stood and recited verses from the Koran. They fell to their knees and bowed forward, pressing their lips to the prayer mats. They prayed in a half-sitting, half-kneeling posture and then stood once more to do it all again—four times.

The sun had set. Fasting for the day was over. Darkness fell. Tourists strolled in the evening breeze that came in from the sea, and they sat in crowded cafés. Little boys selling flowers and cigarettes pestered them. Others begged for money. I was left alone.

I wandered away from the medina, walked along deserted streets covered in darkness. Away from the center of town there were very few lights and the night was black, full of mystery. A young Tunisian was leading a German tourist, trying to seduce her in the seclusion of the darkness. Their lingua franca was very bad English. He was telling her how beautiful she was, and she, looking for romantic adventure and ready to believe any-thing, smiled. He winked in conspiracy at me as they passed.

I wandered back around to the other side of the station and followed the railroad tracks toward the center of town and came again to the railway station. I had thought about finding a phone, calling home, but there was no phone. A man came out and after we chatted a moment, he invited me inside the station to share his dinner.

I had worried that I might have trouble meeting people, but they were as interested in me as I was in them. The world recognizes strangers and men smile favorably on them.

Hassan was this man's name, and for dinner his wife and the wives of the other men working the evening shift had sent along little metal pots filled with warm food. They sat on the floor eating with their fingers and shared among themselves and with me all that they had. There were dates to start with, lettuce and tomatoes and crispy *briques* fried golden. And then a stew with little chunks of lamb.

They were pleased that I had been making the fast. It was a direct line into their hearts. Each man nodded his satisfaction and smiled.

"Ramadan," Hassan said, repeating what I had already heard, "is a way for us to try to appreciate the blessings we have."

It is a sense of brotherhood and oneness, one of the common sentiments of Islamic life.

Hassan was a round-faced, serious man of middle age who did not smile much. When he did, his thin mustache curled up at the ends and pointed almost to his eyes. He offered me a little stool to sit on and handed me a *brique* to eat, a thin pastry holding a raw egg and a few spices inside and deep fried. When I bit it, the yolk broke and gushed. The yellow ran down my hand. I hurried to lick it before it got away. Hassan's lips stretched sideways. His mustache wiggled and curled up. His smile revealed missing teeth. He handed me a towel.

He broke off a piece of lettuce and handed it to me. He gave me a tomato.

"Why do you come here?" he asked.

The grand-tour answer somehow didn't seem appropriate and I said instead, "To live for a time the way other people live. To learn what is important."

"Islam is important," he said.

"That is why I fast."

"The fast will not make you a Muslim."

"I do not want to be Muslim," I said. "I only want to understand Islam a little. I make the fast so that I can know and share what you go through."

The other men continued to eat, but they were listening. Their conversations with each other had stopped and they were quiet, each one ready to carry the banner should Hassan stumble.

There are five things, Hassan said, that a Muslim must do. He must do Ramadan, of course, and he must pray five times a day. Once in his life, but only if he can afford it, he must make

the *hajj*, the pilgrimage to Mecca during the month of Dhu'
l-Hijja, the last month of the Muslim year. He must, naturally,
give to the poor. And once in his life he must profess the faith.
He must understand it and believe it and say it correctly and
sincerely.

"What must he say?"

"He must say, 'There is no god but Allah, and Mohammed
is his prophet.'"

He took a deep breath and looked to his friends. They were
smiling.

Islam is more than religion. It is passion as well. It so
infuses the lives of the faithful that life and religion can hardly
be separated, a sharp contrast with many of us, who profess one
thing but live another.

There was a sink in the corner. Hassan took up the pots
from the other men and turned on the tap to rinse things. The
other men were getting back to work, shuffling papers on desks
and wandering back out into the yard to catch the night air, to
check on things that needed tending to, to smoke a cigarette.
The evening had grown stiller. Hassan sat at his desk and fumbled through the clutter. The telephone rang. He picked up a
pencil and drummed it idly. It was my cue to leave.

The souk gets crowded early. The sun has barely hit the bottom
of the city walls and already along the beach fishermen are
untangling their nets. They are back from morning on the water,
the day's work already finished. The morning catch has been
laid on the levee, and on the flat sand by the ocean's edge fish
lie in long, straight rows. Flies are beginning to congregate. The
sun gleams at the horizon and quickly comes up full and strong.
The town wakens with the rising sun.

In the medina doors are opened to let in the morning's
fresh air. Men bathe in dusty courtyards and get ready for the
day. Goats and sheep forage for food. Little children come out
to play. They run along the narrow corridors and hide in doorways and recesses in the walls. I follow them, but they disappear. Even at an early age, these little children running wild
know every twist in the alleyways and corridors, every scratch
in the wall. The sun has not yet topped the city walls and the still

dimly lit medina is a labyrinth of confusion to me. I wander lost, discovering corners and shops I did not see before.

In the middle of the medina there is a square with a fountain in the center. But the fountain is dry and cracked and lifeless. No water spills from the spigots. No water fills the basin. At the foot of the fountain an old man lies on the ground. He sleeps curled up and drool hangs from the corner of his mouth. He is dirty and he stinks. Flies swarm near his face. His clothes are filthy and torn. He has no shoes. He looks almost comical, and I stop to take his picture. A Tunisian in a blue jogging suit passes. He sneers at me. "Don't they have poor people where you live?" he says indignantly. "We are not freaks, you know."

And he is right. I put the camera away.

At the gates of the old city, men lead reluctant donkeys up and down the ramp from the street into the medina. The donkeys are used as pickup trucks, weighted down with bundles of sticks, loads of fabric and fruit, and everything else on its way to be sold in the shops. Those who cannot find space to rent in the souk leave their loads right here at the gates and do not pass into the old city. Spread along the pavement the entire length of the wall, dates glisten in the morning sun. Children's underwear, T-shirts, and trousers are folded over wires stretched between stands. There are piles of newly shorn fleece, strange candies, bug spray in a mountain of neatly arranged yellow cans. On the front of each can is a big black cockroach, ugly and menacing.

People mill about. They touch everything, as if the value were not only in how a thing looks, but in how it feels. The commotion is intense. Merchants snatch at your attention with loud appeals and promises of good prices. The souk roars with bargaining, buyers and sellers arguing for the best price. The noise is rich.

Down the street the noise is more modern. Black clouds of exhaust rise up and disperse.

In an open space along the wall farther down, cars are parked, ancient Peugeots brought down from France. Some are already packed tight with passengers about to leave. Others wait for a full load. This is the transportation network. Men stand beside the cars and scream out the names of Tunisian cities. They are in a hurry to get your attention. They want to fill each car as quickly as possible. The sooner a car fills, the sooner it leaves.

"Where are you going?"

"Kairouan."

"Farther down, farther down."

There is another little station.

"Is this car going to Kairouan?"

"No, to Sfax."

"Which one goes to Kairouan?"

"Come. I'll show you."

The sky is a pale blue canvas bleached by the bright sun. The sand is a magic carpet of undulating gold blowing in the wind. The air is dry and hot and easy to breathe except for the smelly exhaust of diesel engines. I settle into the back of an old Peugeot, jammed tight between two older Arabs, and we sit shoulder to shoulder, hip to hip. They smell strongly of stale sweat, a fine human smell sharp and stinging, unmasked, unperfumed, unpropitiating. I breathe in shallow breaths. The odors come to me as the smells of my young nephew who, when he's been playing hard, smells like a puppy. I too can smell sweaty from hard work and play, can smell like a billy goat or an aged cheese. I probably do now, but no one is offended.

I breathe deeply now to absorb the ripe smells of the men beside me and intoxicate myself. I perspire heavily in the heat of day and in the oven of this car, and my sweat is absorbed by the cloaks and djelabahs of the men next to me. Our sweat mingles like two rivers coming together and our odors merge and I begin to feel comfortable, almost as if I belong here.

More and more the landscape changes and the scenery becomes otherworldly. More and more women hide themselves beneath their hijabs, as the Koran invites them to do, veils that hide their bosoms and their adornments. They wear heavy black dresses that drag the ground, and their feet, though invisible, are firmly in this one world, tied to these traditions.

In Kairouan and in Gafsa and in Tozeur, women are noticeable because they are not seen. They are hidden away at home, and when they come out they walk the streets in pairs or in threes, but they never walk alone. And they never talk to strange men.

"It is the custom," Akoum says. I have met him walking the streets of Kairouan and he follows me. "The Koran tells women they should dress modestly."

So from puberty onward, women cover themselves.

"The veil," he says, "is a sign that these women are old enough to marry. Women wear the veil as a badge of honor."

The walls of Kairouan are very old, cracking in places and crumbling down. Slowly they are surrendering to the desert winds. Akoum and I sit in the narrow strip of shade made by one of the wall's buttresses and we watch the women walk arm in arm and the traffic chase children across the road.

Inside the medina, the passageways are narrow. I poke my head into shops, peep into windows and doors, stand on tiptoes to look over walls. In the golden light of the noonday sun, a young woman holds her little child in a plastic bucket and bathes him. She pours water from a coffee can onto the child and lathers him head to toe. The child squirms to be free, arms flailing, his body wriggling like a captured toad. He stops shaking when she rinses away the soap. He giggles and throws his wetness, his happiness, his whole body at his mother. She catches him. She snuggles her giggling baby in her arms, rocking him gently.

Around to the right, the steps wind down under an archway. In a dimly lighted shop a man is weaving rugs. A small window and the open door are the only light, but the man doesn't need to see. His hands work from memory. His loom is old and wooden, with so many strings attached it looks like a harp.

Finished rugs and blankets are stacked high in the back of the shop. Big coils of wool yarn in several shades are piled in a corner. The wool is colorful and soft and fine to the touch.

Some of the weavers in other shops make table coverings. Others make garments. Metalsmiths hammer on bronze and brass and carve intricate and ancient designs. Each man working is carrying on the traditions and habits of his father, and of *his* father before him.

Outside the shops younger men stand around in small

groups doing nothing. They are engaged in a newer tradition. One of them asks for money. Another asks me to give him the watch hanging from my belt.

Deeper inside the medina, an army of children follows foreigners here and there. They hold out their tiny hands or little wooden bowls or empty coffee cans, anything they think a few coins might be dropped into. One boy holds out a plastic cup, another just his dirty hand. Akoum shoos them away.

"So many children," he says. "A man in Africa has many wives just so he can have many children. The more children he has, the richer he is. More children to take care of him in his old age."

Even if a son moves a thousand miles away, he cannot escape his obligations to his immediate family. All else assumes a secondary role. Tribe and community are next, as extensions of the family, and last of all, country and race.

Akoum has no work apart from odd jobs. The money he earns helps his father's family. His father has two wives and seven children.

"In my father's time," he says, "a man could have as many as four wives. As long as he treated each one exactly the same. That's a law in the Koran. But those days are gone. In Tunisia now we can have only one."

The Koran insists that "you shall never be able to do justice among women, no matter how much you desire," and Tunisian law has interpreted this requirement for equality among wives as an impossibility. Thus Tunisia prohibits polygamy.

Little by little Africa is changing.

In every town it was the same. The sun went down and the muezzin's chanting drifted across the skies. The square filled with crowds waiting to buy flat loaves of bread from vendors, and I stood apart and watched. The black chech I wore covered my face and hid my beard but did not hide my differences. To the children playing at karate in the square in Gafsa I was a giant. They asked if I was a commando, like the ones they had seen in the movies.

I was like them only in small ways. My skin was too smooth, my eyes too bright perhaps. The sun and the wind had done to others what they had not done to me. They had not carved my face or beat my shoulders round.

I decided to walk across the Sahara. Not the whole thing, of course, but enough to have some idea, to feel the heat and know the thirst that some men know. It was, in my mind, a way to get closer to them and to the land.

The next morning I got a visa for Algeria.

I left the sands of Tunisia and entered no-man's-land, the stretch of territory between the Tunisian border station and the Algerian one.

"Why don't you wait?" the customs man had said. "A car will soon come and you can get a ride."

But I wanted to walk. I wanted to know. One man said it was three kilometers, another said five. I smiled goodbye and started out, forcing myself not to look back. I wanted to focus only on the moment, on the sun and the sand.

The air was dry and still, but the heat moved in waves. If you reached out you could feel the heat striking your arm. My clothes were already soaked with sweat. The heat was like a rippled curtain rising from the ground in the distance. The curtain parted so that I could pass through but closed immediately behind. It was a chamber of heat enveloping, hovering as you walked through it and moving with you. It was translucent, but everything far away blurred in the shimmering heat. It was like looking through an old glass window warped and streaked with age.

Off in the distance little breezes formed swirls of dust that rose off the sand and spun like small cyclones. I held out my arms to catch the breeze. It hit the sweat on my back and the sweat evaporated quickly, cooling for a moment so brief it was hardly noticed. A few seconds later, the breeze hit again, harder this time, pelting me with fistfuls of sand and dust that got in my eyes and that stuck to the sweat already forming again on my skin. I was covered with dirt. For the next ten minutes I cleared sand from my throat.

I didn't look back. I didn't want to know how far I had come. It felt like a hundred miles. I would have been distressed if I had known it was only two or three.

Camels came to the crest of the sand hills and looked down

at me. They were relaxed and comfortable in the heat. They lay on the sand and chewed the shrubs growing there. That's all there was. As far as my eye could see, right to the densest part of the rippling heat rising, nothing but sand and shrubs and camels ranging along the horizon.

In ditches near the edge of the road, cars had been abandoned. Only the shells remained. The rest had been stripped clean of any useful parts. But none of the cars were rusted or corroded, merely dead. In the dry desert heat, nothing rots.

Farther on, lying in the road, was a camel carcass, struck by a car or dead of old age or disease. In the distance it was a full silhouette, but up close it was like the abandoned cars, just a shell, bits of fur and bones and mangled carrion, most of the flesh eaten away by scavenger birds and flies.

The road went round a bend and vanished in the distance, in the haze and in the heat. The sun beat down like a blacksmith's hammer, and my head was his anvil. The winds were his bellows. I covered my head and face with the black chech and crossed into Algeria at Bou Aroua.

A border station and a few scattered buildings, Bou Aroua sat barren on the sand like an old ghost town. A small group of children came into view. They were lifelessly passing a soccer ball around. They stopped to watch a stranger pass by. Apart from the children, not a soul stirred. It was midafternoon. The heat was thickest. And it was Ramadan. Men were debilitated by hunger and heat combined. Life remained still until evening.

But suddenly two old men appeared from the back side of a sand dune and came down to me. They had come straight out of the Bible. One man wore a simple cloth draped over his shoulder and wrapped around his waist. His legs were spindly and he was very old and very thin, his skin very dark and leathery from the sun. The other man wore a dirty djelabah that had once been white. On his head he wore a white chech wrapped loosely. He was even older. They both carried the long wooden staffs of shepherds.

"*Al-salaam alaikoum,*" I said. "Peace be with you."

"*Labass,*" came their raspy replies. "How are you?"

"Grateful to God that I am alive. *Alhamdu l-illah.*"

We shook hands and touched our hearts. Their fingers were bony and craggy like claws, the skin calloused and rough. Their eyes glinted smiles for a stranger, and they machine-gunned me with rapid-fire Arabic until I threw up my hands to beg for mercy and stop them. I didn't know what they were saying.

In French I told them I didn't know Arabic, but they didn't understand me. I asked if they spoke French. They didn't understand the question. They just looked at me and I at them and we lingered like that for a moment, frozen awkwardly, not knowing what to say or do. They wanted to extend to me some hospitality perhaps, and I would like to have accepted, but it was no use. We found no place where our worlds intersected. I gave a gentle wave and moved on down the road. They watched me walk away. When I turned after a short while, they had gone on too, taking soft old-man strides across the sand and through the heat and thinking nothing of it.

The sun was tipping the tops of the tallest dunes by then and hung flat against the pale sky. The wind picked up. More swirls of dust and sand formed in the distance and swept down from the dunes. The soft light of the setting sun diffused and got lost in the clouds of dust. It was the season of the wind, *les vents de sable*, sandstorms hurtling across the Sahara. The road undulated over the hills and disappeared beneath the drifting sand. The sand stung my eyes. I wandered as long as I could, until I could no longer see, and then I sat to rest, lying on the soft, warm sand until a car stopped and offered me a ride to El Oued.

The night air was cooler than the day's. Dimly lighted streets that had been deserted now crawled with activity. A man stepped into the shadows across the street and called to me. I crossed over. With sinister voice he asked if I knew the hour. It was only a formality.

"Would you like to change some money?"

I had been warned about illegally changing money on the black market, and of the consequences if caught. I was a little nervous. This man might have been an informant, he might have been a thief. I looked cautiously around.

"What's the rate?" I said.

"What are you changing?" he asked. "Deutsche marks, French francs, American dollars?"

We haggled for price, three times as good as rates at the bank.

His dark hair glimmered in the faint light coming from down the street. His white pants too. He wore an expensive watch.

I took the bank notes he gave me and examined them against the notes I already had. He made the loudest noise of the night. He laughed.

"Nobody," he explained, "would take the trouble to counterfeit the Algerian dinar. It's not worth the paper it's printed on. Nobody wants it. You can't leave the country with it, and even if you could, foreign banks won't exchange it. It is why the black market exists."

Changing money on the black market, he said, was the only way for many Algerians to get enough hard currency to travel abroad. It also enabled Algerians to buy goods that were not available in Algeria.

"The dinar is worthless," he said. "Algeria can import nothing."

So when he traveled to France, he took with him the hard currencies he had gained from the black market and he spent the notes on televisions and radios and clothes. When he returned to Algeria, he sold them all at enormous profit, enough profit that he could pay black-market rates for francs and marks and dollars, enough profit to allow him to travel and buy more goods to sell at home, enough profit to add to the account he kept at a bank in Paris. One day he planned to leave Algeria for good. For now, he was straddling the two worlds.

And so was I.

The young man who drove me to Ghardaïa told me he was planning to marry. He had picked out his wife-to-be, decided on her by the way she looked. He did not know her at all, had never even met her, but their families had gotten together and worked out the details. They would marry soon. At the end of the month he would be nineteen.

He was a taxi driver and his entire life was the road between El Oued and Ghardaïa. He drove one way each day, and if there were enough people coming back he would return the same day. Otherwise he stayed the night in Ghardaïa, most often sleeping in the taxi. He said he would probably drive this taxi for the rest of his life, or at least as long as the car held together. His older brother drove a taxi. His younger brother one day would drive one too.

"It's a good work," he said without conviction. He leaned back against the car. His arms were folded across his chest and his lips were squeezed tight in a straight line across his face. He looked out over the barren landscape, his eyes fixed, never moving, never blinking, staring at the horizon until it blurred and his eyes watered. He looked suddenly much younger.

"Well, let's go," he said.

As we drove, an intense wind swept sideways across the Sahara. The sand blew through the open car windows and got into our eyes and into our teeth. The great dunes of the desert shifted in the wind and shrank, forming new dunes in the distance and uncovering foundations of discarded glass and plastic, everything well preserved. Automobiles were not the only things that did not rust or rot. The desert had long been a depository for the garbage of El Oued and Touggourt and Ouargla, other cities and towns too, and in the dry desert air, mountains of bottles and cans, shells of old autos, plastic containers, all baked in the sun. They shifted with the sands in a continuing cycle of burial and baring and burial again, treasured layers of trash for future archaeologists to discover and sift through and ponder.

A dry riverbed ran through the deep ravine that divided Ghardaïa. Only a tiny bit of water remained until the next rains. The water lay in stagnant pools brown as cesspools. Where the river had dried completely, trash was piled high. Men sat on the wall overlooking the riverbed and threw refuse into the expanse below.

Above, Ghardaïa rises high in tiers and terraces that climb toward the mosque in the center, its minaret like a candle on an orange and brown cake made of sand.

On the other side of the riverbed, El Ateuf and Melika add to the jumble leaning against the sky. Five cities are grouped here, each one holier and more devout than the next. The riverbed Oued Mzab slices through the ravine and lends its name to the local tribes.

The Mzabites in Ghardaïa are very pious and very traditional. Mzabite women are so devout, so ancient in their ways, that they cover themselves completely, the older ones exposing only one eye to the outside world. When they look around, they cock their heads awkwardly like birds searching for worms, one eerie eye at a time.

I sit on the dusty curb outside a shop and watch them. The shop belongs to Abdallah. He is the friend of Omar in Paris. Following a loose design, I have come here to meet him, to bring greetings from Omar, but Abdallah is not in the shop. So I sit and I wait and I watch.

The unmarried young Mzabite women wear white lacy veils that mask their faces from nose to chin, but they do not hide their eyes. It is in the eyes that mystery and allure come together to work the magic of attraction. To gaze upon them is to see enough; to know them is to want to know more. They are windows into the soul.

But older women walk the streets with nothing exposed. Their hijabs are draped loosely over their heads and held with one hand from the inside, closing them off to the world. No man but the woman's husband is allowed to see more than one eye.

Tradition has it that a veiled woman ceases to be a sex object. She is not defined by the clothes she puts on or how she wears her hair. The veil removes sexuality from normal interaction and is liberating.

But how liberating can it be when a woman is forced to stumble along with one arm carrying the groceries or a baby, the other hand holding the veil closed? How can she even open a door? She is so bound up that even to look off to the side she must turn her entire head and peer.

But the veil is part of an ancient way of life, tied to tradition, tied to religion. It will be a long long time before women are rid of them completely—if ever.

The Mzabites are a profoundly devout Muslim race, but they are not Arabs. They have intermarried with slaves from Sudan and their skin is dark. They speak Berber and keep to themselves. Although they are Shiite Muslims, they venerate a woman saint, Daia, who lived in the caves around which these towns were built. Their rites and rituals are very different and very secret. Arabs are not allowed in Mzabite mosques, and Jews who live here are not even allowed in Mzabite parts of town. In the holy city of Beni-Isguen, no one is allowed to enter without a Mzabite guide.

▲

Abdallah invited me home to dinner, but he did not introduce me to his wife. She stayed in the kitchen, cooking for us. She ate her dinner apart from us, and stayed isolated. None of Abdallah's friends had met his wife. None who came to his house ever got to see her. It was nothing personal.

Abdallah had a daughter and a son. She was seven. The boy was four. The daughter brought our meals to us. She was already being groomed. The son was also being trained in ancient customs. He did nothing.

Abdallah and his family lived in a beautiful compound with lemon trees giving shade to a sandy yard. Date palms reached straight up to the sky and bent just the tiniest at the very top. Their broad leaves cast shadows in the evening's glow.

That first evening we sat in the courtyard and swatted mosquitoes while we ate. The next time we ate in the house.

We started with dates, of course, and drank milk. Abdallah's wife sent us briques and salad and lamb in a stew. We drank lemonade. We listened to music. Later we went back to his shop. He kept it open late into the evening. There was not much else to do in the evenings.

In his shop Abdallah sold clothes—nothing traditional, everything stylish and European. Most of his customers were young girls. Most were Arab girls, not as traditional as the Mzabite women.

One day Abdallah introduced me to Houria, his friend and business associate. She made some of the clothes Abdallah sold in the shop and said she was not a traditional Arab woman.

"I hate Arab men," she said. "I do not like the way they regard women or how they treat us. I will never marry an Algerian."

She worked in what appeared to be a garage near the end of town. She was short and very, very thin. Her legs were like twigs. Her face was stern, framed by black curly hair that made her seem severe. Her hair was very short and wiry. She wore dark glasses in the daytime, which added to her rough appearance.

We had caught up with her at a very busy time. She tried to be polite, but her frown made clear her annoyance. Abdallah had a few words with her privately.

"Tonight," he came back to say, "you will have dinner with Houria and her brother."

"I will?" I asked, looking at Houria.

Houria pursed her lips and agreed.

Her family owned a restaurant. Because it was Ramadan and there was no business, the restaurant was closed. The family was vacationing in France. Only Houria and her brother Hassan stayed behind. Hassan drove a dump truck at a construction site for a living.

That evening I sat with Houria and Hassan and an elderly Belgian gentleman, Monsieur Ledoux, who had lived in Algeria for thirty years. He had no personality and sat quietly sipping beer and eating with us. Hassan watched videos on the television.

Houria served us but did not eat. She claimed to be an untraditional Arab woman, and yet she filled this traditional role.

She told me her name meant "freedom." Naturally I thought she was making reference to her aversion to tradition. But in an oblique way she was explaining why her legs were so thin.

I had asked her if she was so skinny because she didn't eat, or if she didn't eat because she was so skinny. She didn't find my joking amusing.

Later in the evening Houria and I went walking through the palmery. We got lost in the moonlight and in the night air, which was amazingly cool. She told me her parents had named her Houria because she was born the year Algeria won its independence from France.

The year she was born, Algeria and France were locked in the bloodiest part of the war for that independence. Although Charles de Gaulle and France were seeking negotiations with Algeria to end the war, a group of French army generals had formed the Organisation de l'Armée Secrète (OAS), which committed itself to keeping Algeria French. They attempted a coup. It failed. They changed their tactics to a campaign of terror in major Algerian cities and in Paris. There were assassinations and bombings continuing even beyond March 1962, when France and Algeria signed an agreement granting Algeria its full independence. OAS terror continued, but ultimately failed.

In the end, the OAS spitefully resorted to a scorched-earth policy, burning everything they possibly could, destroying crops, and killing over twelve thousand people. Food was scarce. Houria's mother was malnourished when the baby was born. And as a young child Houria had very little to eat.

"That is why I am so thin," she told me.

Paraphrasing Philippe Berthelot: when twelve thousand people suffer, it is a statistic; when one suffers, I suffer.

"I didn't before," I said to Houria, "but now I think I hate the French."

She took my hand and held it.

That night we drove across the desert to Metlili.

The desert at night was more a feeling than a sight. Even in bright moonlight only the craggy shapes and shadowy outlines of dunes and cliffs and palm groves appeared. The sand shifted in feathery drifts across the path of our headlights. The wind pushed hard against us. The tires on the pickup truck were bald, the rubber rotted and full of holes. We slid sideways. The road was as bad as the tires. I would not have been suprised if we had run out of gas. We drove slowly and Houria giggled like a little girl. It seemed almost as if she hadn't laughed like this in a long time.

The laughter continued next day when she took me to the holy city of Beni-Isguen. She wore a yellow ribbon in her hair, tied to a tiny stub of a braid that stuck out like the tail of a wirehaired terrier. The giggles from the previous night were with us still.

Our guide to Beni-Isguen was as ancient as the city walls. He looked like one of the survivors from Noah's ark. He had a long gray beard and carried a staff to keep from toppling over. You could see what a proud man he was. Pride burned in his eyes, and he stood as tall as old age and arthritis allowed. He was bent nearly double.

He took the sacredness of the city seriously. He had once guided the president of Algeria and his entourage through the winding streets of Beni-Isguen, and he proved it by showing us a photo of himself and the president standing side by side. Six times he showed it. Each time he forgot and showed it again. Each time he said, *"C'est le président. C'est moi à son côté—* That's the president, and me beside him."

After the third time Houria couldn't control her giggles. The old man looked at us sternly. No giggling was allowed in the sacred city.

He showed us an ancient well and described for us how the water was once brought up by a pulley. The French word for pulley *(poulie)* sounds a lot like the French word for chicken *(poulet)*. I turned to Houria and asked, "Did he say the water was brought up by a chicken?" I flapped my arms like a bird so she would know which word I had meant.

The old man turned and scowled at Houria, who was laughing wildly. She held her hand over her mouth and her little body shook. She tried hard to stifle her giggles, but it was no use.

We wound our way up the narrow alleyways to the top of the city. The old man was winded by the time we reached the top, so he stopped to have a cigarette. Houria found this funny. She seemed to find everything funny.

Little children emerged from doorways along the twisted, rutted passageways to look at us. A little girl, unprovoked, her head barely higher than my knee, reached up and shook our hands. Her eyes were bright and round, her hair black and silky. She shook our hands and began to walk away without a word. We stopped laughing then, Houria and I. Houria smiled and spoke to the child in Arabic, asking why she had stopped to shake hands with us. All the other children had run away and hid. And I was simply dumbstruck. It was one of those magical moments that somehow bring together bitterness and joy. It was like sitting alone in a quiet place, listening to the sounds all around as the sun goes down, and watching the evening come. The moment seems to last forever and then quite suddenly vanishes away.

I regretted the moment when I would have to leave Ghar-daïa and my new friends Houria and Abdallah. I already had lingered much longer than I had planned and wondered in what ways the journey would be different now, what disaster had been averted, what marvel missed by a day or two. Such is the mystery of traveling, the arbitrary possibilities of life.

Houria came to see me off when the moment of departure eventually came. She gave me a book about Mzabite women and said goodbye. She kissed the palm of her hand and placed it gently against my cheek. That was as great a display of affection as she was allowed. I pressed my fingertips to my lips and held out my hand to her. Then I walked back into the desert.

On my way out of town, a man stopped me. He wasn't very old, but his round face was weathered. There were a few grays in the thin mustache he wore and a deep scar from the edge of his mustache almost to his right eye. He wore a striped djelabah that was dirty and stained with dried blood. It ballooned around his middle and hid his belly, which was round and fat. He wanted to buy my shoes, but I wasn't selling.

"They are such good shoes," he said. "Strong and sturdy. They will last a long time."

I told him no. I told him they were the only shoes I had brought.

"If I can't have the shoes," he said, "how about the pants or the shirt? Anything?"

"If I sold you my clothes," I said, "I would have nothing to wear."

"Yes," he said. "But you can always get more." He tugged at his own trousers. "Look at these pants," he said. "They are nothing. But your clothes are quality. They will last two life-times. The clothes we buy are thin and weak. We are forced to buy what nobody really wants. Don't you have anything extra you can sell?"

I thought hard. I wished I had something to give him, but I was traveling light. I hadn't packed anything inessential.

"I'm sorry," I said. "I can't help you."

"I'm sorry too," he said. "You Americans, you have every-thing." His eyes filled with wonder and then squinted with dissatisfaction. I could not tell where the dissatisfaction lay, with me or with himself and the two places we represented.

"You have everything," he said, "but you share nothing."

"Perhaps that is why we have so much," I said. I was half joking when I said it, but only just.

Desert days are hotter than hell ought ever be; the nights are frigid. I slept the night huddled with three men in the back of an old Peugeot and woke up stiff and disoriented in the red-sand city of Timimoun. The comfort of Ghardaïa had set in and made me soft. The company of new friends brought on a melancholy that made the cold seem colder and the heat a thousand times hotter. A little wind seemed like a sandstorm and a few hours crossing the desert on foot seemed like eternity.

I could have continued south across the *balises solaires*, thirteen hundred kilometers of tracks in the sand to the border with Mali, and then who knows what down to Gao and the river Niger, or I could have made my way east toward In Salah and down through Tamanrasset and down to Agadez in Niger. But I had had enough of the sun beating on my neck and the wind throwing sand in my eyes and in my teeth.

Traveling with no itinerary, no plan, you take life as it comes, moment by moment. Every joy, every sorrow, every surprise. You go where the wind blows.

It was Friday, the Islamic Sabbath. Nothing moved except the sand blowing in the desert wind. I stood at the side of the road and played melancholy songs on my harmonica. When no cars would stop, I walked. Finally, a little pickup truck stopped and I climbed in the back. The driver and his wife were not going all the way to Adrar, 150 kilometers away, but I bounced along with them until they turned off onto a *piste*, an animal trail, and disappeared into the desert. I hiked the rest of the way.

I arrived in Adrar dead hungry and wanted to eat. I would have ignored Ramadan, but there was no place open. The best I could do was find a hotel and wash away the sand on my face. I slept until morning.

But there were no rides going anywhere that next day either.

And then the desert caprices offered me a small marvel. That next day there was a flight to Béchar, and I decided to be on it.

My friend Brian tells a story of how he and another friend were driving across the United States when their car broke down. Neither of them could fix it, and some wizened old man came along and chewed their ears. He compared nowadays to the good old days, the dust bowl days when drought-driven Okies packed up entire families and loaded them onto old crates of cars and trucks and headed west to find a new and better life.

And the old man said, "Grit. That's what we had in them days. Grit. And you young fellows today ain't got it."

And Brian replied, "Yeah, well, they had grit, all right, but we've got something they didn't have."

The old man challenged him. "Oh yeah? What?"

Brian reached for his wallet. "Plastic," he said, pulling out his credit cards.

And when plastic doesn't work, cash will do. I went to buy a plane ticket.

The Air Algeria office was noisy. The heat was thick. The sour smell of old sweat was like a wall. I could have waited one more day or I could have tried to hitchhike, anything rather than drown in that crowd of pushing and sweating madness. But I heard myself say, "Why can't they form a decent line, everybody wait his turn?" and the choice was made for me. I shoved into the crowd of only men and into another world. It was, after all, why I had come: to be with them in this other world. I cast aside my dignity and my gentility and became one of them.

My elbows are pointy and sharp, my hips and shoulders are broad. I am thin enough to wriggle, but wide enough to fill the spaces I occupy. I squeezed between people and spread myself to take up space enough for two. The men behind leaned on me; I leaned on the ones in front. As one man was dealt with and squeezed out, a space opened up and was quickly filled. Before anyone could beat me, I forcefully shoved my way into any space that opened in front of me. I shoved and shouted with the best of them, for it was a different world with different rules and a different order, and I was one of them.

When I finally got to the front of the pack, the ticket agent got up and left. His departure signaled a respite from the shoving. The crowd all at once relaxed. They chatted noisily and in friendly fashion with one another and nobody left the room. When the ticket agent returned, so did the tension and the shouting for attention. So did all the pushing.

I leaned on the desk. Someone leaned on me. Six arms reached around and in front of me and waved in my face like a squid out of control. Each hand held some kind of identity card. You could not buy a ticket without one. I wriggled an arm free and pulled out my passport and threw it on the desk in front of the ticket agent. I nearly hit him with it. And as the other men had been shouting their destinations at him, so did I.

He took my passport and he sat back flipping through the pages, looking at the photo and the visas and all the entry and exit stamps. He smiled his first smile of the day.

"Béchar?" he said.

"Yes, please. One way." I paid the man.

And just as he had done with each ticket sold, he brought out a rubber stamp and pounded on everything. He stamped the ink pad, then the ticket, then the ink pad and my currency form, then the ink and some other form, and he did it with speed and vigor and a bit of a flourish. His smile left him then. He had finished. He handed me the ticket. He put his head in his hand and rubbed his forehead.

I shoved backward and out through the crowd and let out a wild whoop. I had been inside for over two hours. I was absolutely drenched with sweat, tired of the Sahara, tired of the heat and the endless sand and ready to fly to Morocco, to Casablanca maybe, ready to check into a four-star hotel where I could order dates and tropical drinks sent to me, and where I could lounge like a lizard in the sun beside the pool.

But the flight was only going to Béchar.

From Béchar to Beni-Ounif. Deserted streets and a dry wind blowing. Dust and sand settling around my feet, darkness coming. A noisy room full of soldiers, every one of them waiting for the horn to go off. The muezzin chants, and the imam leads prayers on the television. Every soldier in the room, officer and enlisted man, grows quiet and silently mouths the evening prayers. And then the meager Ramadan meal. Dates, a glass of milk, a weak soup. Chicken and rice and a small salad.

And not a woman to be seen anywhere. They eat, as always, apart from the men.

A ride into the darkness with a very old man who cannot see the road or the potholes sprinkled all over it. Half the time he drives on the wrong side of the road. Now he drives at normal speed. Now he slows to a crawl. The sky is black and without clouds, ablaze with stars. In the distance, the gauzy glow of

Beni-Ounif. A small town, a lighted square, a few buildings scattered about, a scummy hotel. More roaches than guests.

In the early-morning haze, mountains rising like ghosts shimmer in the soft light.

The road runs ramrod straight to the horizon, light-colored asphalt gleaming in the morning sun and splitting the landscape. Morocco rises to the Atlas Mountains in the distance, close enough to reach out and touch but hours away. The earth is no longer the soft sand of the Sahara, no longer fine enough to have been ground in the mill of a thousand-year windstorm; it's more agreeable than desert, less barren, less hostile. There are rocks and scrub grass. Camels graze unattended and unmolested. Far off, a boy shepherds a flock of goats. An old man rides a donkey through the valley. The sun rises higher and hotter. The mountains get no closer and seem to recede. The road hums hypnotically. All the way from Figuig to Bouârfa, from Bouârfa to Oujda, and from Oujda to Casablanca, where I would sip those tropical drinks and lounge like that lizard in the sun. Two days later I would be in Meknès, being outfitted and saddled up for a trek in the Rif Mountains.

The wind blows and it is the breath of the unmoved mover. We find ourselves in strange places, doing strange things and we know not why, strange things that seem insignificant at the time and yet prepare us for who we one day will be. French classes in high school. Horseback-riding lessons in childhood. I thought I just wanted to be a cowboy and equitation was as close as I could get. Who would have guessed that many years hence these things would have prepared me for such encounters with strangers?

To paraphrase Harry James Cargas, we each have a certain destiny and the real adventure in life is to discover it; to discover how we may fully develop into who we are.

Suddenly I was part of a group of German and American tourists with whom I had much in common. I found myself realizing that something as subtle as culture could mean infinitely more than something as overt and obvious as the color of my skin.

▲

I was given a horse named Bouârfa, a gray, mixed-blooded Arabian-Berber stallion. The others in the group all sounded like horse-riding experts. They talked about the horses they owned and the exotic places they had been to on riding tours, and all said they wanted spirited horses. But I hadn't been on a horse in ages. When they asked me what kind of horse I preferred, I said: "I want a horse that's old and slow and blind in one eye and particularly stupid." Bouârfa was big and old but he was very strong. I couldn't tell yet if he was stupid.

We would set out on the following day.

While the others toured the medina in Meknès, I took the five-hour bus ride back to the airport in Casablanca to pick up a package of film that had been shipped to me. Because of the heat I hadn't wanted to carry much film with me. Now I wished I had.

TWA had carried the package as far as Paris; Royal Air Morocco brought it to Casablanca. TWA, when I asked, said the package would arrive in three days.

It was a four-hour ride from Meknès back to Casablanca, and another hour to the airport, but when I got to the airport and talked to a man at the Air Morocco desk, he told me I would have to go to the freight terminal.

"Where's that?"

"Three kilometers from here. Take a taxi."

But the taxis wanted to charge me twenty dollars.

"To go three kilometers?"

No one would take me for less. It was a conspiracy. I would walk.

"Go ahead," one driver jeered. "It's closed anyway."

The guy inside hadn't said anything about its being closed. I took a deep breath and went back inside. I could feel the frustration coming on.

I had been afraid I might arrive during lunch. For two hours in midafternoon, sometimes three, everything shuts down—shops, offices, everything. I didn't want to wait that long, so I went back to the Air Morocco counter and explained my predicament, hoping something could be done. I spoke to a woman this time.

"And now I'm told the freight terminal is closed."

"Yes, they're closed."

"What time will they open?"

"They won't open again today."

"What do you mean they won't open again today?"

"I mean they're closed for the day," the woman said. "This is Ramadan."

"I know this is Ramadan. I'm starving to death." The frustration was rising in my voice and I could feel it taking over the rest of my body. My voice was cracking and I was on the edge of shouting. I frowned and squinted my eyes. My vision blurred.

"But what does Ramadan have to do with the airport?" I grumbled.

"During Ramadan, many offices close during the afternoon and do not reopen. The freight offices, for example." She was as calm as could be.

"That's crazy. This is an airport," I shouted. "Airports don't close in the afternoon."

"They do here, sir."

"Then why aren't you closed? Don't you do Ramadan?"

"I'm sorry, sir," she said quietly.

I was going crazy—doubly so, because she was so calm.

"Sorry?" I shouted. "I've come five hours in a bus from Meknès for nothing. And now I have to go all the way back and then do this whole thing all over again. I talked to some idiot on the phone this morning. Why didn't he tell me I had to get here at a certain hour? This place is crazy."

And with that I lifted my arms over my head and pounded my two fists as hard as I could onto the counter. I stifled a harsh scream that growled in my throat and frightened the woman behind the counter. She cowered. I picked up my book and my newspaper and stomped out.

In Casablanca I tried to phone home, but the phones were all *en dérangement* for the afternoon—not working. Totally frustrated, I went and sat at the bar in the Hilton Hotel and sipped Coca-Cola.

At a table nearby, a small group of tourists were making themselves conspicuous in the usual American ways.

I hate tourists for the same reason I hate Coca-Cola. They make every corner of the world a little more American. All over Mexico and Central America you see the too-familiar red and white: *BEBE COCA-COLA*. A little bit of home to refresh body and spirit no matter where you go.

It's a hot day and you've been pushing and shoving through crowds all morning trying to buy a bus ticket. The sun has been beating on your head and you wonder why you ever left home.

Of course, you really didn't. There is always the familiar taste of Coke. It tastes like home. It reminds you how things ought to be, that there are places where lines form in orderly fashion and your turn will come.

Coca-Cola is as soothing as the sudden sound of English in a faraway place. You haven't heard it in months, not honest-to-goodness English unfiltered through translation, the kind where you not only understand the words but the nuances as well, the pauses, the lifting of an eyebrow.

But then here come Mabel and her retired husband looking for a McDonald's. They're wondering why there's no central air-conditioning anywhere, why it takes so long to put a call through, why these stupid people can't figure out how to stand in line.

You want to laugh at them. You want to ridicule them. Mostly you want to avoid them. After all, you're a traveler, not a tourist.

Then someone shouts, "Why can't you people do things the right way," and you realize: They are you. Their complaints are your complaints.

Just that morning you were pushing and shoving in a crowd and complaining to yourself because there was no orderly line. Twenty minutes ago you were wondering why AT&T can't come over here and wire this place, why they can't sell them phones that work.

Their complaints really are your complaints. You want to remove yourself from these people, call yourself a traveler, but you can't. You and they are one. You and Coca-Cola are one. You leave a little of yourselves behind in the places you visit, but mostly what you do is take. You steal away the identities and the cultures of these places and leave behind your own. No matter how lightly you tread, no matter how unobtrusive your passing, you have been noticed and your footprints are wide and deep.

Your clothes are not like their clothes, your face not so beaten by the years as their faces, your back and your bones not murdered by malnutrition. They see you and they want to be like you. You drink Coca-Cola; they want to drink Coca-Cola.

Maybe one day we will all be the same, all eating at Mc-Donald's, all drinking Coca-Cola in our air-conditioned cars, all wearing Levi's. Maybe then too we will see the beginning of the end of starvation and malnutrition, war and racism. When Coca-Cola has a plant in every country, when trillions and trillions of dollars are invested and at risk, perhaps there will be a greater interest in peace and stability. After all, it makes no sense to manufacture if people can't buy what you make. Jobs, money, market.

Who knows?

In the meantime, maybe we need to tread a little more softly.

I was sorry I had gone crazy at the airport.

We rode out of Meknès early, eleven tourists and two guides, thirteen riders and their restless horses stretched out single file, metal horseshoes clopping and slipping on the pavement, stopping traffic, being stared at, not because of the horses in the street but because of the number and colors of the riders.

We were arrayed as if at a dinner party—boy, girl, boy, girl; not by the sex of the riders but by the sex of the horses. If they get side by side, two stallions have a tendency to shout and bite and kick, but somehow they stay calm when separated by mares.

To those stopped in the street and staring, we must have seemed an odd collection of riding habits and hats, blue jeans and jodhpurs and one riding helmet; six women, five men; six Germans, five Americans; three doctors. Our guides were Driss, a Moroccan, and Renate, his Swiss wife. They took turns leading us over the mountains.

We rode at a slow walk until the road and the town were left far behind us. The trail climbed so gradually that the incline was barely noticeable. A horse will stretch head and neck when he is working hard at a walk uphill, but there was no sign of effort. Horse and rider were simply getting used to one another. And the rider was getting used to the romance of riding in another world. This was no pony trek in Ireland, nor even mule riding down a mountain trail into the Grand Canyon. It certainly was not riding in a ring or cantering along a peaceful trail in England or Germany. This was a ride across time and culture.

From front to back, hands went up like dominoes in reverse, a signal to get ready to run.

Off to the left and far away down the hill, Meknès jumbled in the haze like some child's collection of dusty blocks piled high and precariously. Narrow and flat at the bottom like the base of a mountain, the walled city rose in tiers to a broad peak. Ancient cities were built as fortresses behind walls for protection. The higher the city, the easier to defend against invaders.

We rode away from Meknès like a band of warriors out on a raid, breaking suddenly into a trot.

That was the sequence of the ride: a gentle walk to relax the horses, a trot to stretch them out, another walk for them to catch breath. Then those domino hands went up again, and we flew. Three, five, even ten minutes at a gallop. It felt like an hour.

Bouârfa was old. He stumbled often when he walked and several times nearly fell. But he trotted well and he galloped like a dream. He was old and he was gentle, but he was very strong. I had to struggle to hold him back, to keep him from charging to the front of the pack and gone. When he ran, he galloped as if the heart of a young stallion had taken over his body. The old part of him remembered. The heart only forgets what it is good to forget and remembers the rest. Bouârfa forgot that he was old.

There is a surge of joy a rider feels on a galloping horse. The joy comes up from the soul of the animal and into the rider. Horse and rider fuse into one, sharing a sense of joy, the exhilaration of freedom. You can feel his heavy muscles tense and relax with every stride. The horse's hair and your own bristle in the rushing wind. Eyes widen. Skin lathers with sweat. Chests heave. Hearts pound. When the gallop ends, both horse and rider pant for breath.

Little by little our group coalesced. Perhaps it was the beer at lunch or the wine at dinner. Perhaps it was the simple sharing of that first gallop. Common sentiments, common experience, common understandings. We relaxed with each other.

After the first day's ride, my butt was sore. My joints ached. My left knee was bruised and tender. My stirrups were as long as they could go and still they were too short. My knee rubbed badly against my saddle.

Liz, a doctor, supplied gauze pads and tape. Pam volunteered a sock to the cause. She cut off the toe and slipped the cotton tube over my knee for extra padding. We shared jokes and stories and wine. It was as though for this brief moment in time, in a group of strangers, we had found friends.

The black chech around my head flowed out like a mane when we galloped. When I rode at the rear of the column, dust and sand flew in my eyes. I wrapped the chech around my face. I was a Berber nomad.

When we rode into villages, you could hear the people guessing what they thought I might be. Algerian? Malian? Mauritanian? Senegalese?

For the moment it was a pleasure for them not to know.

Because of his beard, Mat was called Ali Baba when we entered a village. To the villagers we were otherworldly and mysterious, as exotic to them as they to us. We felt like gods.

The children begged us for *cadeaux*, for gifts—for pens, for money. The ugliest face of tourism is the way it touches people with envy and turns them into beggars. Too many foreigners bring along candy or drop coins behind them, rewarding the children for their begging, getting them used to it.

The children appeared at every corner of the dusty villages we passed through. They ran alongside the horses. They would follow us right to the edge of the village and sometimes a bit beyond. I turned to Mat.

"Why aren't these kids in school?" I said.

But there were signs of pride in other places. The villages were no more than dust, mud huts blending in with the rocks and crags on the sides of hills. Old people sat and watched us pass. From time to time they waved, but only if we waved first. They were fiercely proud and independent. You could see the stern dignity in their dark Berber faces.

The children had not yet learned pride. They ran behind us barefoot, or else they wore the shreds of old shoes, handed down and oversized, or plastic shoes that had fallen apart and flapped noisily on their feet. They ran across sand and sharp rocks but they never flinched.

I turned to Mat again.

"Don't you wish you could buy them all shoes?" I said.

"And food," he said.

Toward the end of the trip the kids in some of the villages took to throwing rocks at us, calling us names, chasing us out.

A strange relationship exists between giver and taker, an element of resentment that links the need and shame of the beggar with the generosity and superiority of the donor.

Do beggars resent it more when you give to them or when you ignore them?

And how much begging can one man respond to? You can give all you have to the first wave of beggars on the streets of Tangier, and what will you have accomplished? Fed a group for a week, and then what?

We cannot ignore these poor, nor can we save them with a few coins dropped here and there. Perhaps the best we can do is know they are there and feel for them, feel *with* them, and not try to distance ourselves from their poverty.

Ramadan.

For two weeks we rode across the rugged countryside of Morocco. From Meknès to Fez and back. The Jebel Zerhoun Plain on high. The ancient ruins of Volubilis down below. The regal city Moulay Idris, white layered like a wedding cake and stuck into the side of a mountain. Through villages of dust, along streams, and across fields both amber and green of cereal grass and wheat, the terrain changing from rocky hills to champaigns and olive groves. The tall grass became wave after wave of shimmering gold blowing in the wind. Hooves pounding, hearts thundering, lost as if in some romantic dream.

And finally distracted by the odd sights: signs advertising American soft drinks, cables along the side of the road, television antennae. I remembered my first trip to Spain and how different it was from my last. The first time, oxcarts kicked up dust in the streets of Salamanca; old men shared strips of goat meat with me and poured wine into my mouth from goatskin *botas*. But the oxcarts are mostly gone now, replaced by Japanese pickups. Roads are paved, prices are high—old Spain has been cleaned up by the civilizing hand of the European Community and made new. Clean and new and just like France, just like Italy and the rest. It is hard to tell where one leaves off and the other begins. Arrogantly, I resented the changes.

I was distracted by my memories, not paying enough attention to my horse, and angry with myself for my resentment of modern intrusions, my desire for old customs and old ways of living. Who am I to decide how much progress people are allowed?

We were walking down a steep hill, over stones worn slick by Moroccan winds and rains. The horses picked their way carefully. Bouârfa, a clumsy walker anyway, paid about as much attention as I did. He slipped on the rocks and stumbled. He fell to his knees. His head fell forward. He jerked himself to the side to keep from going down. When he did, I tipped over his right shoulder and felt myself falling as if in slow motion.

I tried to grab something, but there was nothing to grab. My left foot came free from the stirrup. I tucked my shoulder and flipped. All I could see was the sky, so brilliant and so blue, surrounding me. My left foot crossed the path of my sight and vanished. All that was left was the big tableau of blue sky and white clouds drifting by.

I slammed into the ground. My back crunched into a huge rock. Bouârfa bolted. Luckily my right leg came free, and I skidded to a stop. I lay with my eyes open. I didn't want to pass out. The doctors rushed to me and told me not to move, but I wasn't very hurt. Only my back and my ego.

The afternoon ride was to make a loop and return to the spot where we had stopped for lunch. We would camp there for the night. I skipped the afternoon ride.

Liz and Gabriele skipped it also. They were both doctors and very concerned. They took turns looking at the swollen place on my back. Gabriele rubbed some kind of ointment there. I felt much better, but I don't think it was just the ointment.

We opened a bottle of wine and talked nonsense. The conversation turned serious for a moment and we argued the existence and weakness of God, the fraudulence and politics of religion. It was a quiet time and we were the last three people on earth. It was a moment that ought never to have ended, a moment that would not have happened if I hadn't fallen. We fell in love with the evening and with the stillness and with each other. The sun went down behind the back side of a nearby mountain. Faint stars glimmered in the dimming sky. The day grew tired and we three new best friends sat in the gentleness of time not moving. We watched the evening come. I hoped the others would never come back.

"This is so nice," Liz said. "I can't describe how nice."
She was right.
"It's beautiful," Gabriele said. "To sit like this and watch the evening come."
I went and wrote that down.

Sitting in the evening shade and watching the evening come. Shadows lengthen and the sky deepens in color. Horses nicker softly and growl guttural noises deep in their throats. They are hungry and tired, but easily contented with grain and fresh straw. From the top of the bluff Africa is serene and all seems right. The brotherhood of Islam pervades the night air.

I sat in the crystal air talking to Mat, one of the Americans, and he reminded me, in case I had forgotten, that all was not right in the world. He reminded me that although Islam, like Christianity, inspires men of different races and beliefs to live side by side in tolerance, men have not learned yet to do so. And in a moment as swift as the flicker of a firefly, he reminded me why I had come. This horseback-riding adventure was merely a diversion. Suddenly its purpose in my life deepened and was made clear.

Mat came of age during a time of American social awareness and upheaval. He had been on the good side in the war for civil rights. He had protested against the war in Vietnam. He was a complex man who, although he was an activist for animal rights, hated carrots and loved to eat meat.

"It isn't death I am concerned with," he said. "But with the quality of life. Inhumanity to animals is not much better than inhumanity to man. And each act somehow desensitizes mankind and spreads like a disease."

He was well informed, intelligent, and conscientious. And he knew where all roads in Africa ultimately lead. South Africa.

"Are you going there?" he asked.

"I don't know," I said. "Part of me wants to. Part of me hates the thought of spending money there and contributing even in a small way to what goes on there. And part of me is afraid of what I will find. What if I love it there?"

"Then that will say a lot about who you are," he said. "Especially if you find yourself hating the rest of Africa."

"That scares me too."

"It shouldn't. There's no law that says you should blindly love the place where your ancestors came from. And there's no law that says what black men do to one another is any better than what white men do to black men, or vice versa or any other way you want to flip it around. Mankind is greedy and selfish and tribal. Men are always looking for ways to distinguish between themselves and others. We define others so that we can define ourselves. And mark my words: when apartheid finally fails, the tribes in South Africa will start fighting among themselves. It's what happened in '47 when Mountbatten ended the raj in India. Hindus and Muslims slaughtered each other in masses. It's what happens when empires disintegrate and the hand that holds things together is taken away. People fight among themselves."

And that, he said, was why he was afraid of black majority rule in South Africa. And why I should be too. Because what black men do to other black men is no better than what white men do, and no better because it is done by blacks.

We rode until Ramadan ended.

We rode until Zonia's horse developed a limp.

We rode until Mat's horse passed out in the heat.

Pam's horse threw a shoe nearly every day.

Gabriele's horse kicked Walter in the shin.

Cathie's young horse fell in love with every donkey, mule, or horse we passed and whinnied like a wild pony, jumped, and bucked.

And I, just to outdo myself, became the first person ever to get seasick on a horse.

It must have been the antimalaria medicine upsetting my stomach. That was the excuse, anyway. I leaned over Bouârfa's shoulder and threw up a rainbow of red wine and orange marmalade.

We arrived at Fez, turned around, and did it all over again.

It had been a good and satisfying time out. It came quietly to an end. It was time for these newfound if not everlasting friends to part. We celebrated the end of our excursion and the end of Ramadan with a lamb roasted over an open fire. We spread a soft evening on a bed of quiet laughter beneath the canopy of a velvet sky sprinkled with stars. One adventure was over. It had been a nice diversion. Now it was time to get back into Africa. Time to find out if there would be common ground among men with black skin as there was among these strangers whose culture I shared. Another adventure was just beginning.

I went back to the airport at Casablanca. Ramadan was over. Surely now I could collect my package.

But the man I talked to said the package had not arrived yet.

"Of course it has," I said. "They told me it would be here in three days, and that was three weeks ago."

He flipped through a stack of order sheets.

"Are you sure that's the number they gave you?" he asked.

"Are you sure you're checking the right manifest?" I asked him.

"Come back in a couple of hours," he said.

A couple of hours! The sun was already high and very hot. I walked back to the passenger terminal, taking the shortcut through the trees and over a drainage ditch and up a high embankment.

In the terminal I ran into the woman I had yelled at before. She recognized me.

"You remember me?" I was surprised.

"You were very upset," she said. "And you were reading a book about Mzabite women. I am studying them at the moment."

Although she was working, Boutni and I talked a little while. I apologized for being so crazy.

"You were certainly crazy," she said. "But I understand. You have to understand that we do things differently here."

"Yes," I said. "I'm learning."

But I was failing miserably. In Africa such a short time and already I was pulling my hair out.

I went back to the freight terminal. They still had not found the package or any manifest to prove its existence. I sat on the apron of the loading dock and waited. Other frustrated men were waiting too.

Sweat rolled down my cheeks like tears. Salt stains from the dried sweat left gray and white blotches on my shirt. My suspenders were no longer the dark blue of a few weeks ago. They had been bleached and faded by the sun and by my sweat.

From then on the afternoon got crazier and crazier.

I jumped up and walked quickly to the counter.

"Oh yeah," the man said. "We finally found it."

But he hadn't thought to come tell me.

"Now you pay one hundred sixty-seven dirhams and we can release the package."

"It was paid for at the other end."

"This is a handling charge," he said.

I paid him. Anything to get my package.

"Okay," I said. "Where's the package?"

"Give this paper to that fellow and he will get it for you."

My package was a plainly wrapped box. I was allowed to hold it, but I couldn't take it anywhere.

A uniformed customs man opened it.

"What is all this?" he asked.

"Film."

"What kind of film?"

"Photographic film," I said. "For taking pictures."

"What kind of pictures?"

"Souvenirs. You know."

He nodded and counted the rolls. He wrote the number down on a form.

I took the sheet inside the customs office. A nasty little man sneered at me and asked the value of the film. I lied.

"Fifty dollars," I said.

He calculated.

"You have to pay taxes and duty," he said. "It comes to . . ." He did his calculations on paper. The pen was low on ink and several times he had to shake it to make it work. "It comes to six hundred forty-two dirhams."

"How much!" I yelped. "That's more than the film is worth." I was glad I had lied.

"You have to pay it," he said.

I dug in my pockets and pulled out all the money I had. It wasn't enough.

"Can I pay you in dollars?"

He scowled at me. "Are we in New York?" he asked.

I blew out a loud breath of exasperation.

"Where can I change money around here?"

"At the passenger terminal there is a bank," he said.

"I have to go all the way back there and then all the way back here?"

"I have other things to do," he said. "If you want your package, go get the money and come back. There is no other way."

I schlepped to the terminal and changed money. Then I schlepped back. When I got back to the loading dock, there were still men milling around, but the customs office had closed. I threw a fit.

"What do you mean the office is closed? That idiot just sent me back to the terminal to change money. He didn't say anything about closing." He could have at least told me. I could have taken a taxi there and back.

"What time did he leave?"

"About five minutes ago."

"Five minutes! He could have waited."

I was talking to a man in uniform. He seemed to sympathize.

"Let me see what I can do," he said.

He left me there steaming. He went to talk to a mousy-looking fellow in a white shirt and glasses. He called me over to talk.

"It might help if you explain to him."

"Didn't you already tell him?"

"It's better if you do."

I took deep breaths to calm myself. I waved the form I still had and told him the story. He nodded sympathetically but said there was nothing he could do. He pointed out a fat man in a wrinkled, ill-fitting suit. He told me to go talk to him.

The fat man told me to come back Monday.

"I won't be here on Monday," I told him. "I'm going to Mauritania."

He wasn't listening. He didn't care where I was going.

"Isn't there anything I can do?" I said.

He just said no. Emphatically. He turned away.

I could see my package sitting on the table where I had left it. They were about to swing the gate down and close off the area. I turned to the guy in the uniform.

"Come on," I pleaded. "There must be something we can do."

He only shrugged.

"I've got all this money I just changed," I said, hinting at a bribe. "Is there no way to solve this problem?"

He pointed to the little guy in glasses again. I went to talk to him once more. He was sympathetic, at least.

"Are you sure there is nothing I can do?" I asked, still hinting.

The fat man had sneaked up behind us and had overheard.

"Why are you asking this man?" he snapped. "Didn't I tell you to come back Monday?"

I snapped back. "Didn't I tell you I'm not going to be here on Monday?"

"Here," he said. "Let me have your paper."

I handed it to him. Finally, it seemed, something was going to be done.

He folded the paper and stuck it in his pocket, confiscating it as if I were some child.

"Now," he said. "Don't ask him to help you again. And don't ask anyone else. I'm keeping this paper until Monday. Come back then."

I exploded then.

"Go ahead," I shouted. "Keep the paper until Monday, you idiot. Keep it until your teeth rot and your hair falls out. Keep the package too. Maybe you can sell the film, you crook. Take the money and buy yourself a new suit."

The uniformed man came and led me away before I got myself in trouble. He walked me back to the edge of the apron. I took a deep breath and held back a sob. The frustration was unbelievable.

Overhead an airplane was taking off. I watched it disappear. I wanted to be on it.

I stepped down from the loading dock and walked back to

the terminal. I went straight to the bar and ordered three Coca-Colas. There was only Pepsi. It was just as good. They were cold and the bottles dripped condensation onto the counter. I lined them neatly in a short row and drank them down one by one. They tasted like home.

I found Boutni at the Air Morocco counter. She heard the frustration and the tears in my throat.

"Sometimes it isn't easy," she said.

Her eyes were beautiful, dark and brown. They sparkled a smile and sympathy.

"It isn't easy for us either."

I tried to forget about the film. This certainly wouldn't be my only frustration. And I knew I would try again to get film delivered. I had that to look forward to.

I looked deep into Boutni's eyes and tried to smile. It wasn't easy. I was back in Africa.

Africa frightened me. And I frightened myself as well. Would I not be able to rid myself of my American sensibilities even for the short time of this voyage? Would I break down and want to cry at every inconvenience, every time things did not go as I thought they should, every time I encountered hardship? I feared that I might not be able to take it, that I might not be up to the task of carrying through to the end. I feared what I might find at the center.

If I knew anything at all about Africa, I knew about poverty and disease. North Africa was the easy part, desert heat and frustration, but closer to home and not quite so ravaged by either pestilence or privation. Farther along malaria was waiting, green monkey disease and river blindness and poverty enough to make angels weep. How would I react to it?

The road south looked suddenly longer, the enchanted forest even more beguiling; the mystery wound tighter around and more difficult to unravel.

The face of Africa has Arab eyes, but now I feared body and soul.

Africa is as big as it is diverse, a creature with eyes still half-closed awakening into the full light of morning, not yet alert, not quite aware, slowly shaking himself awake only to find himself in a cage, wrapped up in djelabahs and business suits,

caught between the four cage walls of Coca-Cola and auton-
omy, Islam and the secular world. And at the tail of the creature, South Africa.

Africa frightened me for what I might find out about myself, and for how I might feel about this motherland.

THREE

TO THE

SHIFTING HORIZON ▶▶▶▶▶▶▶▶▶

Western Sahara
Mauritania

The sun rose over the Sahara and the desert was endless, golden, and soft in the early-morning light, miles and miles of nothing, not a town or a village or a house, just sand from here to the horizon and back. Ridges and rifts that had been carved by centuries of shifting winds were covered over by new sand hills formed since yesterday. Patterns of delicate indentations were etched into the dunes like sandpiper tracks at the shore. In the middle of this nothing, Nouakchott appeared.

Twenty years ago the town of Nouakchott sat in the middle of a grassy, fertile plain here on the edge of the Senegal River valley. The desert was far away. But the desert moves. It is alive and every year greedily gobbles up two hundred thousand new acres. The wind blows. Topsoil blows with it. The overgrazing of camel herds has ruined the land, has made the topsoil fragile and light. There is no grass left to hold it in place. The wind has blown away the soil and replaced it with the useless sand. *Nouakchott* means "the place of the winds."

Sand piles up along walls and fences, and so do the nomads.

The winds have blown them off the land. They have no herds left to follow. The grazing land has disappeared. Life is hard, and getting harder. Men's lives are held for ransom by forces beyond their control. Nouakchott is where they come when they have no place else to go.

A young boy leads an old blind man through the streets. The boy chants a little beggar's singsong and holds out a little wooden container. While the boy chants, the blind man tilts his head toward the sky, lifting his milky, blind eyes as if in prayer, beseeching the gods for a generous man to come and drop a coin or two into the bowl. The coins thud against the wood of the bowl and rattle. The blind man stands perfectly still and never sits down, never lets go of the boy's shoulder. The boy leads him around and then leads him away.

The blind man is old and walks on stiff legs without lifting his feet. His robes are deep blue and clean, and he wears a bright blue chech wrapped loosely around his head. He is one of the blue people, whose cheches and flowing robes are always some beautiful shade of blue. When he moves he is like an apparition.

His chin is dusted with the gray shadow of a stubble beard. His eyes have no pigment and thick globs of mucus hang like tears of paste in the corners of his eyes. He cannot know how beautiful his robes are, but he stands as if he does. He is regal, tall, and slender. He is proud in his blindness and in his begging, holding his head high, tilting it slightly back as if he were able to look down his sharp nose. There is no shame in his begging. He is an instrument of Allah's will, giving men a chance to be generous and letting men see their own good fortune, letting us see at close range how near to misfortune we are, how but for the grace of God we might be blind as this man is blind, victims too of elements beyond our control. Poverty and misery are not isolated here. There is no way to avoid them, no way to pretend they do not exist.

A quarter of a million people live in Nouakchott. Not very long ago there were only five thousand. The rest were blown in on winds that howled across the Sahara. They came to escape the harshness of the desert that swept into the valley like an advancing army to betray them and steal their livelihood. They can no longer support their herds. The desert has eaten away the land where their camels grazed. A way of life has come to an end.

Like other African cities, Nouakchott cannot accomodate the huge numbers of people flooding into the city. There was subsistence back in the village and on the farm, as meager as it was, and there was the support of the family. In the city there is only hardship. There are housing shortages, disposal and sewage problems, starvation. There are no jobs. Men merely starve and wait to die. Garbage piles up high between buildings in the center of the city. A few old goats stand on the heaps, rummaging through them and munching on paper and plastic and straw. This is the waste-removal squad. On the edge of town people live in tents and under tarps and in houses made of cardboard boxes. Sheets of cardboard are propped between rubber tires and covered with tarpaulins and people live there. Out behind the house, a camel digs in the sand to find scrub grass.

Where the town ends, there is nearly nothing. A man digs in the sand with a shovel and tosses each scoop into a screened box. He lifts the heavy box and sifts the sand to find rocks large enough to build with. It is his job. He wears no shirt and his muscles glisten with sweat. He breathes very hard. When he stops to rest, he leans on the shovel. He cannot stand up straight. He is not a young man.

Three miles down this road, three miles that feel like a thirty-mile hike, there is some sort of industry. Dump trucks move occasionally along the road, carrying loads of men sitting on top of the cab or standing on the loads of sand and rocks and dirt and holding on tight. The trucks move quickly. The men bounce around in back. They look weak from the heat.

The heat is numbing, squeezing in from all sides. It takes your breath away. There is no breeze except an occasional warm little wind that carries sand. In Mauritania the *vents de sable* never end. You raise your arms to catch the breeze, to cool off when the wind blows, and it covers you with sand. The sand sticks to the sweat that covers your body.

The sky is hazy with heat. The sun is a blur against a washed-out sky of gray and dull blue. In the air the shifting sand forms into a thick fog. You cannot see very far.

Nouakchott is a low town. Not many buildings stand over

two stories tall. Although the town is very crowded, there aren't many people on the streets. They are hiding from the heat, and the people you do see are desperate for shade. Anything will do, any tree no matter how thin, no matter how narrow the band of shadow cast. Someone will be found lying at the base of that tree in the little strip of shade. On cardboard mats spread at the side of the road, men lie beneath trucks. They look as if they might be working on them, but they are there for the shade. One man lies against the less sunny side of an old car.

Nothing moves. Not much. When it does, everything and everyone moves very slowly. Their blue robes flow in the breezes. The thought of so many layers makes me hotter, but the layers of cloth offer protection from the wind and the sun. Somewhere beneath those flowing folds there must be shade and a slight breeze.

There isn't much electricity in Nouakchott, and no refrigeration. I stopped at a little shack beside the road and bought a big bottle of water that had been kept out of the sun beneath a tarp. But it was no use. The water was not merely warm, it was near boiling. But I was so thirsty I drank down a liter and a half of the hot water anyway, without pausing for a breath.

On the corner, a truck full of soldiers was parked beneath a broad tree. A detail of soldiers was lying on the ground, in the shade. A few were standing. A few others were piled in the open back of the truck bed like a load of sand to be delivered and dumped. The soldiers called me over, and when I crossed the road, a swarm of green uniforms, rifles, and machine guns hovered around me. One soldier pointed his machine gun directly at my chest. He was waving it casually, not aiming it, but I didn't feel any better about it.

"Where are your papers?"

I pulled out my passport.

"Are you Senegalese?" He looked at the picture but he did not know how to read. He studied the passport carefully but he held it upside down.

"No," I said. "I'm American."

He shifted his machine gun around then until it dangled from the strap and hung down across his back.

"American?" he asked. "What are you doing here?"

He was smiling now, almost with relief. I did not understand why and thought only that he was thrilled to see a Blackamerican.

"You're not Senegalese?" he asked once more, and he reached out to shake hands with me.

"I'm not Senegalese," I said, and he was glad.

Mauritania sits on the edge of the Sahara where the line is drawn between black and white. They are all Muslims, but people north of this line are Arabs and Berbers, to the south they are black, and tensions often rise between these blacks and these whites, between Mauritania and Senegal. The whites have the authority and the best jobs. The blacks get the leftovers. They will tell you the Arabs are racist. And although slavery in Mauritania was officially abolished in 1980, many whites—Arabs and Berbers—still have black slaves. Although they share the same religion, religion is not enough.

An officer climbed down from the cabin of the truck. He wanted to shake hands too. He looked at my camera and for a moment it seemed as if he were going to ask me to take his photo. But he didn't. He frowned and scratched his chin with his thumb. He picked his nose.

"Are you a journalist?"

"No, just a traveler."

"Have you taken any pictures?"

Of course I had, but somehow honesty didn't seem very prudent.

"No. Not yet. Why?"

"You are not allowed to photograph here. First you need a permit."

Flies were swarming around us, buzzing in our ears, hovering near our eyes, crawling on our faces. It was enough to make me squirm. I waved my hand vigorously to shoo them away, to try to catch them, to try to kill them, but not one of the soldiers was annoyed enough even to brush the flies away from his mouth. They landed on the men's faces, crawled into the corners of their mouths and right into their eyes. They thought it was funny that I was fidgeting so much.

"The flies don't bother you?" I asked.

They just laughed.

The officer warned me not to take any photos.

The next morning in the very same spot, another group of soldiers called me to them and we went through the same routine. They even looked like the same soldiers, but then all soldiers look alike to me. It's the uniforms and the guns. But I didn't imagine they would have been there all night. If they had been on night duty, wouldn't others have come to relieve them during the day?

I asked why they kept harassing me, why I wasn't allowed to take any pictures. They couldn't tell me, but it seemed as if something serious were going on.

"Because you are not allowed to take photos." The soldier was almost shouting.

"So you said. But why not?"

"Because we don't want any journalists."

"Is there something you are trying to hide?"

He frowned and stared at me.

"What do you mean by that?"

"I mean I am not a journalist. I just want to take a few photos. You know. Souvenirs for friends and family at home."

"Then you will need a permit. You can explain in the office."

He told me where the office was, but of course I had no intention of going there. Perhaps I should have.

Many days ago I had heard there was trouble between Mauritania and its neighbor Senegal. I remembered now the report on the radio saying that the president of Mali had called on his two African brothers to end their dispute. But I couldn't remember when that was or where I was when I heard it.

Already my sense of time had blurred and time itself had become nearly meaningless. I never checked my watch. It didn't matter what day it was. You woke up at the beginning of day, and went to sleep at the end of it. In between you ate when you could and did what you had to do to see you to the day's end. There was no next year here. There was barely tomorrow.

While I was in Mauritania I never heard what the dispute was, and like everyone else not directly affected by it, I put it out of my mind. There were too many concerns more pressing. Day-to-day life was more pressing. Finding enough to eat was more pressing. And the same as everyone else, it never occurred to me that everything, no matter how remote, had some ripple of effect. Even if it was merely being stopped and questioned by a truckload of soldiers. Somewhere down the line, being stopped here would mean something, just as two weeks riding in the mountains meant something.

Whatever the dispute was, life continued. On the streets of Nouakchott the merchants sold oranges. The sun slid across the sky and reached for the ocean. The market became a kaleidoscope of color, mostly blue. But there were other colors too. Orange and green dresses hung for sale and waved in the whisper of a breeze. Red and white cartons of American cigarettes were stacked high behind some of the stalls. Women sat on the ground and sifted through beans and ground nuts. Their breasts hung out of loose wraparounds and flimsy tops, breasts that were stretched beyond belief, breasts that were withered and dried up inside. There was nothing sexual about their nakedness. These breasts were just another part of a human's anatomy, overused like the bent and broken backs of the men carrying loads of stone or hauling goods to the market on two-wheeled wooden carts. The streets were full of them: men bent over and limping, women with bared breasts. Their ages could be guessed, if at all, only in the angle of the bend in their backs, in the number of children they had, in how far their sagging breasts hung.

Before they get old, you cannot tell how old they are. They are almost ageless. And once they are old, they are very old and you still cannot know their ages for certain. There are only young and old here, very little in between.

There was a woman standing near the edge of the road. She was one of the young ones. Ageless in her youth, she could have been twenty or thirty or fifty. And she was beautiful. She wore gauzy layers of green and white that were very clean, and she stood motionless, waiting for a minibus, the local public transportation. As she stood there, the setting sun lost itself in the maze of her robes and dresses. The light bounced around inside and illuminated her skin. Her silhouette was dazzling. The outline was of breasts not yet used as swinging vines for six or seven children. Her belly was round and, though it seemed soft, it did not sag. Her body curved gently. Her black hair shone in waves streaked with the gold of sunlight reflecting off the sand. When she saw me staring at her, she shyly smiled. Her eyes were dark brown, holding the mystery of the thousand secrets she must have carried in her heart. They sparkled like deep wells in the moonlight. And then she looked away. I wondered what she was thinking, where she was going, how she passed her days and nights. I had fallen in love.

I had fallen in love like that once on a bus in Guatemala and would have given anything that day if the Guatemalan woman with her silky black hair tied in two long braids had sat down beside me and spoken. But she never even smiled. This Mauritanian woman at least offered the songs of her heart in a smile, and then she was gone. She climbed on the bus when it came and she rode away, a blossom of softness in the middle of the desert suddenly blown away in a breeze.

At a gasoline station near the airport, a huge parking lot was crowded with cars, white Peugeot 504s, old and beat up, perpetually out of gas. I was there to cut a deal for a ride to Rosso on the border with Senegal, where I hoped I would discover what the tension was all about. Or maybe the frontier would be closed. Maybe I would stumble into a bit of trouble.

I paid for my seat in the car and I waited. The car, of course, would not move until we had a full load. Without eight passengers, the driver wouldn't even go around the corner to fill the gas tank. Why spend the money to put gasoline in a car if it wasn't going anywhere? It wouldn't move until the trip paid for itself and profit. We sat in the hot sun and we waited.

An old woman came begging. She was bent over and wrinkled in a haggish way and she chanted the beggar's tune. I tried to avoid looking at her, tried to ignore her, hoping she would go away. But then I sneaked a secret glimpse.

Her face was old and gaunt, her smile withered and wrinkled, thin and toothless. But there was a dark beauty still in her hair, which was shiny black, streaked gray with age, and sparkling with gold reflections. Her robes and dresses were loose fitting and gauzy, but they were filthy dirty. The light that was caught in their folds bounced inside and showed her silhouette twisted stiff and bent. She dragged herself with her hand out. I looked away.

When I looked again she was still there, and her eyes caught mine. She tilted her head and raised a pleading eyebrow.

She pulled herself over to me and chanted. I remained steady, insensitive to her siren song, looking straight ahead, avoiding her eyes. But then she touched my sleeve. She stroked my arm. Her plea surpassed the ordinary and she made it personal. She touched my heart, stroked my beard, her dirty hand flush against my face. I would have cringed, but she smiled that haggard smile that can melt the cold cold places of any man's heart, and I gave her the few coins in my pocket. She closed her eyes and hummed. Her head shook slowly in some kind of dance or trance. She touched my face again and kissed the back of my hand.

Suddenly everything quiets down and the day becomes very still. The heat reflecting off the hoods of all these cars begins to shimmer so slowly that it thickens and stops moving. Time seems to stand motionless for a full minute. Everyone and everything seems to move in slow motion. It's like those hot summer days when I was a kid. All the other kids had gone off to camp for two weeks or to visit relatives in Kentucky and there was no one to play with and nothing to do and time stood still. The world had stopped spinning and the long days lasted forever.

The men hanging around looked to one another as if they heard something I couldn't. They mumbled to each other in Arabic. One of them finally shooed the old woman away. She had annoyed them more than the flies had. They apologized to me for her existence; she was an embarrassment to them.

The old woman, as she was being pushed away by their insults, kissed the palm of her hand and touched it to the car.

When the car was crammed full we drove south, following a bumpy road that cut across fields of sand. In the stark light, the desert covering was pure white, and the sand looked like snow. High, wide drifts spilled onto the road. The driver, just as a driver on snow would do, slowed to avoid skidding and to keep from getting stuck.

Not far out of Nouakchott a barricade blocked the road. From the shack on the side of the road, two soldiers came out into the sun. We all had to get out and show our identity papers.

Not much farther along, another roadblock, another search,

more examining of papers. The police and the military got to decide who passed and who stayed put. They didn't seem to be looking for anything special.

The Africans in the car never uttered a word of complaint. Five, six, ten times we had to stop and climb out into the heat. Each time the search seemed to take a little longer. And no one ever complained. The Africans sheepishly acquiesced and did what they were told.

I was silent too, but my mind was shouting.

At one checkpoint the soldier was napping as we pulled up. He rolled over and crawled off his cardboard mat. Without leaving the shade of his little concrete shack, he peered into the car with squinted eyes and gave a cursory wave, sending us on.

Maybe the roadblocks were just to give the soldiers something to do, keep them busy. This soldier was already busy trying to sleep. He would leave it to the next roadblock to stop us and check us more carefully.

There weren't many cars on this road, but there were people walking, approaching the road out of nowhere to walk along it for a distance then disappear into the desert again behind another sand hill. It was an image centuries old. Nomads in the desert.

A passenger taps the driver on the shoulder. The car stops. There is nothing on the horizon for miles around, but the man gets out and closes the car door. Somehow he recognizes a certain pile of rocks, a shifting of the sand, a shrub. He knows his bit of the desert as well as any man knows his own name. He knows this is where he gets out. Something is out there somewhere, his family, his herd, his tent. He knows where. He hitches the robes around him and crosses the road. After searching a long while I can see a little path in the sand. The man starts down it and heads for the horizon. There is nothing out there but shimmering waves of heat.

Farther on, camels graze in the sun. Each one lies in the shadow the next one makes. They lean against one another. Nearby, a tarp is stretched close to an outcropping of rocks. A family lies inactive in the small patch of shade. All around them is nothing but sand and sun and the stranglehold of this heat. But somehow they survive. They cling to life. It is as precious to them as to those who are richer. There is life in this desert. Everywhere you look there are signs of life. And in such simple things as a man's returning home, they find joy.

In the car the man beside the window refuses to open it. If he rolled it down, the wind would blow the dust and the sand in, stir the heat and make the car hotter.

At some point you just get used to the heat. Man is an adaptable beast. There is little, it seems, that he can't endure. But so far I haven't reached that point. The feeling of suffocation has ended but I still drip sweat. I'm dying of thirst.

We pull off the road and turn down an embankment into what seems like a ditch. Other cars are parked here, waiting to fill up for the return trip to Nouakchott. This is Rosso, another dusty town on the edge of nothing, a few low, clay-colored buildings huddled against the wind. Where the pavement of the main road ends, there is dirt packed hard and worn into a path by the endless walking and by the horse-drawn carts. The earth is a different color here, no longer that fine white sand but rocky and clumped together, an amber soil. The land is trying to hold ground here, hold back the advancing desert.

In town, two-wheeled carts are used as taxis. An old horse, the cart even older, two unsteady wheels wobbling off-balance, and always the feeling that you're about to fall off. The driver beats his old horse every now and then just to get it to break into a trot. He beats the horse with a long switch. The horse tries, but the trot is feeble, the gallop not there at all. The burst of effort lasts only a few seconds.

I am as tired as the horse and twice as hungry. More than anything, I am thirsty. The driver of the rickety old cart promises me a place to eat that is air-conditioned, and I have visions of walking into a frigid little room and shivering, the sweat on my back turning icy cold and giving me a chill. But the air-conditioning turns out to be a ceiling fan stirring up the flies and moving the heat back and forth. The little room is a broiler. The heat slaps one side of my face and then the other. The flies move with the heat, landing first on one side of my face and then the other. But the miracle of electricity buzzes in the walls. The drinks are refrigerated. They are cold and wet and stinging with carbonation. The first I drink in about eight seconds. The second takes a little longer, but not much.

The man in the kitchen brings me a kind of chicken stew with rice and another cold drink. The chicken is tough. I can't cut it with the knife I've been given. I tear it with my fingers and gobble it down. The rice is gritty and pasty but absolutely delicious. I'm ready for a second helping. Hunger makes palatable even the worst food, turns the simplest meal into a feast.

I slouch in my seat as if I've had a massive meal. I stretch out my legs and cross them at the ankles. I sit relaxing for many long minutes.

Outside there is a strange sound in the air. The muezzin is chanting in a crackly voice from the mosque tower. It is time for prayers.

When I pass the mosque, men are already sitting on the side of the road. They are washing their feet with little plastic pitchers filled with water. They wash their faces, necks, and hands. They roll out their prayer mats and watch my passing with slight suspicion, wondering, no doubt, why I do not stop to pray.

The atmosphere is heavy with prayer and heat.

I was searching for the frontier. As I walked down the road, a man walked toward me. I stopped him to ask directions. He spoke no French but nodded. No matter what question I asked him, he nodded enthusiastically.

Another man followed him. He told me yes, I would reach the frontier if I continued down this road. He said he didn't know how far. After I had walked a little farther, I turned around and he was still there, still standing in the middle of the road, still watching me.

From a dusty compound surrounded by a high wire fence, a soldier called me over. I put my bag down.

"No, no," he shouted. "Bring your things.

"Where are you going?" he asked in an irritated voice. "There is nothing down this road."

"I'm looking for the frontier."

"What frontier?"

"The border with Senegal. That man who just passed, he told me to continue down this road."

"The frontier is not down this road. You're going the wrong way."

He asked, of course, to see my papers. I handed over my passport. Right away the soldier smiled and invited me inside the little hut. He offered me tea. There was a second soldier inside.

They boiled water in a little pot over an open charcoal fire in the middle of the hut. The smoke billowed out through a hole in the ceiling. No one spoke as we sat together on the dirt floor. The soldiers were engaged in a little ritual, pouring the tea into a little glass, pouring that back into the pot, and repeating the process. We drank three cups of tea each and then I got up to leave. And that was all. Tea and a smile and a wave.

"Next time, just ask where is the frontier. The closest one."

They pointed me in the right direction.

The Senegal River flows through the valley just over a nearby hill. On the other side of the river lies Senegal, the starting point for many Africans stolen and shipped as slaves to the Americas. I have been told by many people who know Africa that I resemble the Senegalese.

There is in all of us some profound craving to know where we come from. On the grandest scale, we seek to understand the origins of the universe, the evolution of mankind. At a simpler level, an adopted child wants to know the woman who gave him life and birth. We trace family trees. We visit the neighborhoods where we lived as children. We look back as far as we can.

On the other side of the river quite possibly were the origins of my family.

On the other side of the river children were swimming. Faintly I could hear them screaming joyfully at one another, sounds of warm fun, joy and laughter.

From the east, from the flesh of Africa, the river ran like a bleeding vein, its blood the color of steel.

I crept through a vacant lot between two old buildings and leaned against a wall. The river opened before me, a beckoning embrace. Across a wide field of dry grass and shrubs, a crooked path ran from the river to me. Men were bathing naked at the river's edge. The vista was an ancient sight of rituals performed for a thousand years, pirogues—dug out canoes—carrying passengers and cargo from one side of the river to the other, men fishing the shallows, men bathing. Before me lay the simple beauty of Africa in all its quiet grandeur.

Here along the wall where I stood there was a harsher reality. A small mountain of garbage, paper, plastic, and bottles had been discarded and left to rot. Signs of modern life driven like a wedge against the ancient vista.

A young man who had been bathing came up from the river. He watched me take a few photographs, then he left and returned a few minutes later, pointing me out to the soldier who had come with him. The soldier yelled, but I only waved. I turned away, ignoring him.

The soldier came to me.

"*Bonjour,*" said I.

"What are you doing?" said he angrily.

"Not much." I didn't look at him, didn't want to acknowledge his authority. "How are you?"

"You are taking photos. Are you a journalist?"

"Not me."

"Then why are you taking photos?"

"Just a remembrance."

"What are you taking photos of?"

"The river. Is there something wrong with that?"

"You'll have to come with me."

"Of course."

"Photographing is not allowed."

"Of course not."

"Come," he said.

He dismissed the squealer, to whom I waved once more. I followed the soldier to the customs compound.

The compound was behind a wire fence half hidden by a hedge of trees. The trees were withering, turning brown and nearly leafless. The courtyard was a narrow plot of dust and sand; the building was baked mud. Inside, lying on the floor behind the counter, were two soldiers. They did not at first know I had been arrested.

Slowly one of the soldiers rose and stretched and came to the counter. He opened a big ledger, asked the questions that customs agents ask, and he wrote the answers: destination, reason for being in Mauritania, nationality. I laid my passport on the counter and the soldier wrote my passport number into the ledger.

"American?"

The soldier still lying on the floor perked up and stood. "You're American?" he said.

They would have been pleased to talk to me, but the commandant came in and he was very serious, with a great need to flex his muscles.

"You," he said. "Are you a journalist?"

It was hard to decide, but either journalists could get away with anything, or they were continually harassed and always in danger of being jailed and having their equipment confiscated. But I realized now that this was no game, that I might lose my camera.

"Photographing is not allowed here," he said sternly. "Let me see that camera."

He examined it as if he thought it might be a weapon. Then he handed it back.

"Where are you going?"

"To Senegal."

"Why were you walking down this road?"

"Someone told me this was the road to the frontier."

"It's not. Senegal is across the river."

"I know that now, but how was I supposed to know?" I was getting irritated and started to raise my voice. And I wanted him to know I wasn't afraid. "I asked a man I passed and he said the frontier was straight along this road. Then I got stopped by some other soldiers who pointed the right way. They didn't give me any problems. They just turned me around. So why do you want to harass me? Is it a crime to make a mistake?"

It might very well have been, depending on the mistake. The commandant never smiled.

"You have to come here first," he said. "You have to get your passport stamped."

"I thought I did that at the frontier."

"This is the frontier," he snapped. He took my passport and examined it. "You are American?" he asked. He seemed to soften and quiet, but only just a little. His severity was a little less rigid now, but I could not tell if the change in him came because I was black and American, or simply because I carried a U.S. passport.

"Yes, I'm American," I replied, pushing him a little. "Isn't that what the passport says?"

He handed back the passport.

"You have done a very bad thing," he told me. "You will be sent out of the country."

"What do you mean?" I asked, hoping he was not threatening to have me sent back to Nouakchott and then flown out from there—perhaps back to the United States. "I'm leaving anyway."

He ignored me and called out. Another soldier appeared. The commandant gave him his orders and he took the camera.

"Follow him," the commandant said. "You must leave the country. This man will escort you."

"What about the camera?"

"It will be given to you, but you are not to take any more photos. Understood?"

The two soldiers behind the counter were leaning on it, listening to the entire exchange. When I looked at them, they shrugged as if in apology. I smiled and they waved. My escort took me by the elbow and led me out.

I stopped smiling now, the smile being replaced by a quiet anger rising from my belly.

I was not angry about being deported but about something else, I wasn't quite sure what just then. Perhaps I was angry about the general unfairness of earning a certain measure of respect because of the passport I carried, a passport that was a barrier keeping me from knowing certain fears and degradations, keeping me safe. I couldn't put my finger on it, but in the air there was a certain angriness not entirely mine.

I blamed it on the heat, told myself that the desert and the sun had burned holes in my soul, but as I looked then across the river and faced black Africa I was confronted with the realization that those passing through Senegal and bound for the Americas had been in chains, and I knew then that the holes were being burned into my soul by the mingling in my blood of the acids of various strains of my African ancestry, and deep in the consciousness I shared with my forefathers I remembered how others among my peoples had turned tribal and fought among themselves, collaborated with what should have been the common enemy, and enabled the white man to buy and steal and enslave my African ancestors. As I was escorted out of Mauritania I was outraged, for I could see in a small way how slavery could happen, how many horrors can happen. Men following orders, hiding their humanity.

At a wooden stand selling bottles of soda floating in a bucket of melted ice, I stopped to buy a cold drink for myself. I offered to buy one for my escort, but he refused with a wicked stare, full of suspicion and contempt. To him I was a criminal who must not be talked to or smiled at, must not be treated with civility. He had his orders. He was rigid and stern and unfriendly, his green uniform cloaking anything human in him.

I took my time and drank the soda as slowly as I possibly could, just to make the soldier wait. When he had waited long enough, he grabbed my shoulder and shoved me forward. I knocked his arm off my shoulder.

"Let's go," he ordered, and led me down to the river.

And that was how I came to be deported from Mauritania.

There was no bridge between Mauritania and Senegal. To cross the river I climbed into a pirogue. An old black man paddled me across.

The pirogue was the gray color of a dead tree, pointed at one end and blunt at the other. It had been hollowed out and sanded smooth inside. There were no seats; you crouched or you knelt and held the sides of the canoe.

The river beat against the sides of the little boat and violently rocked the boat side to side, but the old man never got nervous, never sat down. He kept his balance, standing upright to paddle the canoe, and did not flinch at the pitching of the boat on the waves.

The waves were high and the river was very wide. The mouth of the Senegal River was not far from where I crossed, to the west and south, just around that bend. The old man paddled furiously to keep us from getting caught in the current and sucked out to sea. He aimed the boat more upriver than straight across and the crossing took time. The river splashed into the boat. The water was cool against the heat of the day.

Off to the right the river widened still further, disappearing around the bend and emptying into the sea. Mauritania moved farther and farther into the distance behind us, and with it Arab Africa. I did not care to turn around. Senegal lay before me, the beginning of the road into the heart of Africa. My mind looked only forward.

Children frolicked in the water near shore. Men sat in the shade away from the river. There were trees, but the ground was parched. A slight breeze kicked up a swirl of red dust. The earth was not quite sand, separated from the desert by this river, but the dryness continued. The ground was not quite dirt, either, but fragile and brittle dust.

But the rains will one day come. When they do, the land will flower green and fertile. The earth will become mud and hold in place for a time. The world once again will seem abundant, but only for a time so short and so delicate that when the land dries again under the sun, the memories of bounty will be faint and the fertile time will seem as distant as a dream. The wet seasons had been sporadic lately. The sky had refused to rain. The land was baking, was brittle and cracked.

I asked when the rainy season usually begins. The answers were vague, uncertain, as if to say: *We don't really remember. And what does it matter anyway?* "The rains will come when it's time for them to come," I was told. And the people will wait for them. If the rains don't come this year, they will come next year, or they will come the year after, or maybe the year after that. And the people will be here waiting.

At the little border town on the Senegal side, a small group of men stands where the road begins at the edge of the water. They look out across the water and they wait. The faces of these men are carved with lines drawn by wind and sun and by eternal waiting. The waiting they can handle. The wind and the sun they are used to. But in their faces rises an expression of pain and bewilderment that is almost anger. They stare out across the river to Mauritania. Something about these days is new to them and makes no sense.

One of them asks me: "Was there any trouble?"

"Not really," I answer. "Why?"

"Because you are black," another says. He is young and anger simmers in his eyes. "The Arabs are racists," he says.

But one of them takes my hand to shake it.

"You are American?" he asks. "Welcome home. We are happy that you have come."

FOUR

BEGINNINGS

OF BROTHERHOOD ▶▶▶▶▶▶▶▶▶

Senegal

The young man's house was four walls of mud and concrete. An opening was cut in one of the walls, but there was no door to close. It was cooler inside the house than outside in the sun, but not much. The house was an oven. Flies buzzed in small swarms hanging lazily in the heat. Two men slept on the smooth dirt floor. One of them awakened to greet me, and then lay back down and went to sleep again. I sat on a wood slat laid across two concrete blocks.

Outside in the heat a man roasted some kind of meat over an open fire. Another man squatted over a little charcoal burner and fussed with a teapot. Nothing else moved except the lizards, which moved like lightning in and out of the cracks. Inside the house, they clung to the walls and remained still for only a moment. Their heads bobbed up and down. The lizards on the floor were dancing, bouncing on their forelegs, doing push-ups. Their little tongues whipped out to taste the air, to smell for prey, to feel for danger. In the thickness of the heat the flies hovered and the lizards waited until they drifted too close. Then they had them for lunch.

The little lizards never stayed long in one place. Any movement from any corner of their senses and the lizards were up on their three toes and darting nervously for cover. They scurried up the wall, dived into the cracks and out of sight. They moved so fast my eye could not follow and when I looked, they had simply vanished, blended into the dust color of the wall, the same dust color as the lizards, the same dust color as the roads, the same dust color as everything.

The meat roasting outside was done. The man offered me a piece. I shooed the flies off and ate it.

Africa.

Black Africa. A quiet sense of elation and something akin to relief swept over me. It wasn't exactly like coming home, but perhaps simply the bracing awareness that upon this same earth a man who looked like me had walked centuries before me. What he saw and what he did was planted in my genes. Something in the soul does not forget. I was in black Africa at last and all the rest had been a prelude to getting here.

The face of Africa has Arab eyes. The great Arab empires that reached deep into the body of black Africa left imprints of Arab customs and ways of thinking. But the skin of Africa is brown, rich and dark. Now I was in the body of Africa and looking for heart and soul. I smelled the earth and listened to the wind and felt for the rhythm of Africa coming up through the ground like a heartbeat, making a joyful sound like music and laughter, and another one as sad as a moan. I was at once thrilled and anxious. My heart raced with a rich rush of excitement mingled with fear.

In the imaginings of every person with black skin, Africa is a place of wonder, a place of return, rumored since childhood and seen as a place filled with promises of black dignity and rich with a sense of belonging. We cannot help but approach it with anticipation.

Somewhere between the blackness of my skin and the whiteness of my culture I am trapped. I am a victim of education, cultural assimilation, and good fortune. I know the right forks to use, the right wines to buy. My white friends, so they say, never think of me as being black—as if there were some-thing wrong with being black, something to be ashamed of, as if it were some kind of illness maybe.

"I never think of you as being black," they say. *I never think of you as having only one arm. I see you as a whole human being.* As if having one arm or being short or stuttering lessens your humanness, your wholeness, your value.

They mean it as a compliment, I know, but what they are saying is that if I changed the color of my skin I could be one of them.

But I can't change the color of my skin.

When I was a little boy sitting in the barbershop with my father and listening to adult conversations, the men sitting there always described people in terms of color before they mentioned anything else.

That dark-skinned boy who walks his sister to school.

That brown-skinned man on the corner.

Conversations of strangers, family, friends were all sprinkled with these little dabs of color.

"Melba, Bonita said you're black." It was a great insult, words to fight over. The darker you were, the lower your status.

Until Ronnie Brown issued those same fighting words, called me black, and added a twist. "Be proud to be black," he said. "It's nothing to be ashamed of."

It was 1966. Ronnie Brown was twelve years old. I was ten.

On a Sunday morning a long time ago, Malcolm X was preaching in a mosque in Harlem. In his sermon he described the smell of black people, the look in the faces of black people, the walk of black people, and he told the black people gathered there how black people felt and what caused them to feel that way, walk that way, look that way.

The hardship of Africa was in our blood. The chains of slavery weighed heavily upon us. We had lost our names and our history, our ancestors and our dignity and a sense of ourselves. We had learned over too many years to dislike ourselves.

I would like to be a little boy who still believes he can be loved, hated even, for what he does and says and thinks, for who we are comes primarily from these. I would like to believe that color is meaningless. But it's not. And I'm no longer that little boy. In this world we have made, color corrals us and defines us long before we have a chance to speak. Color alters the way we are perceived and even the way we perceive ourselves. Color re-creates us and is too important to be left to little boys who will only get it wrong.

(When asked to match baby pictures with pictures of the same people as adults, small children in one experiment picked this man's photo and put it alongside this little boy's photo, this woman next to that little girl, and did it all with such childish reasoning that there was no regard for color. For them it made sense that white children could grow up to be black, and vice versa. They were too young, too innocent to know and would have to be taught.)

I was happy to be black in Africa. It wasn't home, but simply the land of my ancestors, a faraway land of myth and magic. By the smell and feel of these places I now walked, I would know that my ancestors had walked this land before me. And surely it would be no crime here to be black.

Along the river, the land has been flooded. Rows and rows of rice grass grow up out of the marsh surrounding the irrigation ditches. The land stretches green to the horizon. Away from the river, the landscape is flat and barren, dusty brown fields and leafless shrubs. The land is stark and dismal, endless miles of nothing but parched earth and low bushes. The loamy soil is lifeless and dry and swirls up in ocher coils of dust at the side of the road as cars speed by. Occasionally a head will appear from its resting place against the trunk of a tree, and a man will come up from the shade to see who passes here.

How long has it been since men used to lie low against the trunks of trees to hide in ambush against antelope and elephant, or dive into the bush to escape the jaws of a hungry lion? But there is no game here anymore, no elephant, no lion, no antelope. They have been hunted to the edges of extinction, driven away by man and by drought. Dust and dryness abound now. The shrubs and bushes scattered about the landscape are only sparsely covered with leaves. What have we done here? The face of Africa is devastated, almost as if in retribution for some sin.

But in the middle of the desolation stands a massive prince of a tree, a baobab tree. It doesn't stand very tall. It is not a majestic tree like some forest pine. But it is as solid as hope and as steady as the time-proven wisdom of old age, standing not in a grove of trees but isolated and lonely, like an old man who has outlived his friends. The tree's bark is an old man's skin, gnarled and twisted, fibrous and wrinkly. It is a tree that lives a long long time. Like an old man, it knows the tricks of survival. The baobab tree can hold twenty-five thousand gallons of water in its storage tissue, holds them like an old man hanging on to memories.

I put my camera down and sit in the shade of this baobab tree. A sound like thunder rumbles over the landscape and echoes through the skies.

It is the sound of thunder promising rain to cleanse and rejuvenate, to turn this dust into fertile soil. But the skies are clear.

It is the sound of hunger rumbling in too many bellies.

It is the sound of waiting like nowhere else on earth, waiting for the rain, waiting for deliverance, waiting for death, waiting waiting waiting.

It is the sound of time passing.

In the shade of the baobab tree, Africans huddle in groups waiting. Two old men play cards on a short bench. A young man shuffles through the heat and boredom, lifelessly selling T-shirts and toothpaste and candy. His slip-slops are torn to shreds, tied with string to his calloused feet. His feet are covered with dust. His toenails are as thick and hard as the hooves of a horse. His skin is fiercely black.

The T-shirts he sells are emblazoned with images of a Blackamerican rock star. The torn shirt he wears bears the name and emblem of an American university. Joking, I ask him if he went to school there, but he doesn't know that I am only having fun with him. He tells me he stopped going to school when he was nine years old.

"I pass my days walking up and down this street," he says. "I try to sell enough to buy rice and sometimes a chicken."

Today everyone ignores him. He hasn't sold anything all day.

The cardplayers continue their game without looking up. Others lie in the dust and sleep in the shade. One man digs in the dirt with a stick.

A few women appear but they talk only among themselves. We are waiting for a ride to Saint-Louis.

A great uneasiness stirs in my bones. An eerie sense tells me that I have been here before.

When the French came to Africa, they settled first at Saint-Louis. By coincidence, I grew up in an American town called Saint Louis. But it is not that simple. This place is weirdly familiar to me suddenly. The feeling is like a cold and clammy hand grabbing my shoulder in the darkness.

When the slave markets were thriving in the Americas, this African Saint-Louis was one of the collection points, the last smell and sight of home before being caged in the dark holds of sailing vessels and shipped to a new world. The fear I feel is the fear those slaves felt. I feel the same icy panic in my bones.

I have known this feeling before. In a small ghost town in France. Oradour-sur-Glane. A town full of ghosts. Deserted streets and screams of terror. Visions of the town on fire. The smell of charred human flesh. Sounds of firing squads and children screaming.

In Oradour in 1944, the French Resistance killed a small group of German officers. In retaliation the German army lined up every man, woman, and child in the town and put them all to death. The town and all that was in it was put to the torch. As a reminder of what horrors we have done to one another, the town stands today almost exactly as it did two days after the slaughter, not a single stone replaced or a roof rebuilt. Only the plaques put up to explain and to remind. There are the stone shells of houses burned to the ground, the church where the children hid before facing the firing squads, the rusted remains of an old car sitting on a corner outside a shop. Perhaps the driver had run into the bakery to grab a loaf of bread. Maybe he left the engine running. The Nazis were waiting for him when he came outside. He would have dropped the bread, of course. He wouldn't need it now. And time came to a standstill.

The fear that seized Oradour seized every African village where men stalked in the night, burned homes, and lined up the young and the healthy. The old and the sick were probably lined up too, before they were slaughtered. The forests on those nights were alive with terror. The roar of the lion and the sounds of thunder were drowned out beneath the wailing.

Because I am black I feel the pain of Africa. Because I am human I feel the terror of French children in Oradour, the suffering of Jews in Auschwitz. I have been here before.

Teilhard de Chardin, French theologian and philosopher, called it the *noosphère*. Carl Jung called it the collective unconscious. They are the same. They are the foundations of *déjà vu*. They are layers of awareness, a bubble of consciousness into which are deposited all matter, all action, all thought. By this collective unconsciousness we are all connected, all that is and all that ever was. We and all we do are teardrops falling into an ocean, the ripples on the surface of the water when a stone is cast. We inherit other people's pain and other people's hate. We pass on our love, our hope, our everything.

Old Saint-Louis was built on an island that lies in the mouth of the Senegal River. One side of the island is connected to the mainland by Pont Faidherbe, a fairly modern bridge of steel and concrete. In the daytime men and boys with nothing else to do come to the bridge and throw long fishing lines down into the water. The bridge hums all day with autos buzzing over the metal grooves in the roadway. Pedestrians hurry mornings from the mainland to work on the island, and then back across to the market and home in the evening.

On the mainland side of the bridge there are houses and a market and the railway station. It is the part of Saint-Louis that has risen to meet the tide of job-seeking villagers moving down to the city since Senegal's independence from France. Saint-Louis is the seat of regional government. Bureaucracy means jobs.

But jobs or no jobs, Saint-Louis is above all a fishing village. On the far western side of town, a bridge passes over a narrow inlet and the city is connected to a flat sandy peninsula that is not very wide. On this narrow strip of land the fishermen live, and each evening their wives come down to the sea to watch the sun sink in the west and to wait for the fishing boats to bring their husbands home, and the catch of the day.

Anxious women chat nervously. They keep their eyes on

the far-off line where the sea joins the sky, waiting for the boats to appear. The sea breeze breaks the heat. The salty ocean spray stings the eyes. The women look as if they have been crying.

The boats finally appear. One by one they break the shimmering line of the horizon. A collective sound of relief escapes the women, as if they have been holding their breath, but then a new anxiety surfaces, for these seas are rough and the fishers are still a long way off. Too often men die on the water, and when they do, the lives of these women abruptly stop. So they wait anxiously, holding their breath again. The boats coming in rise high on the crests of waves for only half a heartbeat. Then they disappear for long seconds in the deep troughs. You can hear the quiet gasps.

The boats start to arrive and the scene enlivens. The women rush down to the water's edge. They help with the loads of fish, sorting the catch, gutting the fish and scaling them, preparing them for market. They holler prices and bargain with shoppers in a hurry to buy and eager to cut out the middleman.

The sun goes down and the fishermen secure their boats in the half-light before night. The fish not sold on the beach are carted off to market and sold to merchants who will resell them tomorrow. And tomorrow it will all happen again just as it has today, just as it happened yesterday, and the day before that, and as it has happened for many many years.

I stroll in the evening past the big market and the post office, the old governor's mansion and the former colonial buildings that now house functionaries and accommodate the local government and soldiers. Past and present come together here in the old colonial parts of town. They are the links between past and present, links that are apparent and eerily felt. A father sitting on a log, telling stories to his children. An old woman's ancient songs. Relics of a colonial past maintained and still in use. My father's old neighborhood. Everything the same, but everything different.

In the older residential areas, many of the houses are caving in. The stone walls of courtyards are falling down. In the courtyard of one old house, a baobab tree grows, its branches entering the crumbling walls and reaching up through holes in the roof of the house. Farther on there is a Catholic church lit up, all aglow with candles and singing. A nighttime baptism is being celebrated inside.

Just beyond the plaza where lovers walk arm in arm, a military building lurks in the darkness, the limits of approach clearly marked by the scowling faces of the soldiers surrounding the place.

On the stone outer wall of the building there is a poster, a drawing of a healthy man standing beside a visibly weakened and sick man who stands next to a skeleton. The caption is simple: AIDS KILLS. There is a brief explanation in words and small drawings about the precautions against getting the disease, but no one stops to look or read the poster. No one wants to be on the same side of the street as the soldiers. Lovers cross the street to avoid them. They hold hands, stopping to kiss beneath the trees filling the square.

And now it is night.

On the corner an old black woman sits in the shadows. She is doing something with her hands, but I cannot see what, peeling potatoes, scaling fish perhaps, shelling nuts, or just sewing. She is hidden except for the light color of her dress catching the soft glow of a lamp shining through the curtains of the window above her. The light flickers as the curtains flutter against the breeze. There is no other light apart from a streetlamp away in the distance. All around her is darkness. And in that darkness she rocks gently forward and back, but not steadily. She moves to a syncopated rhythm, almost erratic but very delicate. And while she does whatever she does there in the near-darkness, she sings a song that rises in the cool, quiet night. Her song is a soothing breeze at the tail end of a hot day, a song that echoes off the wall of deep African blackness, bringing back memories. Her singing runs high harmony to the distant deep whisper of the ocean, and if you close your eyes you can hear the low, intermittent, and swooshing counterpoint of the sea.

The song is not French but Wolof perhaps, or Tukulör. Maybe she is a Bassar woman, a nomad like her people, here now, working in the street by night. When the morning comes she will be packed up and gone.

I have with me a very small tape recorder. I lean against an opposite wall and switch on the machine. Here in the night I steal her voice and carry away a little piece of her soul.

▲

In bed I listened for the hypnotic rush of the sea and fell asleep. Suddenly, deep in the night, I woke up dancing. I was sitting up straight and I was bouncing, sleep-dancing in my dreams, to music I could not hear, to rhythms I could only feel.

Africa.

I put in a phone call to the United States. The call went through in only fifteen minutes. I wanted to share my moments of joy with my friend Harry, but Harry wasn't interested in my sleep-dancing. He asked if I had found out what all the trouble was about.

"What trouble?" I asked.

"Senegalese are being slaughtered in Mauritania," he told me. "Their throats are being cut and their bodies hacked to pieces with machetes."

It was impossible news. I wanted to scream. I wanted to tear my room apart. I wanted to vomit. I felt the anger of a man who has just learned some member of his family has been taken hostage and shot, eyes gouged out, body mutilated.

The song of the old woman had not been a lullaby after all, but a deeply felt lament, sad and bitter, bemoaning the fate of her people.

Ibrahima Guèye sits outside the post office from sunup until well past dark. He sits on the curb and waits the day away. The booth behind him, where he sells carved figurines, traditional musical instruments, drums, all sorts of tourist junk, he calls his minigallery. He tries to interest me in something, but I am in no mind even to pretend. Failing that, he invites me to sit and he offers me tea.

Ibrahima wears dark glasses and I cannot see his eyes. He hides his thoughts. He is quick to smile, though. His teeth are stained yellow from tobacco and they are brown and rotted. His skin is rough and very dark. He stands now to ballyhoo at the passing women and to a group of young French girls who are easily persuaded to buy the things that he sells. Everything seems quite ordinary, quite the same as it would have been two months ago, the same as it will be two months from now.

Two regally dressed women in flowing robes of gold and

crimson come to talk to Ibrahima. They stand noble as statues above me. One of them chews on a stick and brushes her teeth with the frayed end. When the splinters and pulp collect in her mouth, she spits them out like a rube chewing tobacco. Her royal air vanishes.

They have come to visit with Ibrahima, to show off their flamboyant new dresses, and to laugh. When they laugh, they really guffaw.

Ibrahima invites them to tea and introduces me as his American friend. They are not impressed. They offer limp hands for me to shake. From then on they ignore me completely.

The man in the next booth over leans out to give Ibrahima a little charcoal burner. Ibrahima lights the fire. He pours water into a little metal pot and stuffs it with loose leaves of tea and lots of sugar. When the tea has boiled, Ibrahima pours the tea into a small glass and then back into the pot. He repeats the pouring several times, each time with a great flourish, each time creating more and more froth on the tea. He tastes it and repeats the pouring, tastes it again, and finally decides the tea is ready. He offers me a glass.

Three rounds of tea are made and shared all around. Ibrahima's younger brother disappears around the corner with a glass of tea for someone. When he returns, his glass is the glass I use for my second round.

When the tea is done and the two women have left, I finally ask Ibrahima if he knows what has been going on. He answers with less animation than if he had been giving football scores.

"The Mauritanians are killing Senegalese," he says.

I am agitated and angry, as much at him for taking it so casually as with the Mauritanians and the gods with whose permission such things are done. I nearly shout at him.

"I know," I say. "But why?"

"Because the Arabs are racists," he says, and that is enough for him. He needs no further explanation. He can do nothing about it, has no control over it. He has no voice in who is and who is not racist, no say in who does and who doesn't die. He has enough problems selling souvenirs to tourists, trying to earn enough to feed his wife and his children and help his father feed his brothers and sisters. It is the way life goes.

▲

The Senegalese national anthem sings of brotherhood. "The Bantu is a brother," it says, "and the Arab and the white man." But there is no unity in Africa.

Forty thousand blacks—Tukulör, Fulani, and Wolof—were forced out of Mauritania. Hundreds and hundreds were killed. Their throats were slit and their heads cut off. Women were disemboweled. Men were castrated.

In Dakar, the Senegalese responded in kind to the grisly stories coming out of Mauritania and went on a rampage of retaliation. Crowds crazed with anger flooded the streets. They rounded up Mauritanians to lynch them, to club them to death, stone them to death, burn their bodies and pillage their shops. Their shops are boarded up now. Mauritanian shopkeepers are gone from Dakar. Thousands and thousands of Mauritanians fled into The Gambia. Thousands more were evacuated to Nouakchott. Very few remain.

One eighty-year-old Mauritanian man stands outside his boarded-up shop. He weeps silently, but without shame. His wife stands beside him in shock. They have been in Dakar for fifteen years. They sold candles in this shop, and rice and cooking oil and matches and cigarettes, plastic pots and metal bowls and toilet paper. Now they will be going home.

"To do what?" I ask.

"To start over."

Most of the shopkeepers in Senegal were Mauritanian. Most have closed up shop. Most have gone home to start over.

From the other side of the border comes a river of Senegalese refugees. Forty thousand fled or were deported. They were the lively black fishermen who sold fish on the beaches near Nouakchott. They were the carpenters, the taxi drivers, the laborers. Now they are gone.

The story in Dakar tells of Mauritanian camels that strayed—deliberately led, some say—onto land claimed by Senegalese. Two Senegalese were shot, either by Mauritanian herdsmen or by Mauritanian soldiers. No one knows for sure. Angry Senegalese in Dakar looted a few shops. In Nouakchott, organized bands of Moors roamed the streets in search of Senegalese and other blacks to kill, it didn't matter whom, it could have been me, stabbing them, clubbing them, hacking them to pieces, cutting off the testicles of young boys, slicing off the breasts of nursing mothers, gutting people like fish and leaving bodies and entrails for the flies to eat.

My knees tremble with fear. One of the dead men lying gutted in the road, flies buzzing over his face, roaches crawling in his ears, could have been me, my skull bashed in, clubbed by mistake, stabbed dead and mutilated because of the color of my skin.

If today had been a week ago, instead of being deported I might have been killed. If today had been two hundred years ago, the slavers might have caught me, manacled my ankles, chained me to the wall in some holding cell, and stuffed me in the damp musty hold of a ship bound for America.

It could have been me! It *was* me. They are all me.

The Bantu is a brother, and the Arab and the white man. There is no greater truth. And no greater lie.

There is in Africa a political association called the Organization of African Unity. Its stated purpose is to promote brotherhood among African nations, a sense of unity. It provides a stage for dealing with the problems that face Africa and hinder its progress as a unit, or as a collection of individual nations. It deals with political problems and problems left over from the colonial era, border disputes, war and drought, human rights violations, famine and starvation, economic problems, crises.

With the single exception of the Republic of South Africa, every nation in Africa is a member and has a voice in the OAU. But in the charter of the OAU is the explicit requirement that no nation interfere in the internal affairs of another. Even verbal criticism is considered interference. The OAU, therefore, lacks any real means to settle disputes, to end wars, to solve problems. The OAU lacks resolve, and each country proceeds as it wishes.

The unity the OAU fosters is restricted to the leaders of African nations, a brotherhood of thugs guarding their positions and powers, for in every national palace or chief executive office, save only a few, some general or colonel or captain who overthrew the last colonel now awaits his own turn to be turned out and imprisoned or assassinated. The OAU is a powerless league mostly of dictators leaving one another alone and promising noninterference. It has nothing to do with brotherhood among the peoples. The people have no voice.

▲

The African sun climbs high in the afternoon sky. A hot wind rises from the ground and swirls upward through the tops of the leafy trees. The heavy branches bend first one way, then the other, swaying and creaking, the leaves fluttering and swishing together. The harsh light from the sun shatters into sparkles like little beads of glass glittering in the treetops. The hot, dry wind carries with it coils of dust and sand spiraling skyward like little cyclones. There is not a hint of moisture in the breeze, nor anything cool or refreshing. The heat reaches deep into the shade and settles everywhere like a bad smell that stings my eyes and brings them to tears.

In Dakar many shops are boarded up, their windows broken out. Light-skinned Lebanese merchants walk nervously. There is a weakness in their knees. Their eyes dart quickly and anxiously about.

A week ago they would have invited me into their shops to drink tea. They would have lingered on the street to chat. Today their answers are quick and curt and they hurry on. They avoid all contact with strangers. In their eyes is the terror of resembling marked men. They know how easy it is to be mistaken for someone else, cut open, and hacked to pieces.

A Lebanese merchant nervously explains.

"Mauritanian, Lebanese, it's all the same," he says.

He sells sandwiches in a shop along the avenue Pompidou. His droopy mustache twitches. His watery eyes edgily search the passing crowds.

"When you're looking for someone to kill," he says, "light skin is light skin."

As he waits for his next customer, he moves away from the counter and stands anxiously in a corner where he can watch the shop and the street. Any sudden movement will send him scurrying into the back room.

For black Senegalese, life settles quickly back to normal. On the corner across from the crowded and noisy madness of the market, a young man sits stoically on a wooden crate and has the gray dyed out of his hair. The man working on him wears black rubber gloves and smears onto his victim's head a thick black mixture like liquid shoe polish. He invites me to be next.

Nearby, at the end of rue Vincens, a woman cooks on the pavement beside her home. She lives in a shack made of cardboard and paper and sticks, held together by string and supported by a mound of large stones at the base of the walls. It sits on the pavement and is held in place by a large sheet of black plastic draped over it and secured by a few of the large stones. It is her home.

She isn't very old. She wears a colorful print dress of purple and pink and white, but the dress is dirty. Her head and part of her face are wrapped in a red turban. She glances up and reveals her watery eyes and her broad nose and two scars on either cheek. Squinting hard, she looks around as if to stop anyone from staring. Then she goes back to her cooking.

She has surrounded her shack with buckets and bowls and the cardboard boxes she uses for tables. They are also the replacement panels for the sides of the little house she lives in. At the moment she is cooking on a little charcoal fire, squatting before the fire and pouring water from a pink plastic bucket. No one stares at her. No one even looks twice. People who pass by walk on with hardly a glance. Each one has seen it all before, will see and suffer it all again.

And all is back to normal. No one shouts angry slogans. No one speaks openly of murder. The streets are not stained with bloody reminders, no signs of horror. There is no dried blood on the walls, no torn fingers lying on the pavement. It is only in the eyes of people passing that a certain sadness seems to lie.

Their eyes are bloodshot and watery, probably from the heat of the sun, but it looks as if they've been crying. They walk slowly with shoulders sagging more than usual. Tired maybe, or hungry. Their eyelids are heavy and droop with fatigue in the middle of another long day, or maybe from fear and shame, from memories that will not easily fade.

In the gutter near the corner lies a bent knife blade. Farther on there is a broken toy.

In the heat of early afternoon I sit in a circle of five friends who are gathered in the courtyard of a bar to share a meal. They plunge their hands into a bowl that steams with rice and bits of tomato and a very large fish that was cooked whole and stares up with one eye, like a man lying dead on the street. I watch as they pick the flesh off this fish. I am afraid to eat, afraid it will taste like corpses.

Music plays in the open courtyard, where two Europeans sun themselves at a table and wait to be served. They will not be served soon, for these are the owners of the restaurant I am eating with, and the Europeans will have to wait until we finish our meal. They sit relaxed and unhurried. They are on holiday.

The Africans talk about them in words I cannot understand. They smirk and laugh and point with their chins at the Europeans. They are happy to make them wait.

A man in a striped shirt sits opposite me. He looks up from the bowl to answer the question in my eyes.

"For them doing nothing is a luxury," he says. "For us there is no other choice."

It is a day like all days, slow moving and hot. The sun beats down, reflecting off the pavement and walls, bouncing into corners of shade and spreading the heat. Half the courtyard is shaded with leafy trees, thick and low to the ground, and when the wind blows and rustles through those trees, it rumbles like thunder.

The Europeans sit sunning themselves like royalty, and a quiet anger simmers behind the eyes of the African men watching them.

"We like to make them wait," says a woman in a pink camisole. The others laugh a little, but a man in green stops their laughter and sobers them just a little.

"We have this need," he says, "to exercise our control. Otherwise we have nothing; we *are* nothing."

The European woman is a thin and striking blond with her hair tied in a bundle on top of her head. Her neck is exposed to the sun and to the slight breeze. She wears a soft cotton skirt hiked up to her thighs. Her legs are wide apart but moving side to side to create and catch a breeze beneath her skirt. She kicks off her shoes and wiggles her naked toes. One arm on the table in front of her, the other in her lap, she tilts her head back to catch the sun on her face and throat.

Her companion sits quietly beside her. His legs are stretched out straight and crossed at the ankles. He slouches in his seat. He has removed his shirt to catch the sun on his chest, to darken his skin, so that when he goes back to France he will be able to joke about being nearly as dark as the natives.

But he will never be like the natives, will never be like them at all, for he makes it clear that he owns this world and all that is in it. He is comfortable here and everywhere he goes, basking in the glory of conquest. He brings with him Mungo Park and Christopher Columbus and Hernán Cortés; Beethoven, Shakespeare, Rodin. Not even the remotest cranny of any faraway land remains completely untouched and unconquered by his kind—without envy of them and their power, their freedom. These people can never feel out of place no matter where they go. The world knows them.

The man beside me speaks again, the one in the green shirt. His face is puffy and soft and round. His lips are thick and dark, his nose broad and flat. Around his eyes there are creases from squinting in the sun, perhaps from pondering, perhaps from worrying. The skin of his face is scarred from shaving with dull razors.

"It is maddening," he says. "We get much from them and we love them. They have everything and we envy them. But they have stolen our spirit and left us wanting. We hate them because they have taught us in small ways to hate ourselves."

The others are still. They lean with elbows on knees over the food bowl, now empty, and they listen.

"Our ancestors are the conquered ones," he says. "They watched these conquerors come. They watched them kill and take, and they helped them to own us, to buy us, to sell us, to own our land and our flesh and our spirit. They surrendered to the conquerors and helped the conquerors to defeat us. And now the watching continues, and so does the surrendering."

He purses his lips and stretches his face, but in his eyes there shines no resistance, only a quiet acceptance. He squints from the hot light in the courtyard. And although the distance is not very great from where we sit in the shadows to where the Europeans sit in the sun, he shields his eyes with a hand over his brow, peering as if into the faraway distance.

In 1885 at the conference of Great Powers in Berlin, Africa was divvied up among the European governments. There was a brief push by black leaders for some sort of pan-Africanism, unity among all Africans, but by the 1940s the move was toward independent nations. In June 1977 the colonial era finally ended. When it left Djibouti, France became the last European power to pull out.

Perhaps not so ironically, France remains the major foreign force in Africa.

Trade routes and natural resources were why the Europeans had come in the first place. Export markets and influence are the reasons they are still there. And they are very much still there. Especially the French.

If there is a complicity, a tacit alliance between slave and slave owner, there is an even unholier one between *former* slave and *former* slave owner.

In 1988 more African heads of state attended the French-African summit meeting than went to the twenty-fifth anniversary meeting of the Organization of African Unity earlier that year. The delegation to the summit included not only former French colonies, but former British colonies as well, former Portuguese and Belgian and Spanish colonies too. Many of these countries have been begging for admission into the franc zone, begging in a way for continued colonial—or neocolonial—ties to the old slave master.

The franc zone was established at a time when both France and Africa needed hard currencies for development. Local African currencies in the French colonies were done away with in exchange for the African Financial Community franc—the CFA. It is backed by the French franc at a constant exchange rate of fifty to one, and is nearly as convertible in French banks as dollars or deutsche marks—unheard of for an African currency.

Initially the foreign money earned by Africa's exports ended up in France's central bank and was used for France's development, not African progress. Instead, France shipped to Africa CFA francs, which could be used to buy the French products that would aid African development. But since CFA were convertible only *in* France, they could be used to buy goods only *from* France. Still, it was better to be able to import from France than not at all, a lesson other African nations have learned too late. Their shelves have been bare long enough, and now they are negotiating for admission to the franc zone.

There are French tourists in Africa. There are French military advisers and, in many African countries, French troops. There have been seventeen French military interventions in Africa since 1960. Many African heads of state owe their existence, their survival, and their allegiance to France. In 1987 alone, France donated $2.5 billion in African aid.

It is as though France had never left.

Out in the harbor Gorée Island sits like a scab on the smooth skin of the evening sea, raised like a welt, ugly and dark in the distance and misshapen. In the daylight and up close the island is as pretty and precious as a prize, its low buildings glimmering faintly pink in the newly risen sun. Flashes of blue from the sea and from the sky sparkle under the arches. Greenery blossoms along the narrow walkways. Bright red flowers peep around corners and over garden walls. The tops of the walls sprout a cascade of red and yellow flowers spilling over the edges and hanging down. The walls are alternately rough stucco and shiny stones worn smooth and mortared into place. The pathways are sand and light-colored pebbles ground fine and level by aeons of wind and rain, by centuries of footsteps crunching back and forth from one end of this island to the other.

There is no fresh water on the island, nothing but a trickle from a spring and a few spent wells, but there is a river of blood. A river of tears. A river of history. Gorée Island was an important slave station.

The island was barren when Portuguese navigators arrived in the fifteenth century. It was isolated and uninhabited and sheltered by the peninsula jutting out from the mainland. Ships could be harbored there, take on stores or repaired there, and remain safe from tidal waves and hurricanes. It became a European outpost.

Almost immediately, the trading of slaves began. Humans were bought and sold the same as gum and hides, gold and wax and cloth and ostrich feathers. Long before Columbus set sail for the Americas, slave labor had been used to work sugarcane plantations in Spain and Portugal and in the Atlantic islands— Cape Verde, the Azores, the Canaries. From a trading post along the Volta River on the mainland, the Portuguese supplied the islands with slaves. Between 1450 and 1500, over 150,000

African captives were bought by the Portuguese. Most of the slaves were handled and exported through Gorée Island.

Traders went deep into the African kingdoms to persuade and encourage villagers to trade humans for salt and tobacco and whiskey, powder and ammunition, trinkets and cowrie shells, glass bottles and cups. African princes and tribal chiefs sold brothers and friends for buckets of beads and armloads of blue cloth and serge.

One by one, slaves were paraded and examined for musculature and teeth, arms and legs and eyes. They were made to run and jump and speak. They were sorted and put into irons. Heavy iron collars were bolted around their necks and attached to six-foot chains to hold them in place. They were put to work on Gorée breaking and hauling rocks for construction, rolling water barrels, and unloading boats. In the night they were packed together in detention quarters, with no light and very little air. In the morning they were let out and led back to the work sites. Slaves resisting their capture were locked behind bars and kept in damp darkness until they could be loaded into the holds of ships and branded with the initials of the export company that owned them.

Slaves that revolted were either shot or stretched across large blocks of wood and chopped into pieces. Those who didn't rebel were crammed together and chained belowdecks in the cargo holds of ships. The voyage across the Atlantic lasted two months. The cargo holds were dark and damp and filthy, reeking with the stench of sweat and vomit and human waste, and packed tight to allow the merchants to deliver as many slaves as possible for the lowest cost. Many did not make it alive. Between two and six million Africans died before the ships ever reached the Americas.

In time a new society arose on Gorée. Free black men came to the island and brought their own slaves with them. They shared the island with the same men who had bought and sold their brothers and fellow tribesmen. And as tropical diseases and difficult conditions kept European women from the island, soldiers and traders took as concubines and wives local women and slaves. Their mulatto children, called *signares*, became intermediaries between the slavers and the tribal chieftains on the mainland. These signares profited hugely from the slave trade. They owned slaves themselves, and other properties. Their straw huts were torn down and rebuilt in stone. They paraded the streets wearing gold jewelry, wrist and ankle bracelets, precious gems. And Gorée prospered.

But in the nineteenth century, the trading ended. Gorée's prosperity eventually ended too. Only a thousand people live now on Gorée Island.

From the top of the only real hill on the island, Gorée is just another quiet place, a collection of tile roofs in various shades of orange and red and rust. The walls in the distance are sand colored. The dark green trees are bunched so close together they are like a forest. You cannot see the pink blossoms or the purple flowers. You cannot see the clinging vines or the low shrubs.

Amid all the color, the old slave cells are somber now, monuments to a history long forgotten in the never-ending onslaught of life.

The late-afternoon sun shimmers down in waves bright and warm, bouncing off the leaves in the tops of trees and transforming them into a thousand ghosts, green and fluorescent. The breezes that earlier billowed in the trees now whistle softly for a moment, then stop. Everything is still.

The boulevard leading up from the harbor is spotted in irregular patterns of white light from the sun and black shadows falling from the thick trees that line the road. Up the hill, Dakar puts on a cosmopolitan face. Place de l'Indépendance is a grassy mall with benches all around. Today it is decorated with airy tents and display booths for some sort of francophone convention, an enormous assemblage of delegations from French-speaking countries. A motorcade screams by as some foreign dignitary and his entourage pass. Sirens blare. Pedestrians scamper across the road.

Around the square, Dakar is an urban zone of high-rise banks and office buildings, some of them fifteen stories high, hotels and apartments, plainly built and inelegant. At one end the dome of the Catholic cathedral towers above the street and glints red in the afternoon light. Nearby on a rising bluff the president's home stands like a royal palace, guarded by soldiers crisply uniformed but friendly. They cheerfully give directions.

The entire area is lively with movement and yet there is a casualness. Businessmen wear suits but no ties. Their collars are open to catch what little breeze stirs as they pass back and forth between buildings and banks. They carry briefcases and portfolios under their arms.

Along avenue Pompidou there are outdoor cafés where Europeans gather and sip cool drinks. Young African boys hawk newspapers up and down the street; old women sit on the ground and shell peanuts or hold up the things they sell, offering them to passing tourists.

I walk with my new friend Mamadou, who came to me as I was strolling down by the harbor. He was grinning from ear to ear, teeth glowing brighter than white against his dark skin. He reached out his hand to me, grabbing mine even before I could offer it. He held on to it all the time we talked, even as we started to walk. He let my hand drop only when he wanted to show me the wad of business cards and scraps of paper he carried in his pockets. On each piece of paper was scribbled the name and address of someone in America.

"One day when I go there," he said, "I will have many friends."

He tries to engage me in conversation, asking me about America, wanting to know if everyone there is rich.

"Not everyone," I say.

"Not rich, maybe, but everyone has a home and plenty to eat?"

"Not everyone."

"But there are no beggars on the street," he informs me. "And work is easy to find."

He wants to hear that America is paradise. He wants desperately to go there.

"And racism no longer exists?" he asks.

"It's perhaps not as bad as it used to be, but it exists. I guess it will always exist. In a way, it's natural, I suppose, to want to keep something in the family. You know? So there are those who give the money or the job to their brother, or to their wife's brother, or maybe to someone who went to the same school, or someone from the same hometown, a fellow countryman, someone of the same race."

I try to think of a way to say *old-boy network* in French, but I cannot.

But Mamadou understands.

"Yes," he says. "It happens like that here too."

In Africa it is called *tribalism*. Racism doesn't rest on white shoulders alone. It exists wherever some men have what other men want—power, money, jobs, women, food. As long as there is a way for them to keep things for themselves and for others like them. We hunger to belong and we search for ways to identify the ones who are like us and the ones who are not. Race, color, family, tribe, and religion. Same school, same shoe size. We always find a way.

A young man sits on the low stone wall that surrounds the place de l'Indépendance. He wears a flat tweed cap and his trousers are shredded at the hems. There is a hole in his right knee. On his dirty feet he wears black slip-slops with one strap ripped through.

His hair is cut close, shaved almost. There are two dark scars on his left cheek, two scars in the same place on his right. They are tribal markings of the Fulani. His eyes bulge with anger and despair. They threaten, they plead. They lock on to me and I feel them following me like a heat sensor on a missile.

I know he is going to beg for something, and I try to ignore him. But when he calls me I cannot help myself. I go to him, sit on the wall beside him, and we shake hands.

He holds my hand as if we were lovers in a park. This is not strange. On the streets of North Africa men walk together holding hands. In black Africa too. Rarely is any such display of affection shown publicly between a man and a woman, but men hold hands in Africa. I am not surprised by it anymore, but when some man I have just met takes my hand and holds it for moments that seem too long to me, I squirm just a little.

The initial discomfort soon passes. I stop glancing nervously around to see who is watching. I look instead at the bloodshot eyes of the man still holding my hand. Beneath his anger there is a deep tiredness as sad as Mbaye's in Paris. Here is a man lost. He has no voice and is reduced to asking strangers on street corners to listen to him. He has been sitting here a long time, waiting for me.

"It is not right," he says. "It isn't fair. I am not a stupid man. I did not come from the bush. I am educated. I know about computers. I know about a lot of things."

His voice begins to strain.

"I don't want to sit here on this wall all day watching the cars go by, doing things I despise just so I can eat. I don't want to beg. I want to work. I want a job. I don't want anybody to give me anything except a job. Nothing else. I'm a good worker, a hard worker. I'm intelligent."

The pleading turns to anger.

"I'm not lazy. I'm not like those people from the bush. They can't do anything. They don't know anything. They're from the bush, man. Stupid, stupid people from the bush, from the jungle, but those are the people who get the jobs."

Angrier and angrier until he is almost shouting, repeating himself and bobbing as he talks, looking at me so hard that he looks right past me.

"Nobody gives you a job because of what you can do. You have to be from the right tribe, the right village. So we get these stupid people from the bush doing important work, and that's why nothing works right in Senegal. That's why people from France are running our businesses and our lives. The government steals from the people so they can have palaces in France. They take what little we have and buy big cars for themselves and their friends. They leave us to beg on the streets, with shit to eat and houses made of paper. That's why I want to go to America. Can't you help me?"

The final plea he whispers. His head hangs down and he averts his eyes so I cannot see his shame. When he turns back to me his eyes have narrowed to a hard squint of anger. Too soon he gives up. His eyelids become heavy and he looks about to cry.

Mamadou and I cross over to the crowded world of the Sandaga market, where sunlight brightens everything. The streets are narrow and crowded. The market overflows with people. We are swimming in a sea of black faces. There is much movement, but nothing really happens. The same people pass, first going one way, a few minutes later going the other. They roam back and forth all day with nothing else to do.

Outside one of the stalls, men sit on broken chairs held together by pieces of string. To make a bench, someone has nailed a plank unevenly to blocks of wood. It wobbles. The shack is made of cardboard boxes flattened out and pressed together. Inside a shop a man makes and repairs clothes on a very old mechanical sewing machine, his feet working the pedals that make the clackety machine rattle and run. Shoppers look but they seldom buy. Mostly the people who pass stop only to chat and visit, the same as Mamadou and I. Later we sit on a bench in the shade of a different stall where Mamadou's brother sells batteries and handkerchiefs, pots and plastic pans. We watch the crowds milling by.

Soon an old man comes along. He walks slowly, like royalty, stopping in each stall he passes. He is known by everyone and greeted with great respect. When he comes to the stall where Mamadou and I sit, Mamadou stands and shakes the old man's hand. The old man stands regally aloof, looking all around with his hand held out and his nose in the air. Though he never looks directly at Mamadou, the young man's face is alive with respect and lighted with joy at the greeting. Mamadou bows and touches his forehead to the man's hand, repeating this gesture several times before offering the man a seat. The old man sits in the shade beside me and rests a few moments before carrying on. Mamadou introduces me with pride as his American friend and then stands silently beside the old man. The old man is not impressed. He is the important one here. He is the one people bow to.

When I was a small boy there were always old men sitting outside the barbershop where I used to get my hair cut. I remember them now. They would have liked it here, sitting in the shade of an African market and watching the traffic pass. Those men would sit for hours with nothing to do, nowhere to go. Sometimes they would sit and talk, telling stories, telling lies. Sometimes they would just sit quietly with nothing new to say. They had said it all before. They had heard it all before. And then someone would pass that they recognized, someone in a new car, someone in an old suit, someone they could laugh at and talk about.

Time had a way of stretching out and standing still for them then, making the days longer and their lives longer too. And I used to wonder how in the world they could sit like that all the time. I was a young boy ripe with energy and bursting with plans and dreams of many tomorrows. I never stopped to think that longer days and longer lives might not be the blessing they seemed.

Those old men commanded a certain respect from me, the respect all kids had for old people then. One of the old men sitting there would call out: "Hey, young blood! Run up to the store and buy a pack of cigarettes for me." Or some old lady would send one of us to the corner to pick up a can of soup. She knew us only as "sonny" or "little boy," and we knew her only because we had seen her a thousand times before, sitting and rocking in the summer sun on her front porch as we passed on our way to play ball. And though we were in a hurry to get to the playground, we would run to the store for her and for the old men, hoping for a coin or two, maybe enough for a cold soda. But even if there were no reward, we went anyway. We went out of respect, the pension they had earned just by living so long.

For us there were a thousand tomorrows to sift through, to plan for, to dream about. We could get tired just thinking about all the living we would do before we were old enough to sit for endless hours watching traffic go by.

Here in Africa even the young somehow seem old, and they do not mind sitting for those endless hours. Young men sit beside old ones. There is nothing to do but watch the people and the days passing, listen to the wind, and wait for something to happen. Lives here are shorter in time, but they are infinitely long in the emptiness of the days.

If you live in Africa and you survive your fiftieth birthday, you are an old old man. Ten percent of the babies born don't even last the first year of life. In Mali, 50 percent die before they are five.

The old man sitting beside me, then, is ancient, the respect for him a greater reward in this place where the young seem so old and where it is no easy task to earn an old man's age. Surviving is not without effort and a great deal of luck.

If you earn a thousand dollars a year, in some places you live very well, in others you are wealthy. The camera swinging from my shoulder is more than a year's backbreaking wages for some.

Beside me on this bench sits the prebirth of the blues, and if I were a singer of the blues I would sing sad songs about the waiting, about having nothing to do. Here beside me is the prebirth of the nearly endless patience afflicting black people. This is how and where we learned to wait and to ask, *How long, oh Lord, how long?*

A luxury hotel stands on a hill that is landscaped like an English country garden. A lush lawn and shrubbery rise in tiers up the hill. A curved walkway snakes across the grass from the hotel to the street. Low bushes and flowers grow alongside the walkway. A black gardener waters the greenery with a hose. He stops to take a drink of water.

Across the street the property of the hotel continues down to the sea. An enormous patio spreads across the lawn and opens on a swimming pool. A guard at the gate stops me when I step inside to have a look. Mamadou waits timidly in the street.

The guards are black, the gardeners are black, a man picking up trash is black. All the folks lounging like lizards by the side of the pool are Europeans. They sip tropical drinks and bathe in the sun.

"Why can't we go in?" I ask the guard.

"You have to be guests of the hotel."

"Come on. We just want to have a quick look around. We won't stay long and no one will ever know."

But he is devoted to duty and even a bit huffy.

"You cannot go in. And that's all."

Mamadou calls me with a modest wave of two fingers. He shakes his head as if to tell me that this is not how things are done. He doesn't want to cause trouble.

"Come on," he says to me. "Let's walk over this way."

If he sees anything ironic in the situation, he says nothing.

I frown at the guard and shake my finger at him.

Farther along this row of luxury hotels, a path dips sharply downhill to the beach. The sand is oily black in many places and littered with debris: cans and plastic bottles, driftwood washed up by the surf, tree limbs and shrubs thrown into the ravine by the gardeners pruning bushes and landscaping the terraces. The beach is crowded with black children running along the shore and dashing into and out of the playful surf. A few swim in the bay. Some adults lie on the beach, quietly getting darker in the sun. Others sit fully clothed, looking forlornly out to sea.

At the end of this narrow strip of beach a pier juts out into the water—an outdoor deck for European vacationers who eat and drink here and bathe in the sun. They are a mélange. Old men with gray-haired chests wear the skimpy bikini bathing suits of younger men. Their skin sags. Their soft bellies bulge over the tops of the suits. Long-legged blonds bake their naked breasts in the sun. Their hair is piled high on their heads; their bodies glisten with suntan lotion; their bottoms are barely covered in bikinis every bit as skimpy as the old men's. They use the pier as their private sun deck. Most locals cannot afford to eat or drink here. They come to the base of the pier to squint in the sun and see how these others live.

Waiters carry drinks, light meals, and sandwiches to the sun worshipers, who lie about like bored princes and queens. The servers are black.

I cannot help but notice the inequity. I think I am becoming a racist.

"Mamadou, are you thirsty? Would you like a cold drink?"

"We might be able to get one on the corner by the bank."

"No, I mean here. Do you want to sit on the deck?"

How many times has he passed this place and glanced out to glimpse paradise? Perhaps he even promised himself that one day he would sit out there and sip sodas, have lunch, spend money. The notion would flicker past his eyes too quickly for him to mouth the words, so unlikely was the possibility.

In his eyes flashes a tiny sparkle that quickly dims. He smiles nervously.

"No, let's go," he says.

"Come. Let's sit and relax a little. I'm tired."

Mamadou gives in. He nods. Once he agrees, his nervous smile broadens into a great grin and he leads the way in.

The first waiter turns to greet us and stops, a little stunned. The other waiters react as if on cue. Each one at the very same time as the others slowly turns to watch us pass. Suddenly, even I am a little nervous and doubtful. I tug at the waist of my pants and summon up my bravado. I saunter in as if I, like the Europeans, own the place. We sit in the shade of an overhanging canopy.

A waiter sneaks up to our table.

"What can I bring for you, gentlemen?"

Mamadou wants nothing to eat and only a soda to drink. I ask for a gin and tonic.

A dish of peanuts is laid before us on the table. Mamadou sits up straight, but I slouch in my chair and let the sun fall on my face. Between sips I hold the cold glass against my forehead to cool me. The condensation runs down my arm. The sea breeze blows warm and steady from the west.

The deck reaches out over the water. The sea is calm and green. Farther out the water breaks blue and white in gentle crests. On the bleached wooden deck, fleshy bellies, wide hips, and pale, naked breasts sprawl on white plastic beach chairs. Men and women sip drinks and read, or they simply lie quietly, and do nothing at all. There is no conversation among these pale strangers.

I do not want to be like them, but in many ways I already am and cannot help it, more like them than like these others whom I so visibly resemble. It is odd.

Over the red and white metal rails of the deck, black children a world away continue cavorting in the water.

The sun sits low in the sky and slips slowly toward the horizon. It is a blaze so bright it erases the blue from sky and sea.

At the end of the deck there is a ship's wheel, a decorative addition that faces west. A young man stands at the wheel, his hands on the wooden pegs as if he were steering this deck and its passengers out to sea. In the haze of distance Gorée Island rides on the waves and on the wind and holds steady in time. It bobs up and down on the sea but never completely disappears.

Mamadou and I sit quietly, waiting for the evening to come, waiting for the sun to sink into the sea.

In the outlying areas of Dakar, the paved roads lose their city smoothness. They are rutted and dotted with potholes. There is no pavement at the sides of the roads, only gravel and dirt the orange color of rust. Shoes have disappeared, even the slip-slops. Men and women walk barefoot.

In the heart of Dakar a bus stops and I get on. I don't know where it's going. I'm not heading anywhere in particular, just going, just looking, just trying to understand a little more.

The bus rattles to a stop and farts a large gust of sooty exhaust. I hold my nose and squeeze in the back door along with the enormous crowd.

Near the door sits a man in a caged booth. People pay him as they get on and he in turn hands them little white tickets. Periodically inspectors will get on, shoving through the crowd and checking tickets. Anyone caught without a ticket will be dragged off the bus and embarrassed. He will be dealt with most severely. The fine makes the risk almost unacceptable. The bus ride costs only thirty CFA.

I stand in the line at the cage and wait for the man inside to tell me how much to pay. He never tells me. I never pay. Thirty CFA *is* thirty CFA, after all. Each coin is precious.

The man in the cage gives me the evil eye, but he says nothing. It's not his job to make me pay, nor to warn me about the consequences.

At each stop more and more people jam aboard. I am shoved deeper into the crowd, farther away from the doors, farther from the man selling tickets. Fear nags me and I consider paying, but now it would be impossible to get back to the cage.

The air is thick and moist and stale with sweat. The bus smells of mildew. As people get on and others get off, I move closer to the window. The air outside is clouded with soot and exhaust. I cannot stand up straight because I am too tall. At the side of the bus, the roof arches down. I have to hunch over to fit. At every rut in the road the bus runs over, my head bangs against the metal roof. If I lean too far forward, my face is jammed into some lady's armpit. And at every bus stop is the threat of a ticket inspector getting on.

Dakar raises from the plain, a low, crowded place radiating from the center of the city and extending far to the northeast. The earth is the ocher dust of the desert and the red laterite of rocky soil rich in iron. The city is gray.

From the tops of the undulating hills the city appears as a crazy jumble of shacks thrown one on top of another in chaos. From street level the view is different. Dakar is poor, but not painfully so. The homes are small, made mostly of concrete, and there are many shacks. But the streets are wide and shady, a blessing in the heat that makes men and women slow moving and motionless. They sit in the shade or stay in the house.

Not so the children. They feel no heat. For them there are open spaces and fenced-in compounds on the corner where they play running games. They chase one another with sticks. They kick a ball around in the patch of dirt surrounded by overhanging trees. It is a serene existence.

But at the next corner serenity vanishes. A crowd of uniforms waits for the bus to stop. When it does and the doors open, two men fly off. They leap too slowly and fall into the arms of the waiting bus inspectors.

The panic in my eyes is a dead giveaway. The man in the cage smiles, but says nothing. It is not his job. Two inspectors climb on the bus and begin checking tickets. I move away from them, edging toward the front of the bus. Two more inspectors get on in front and move my way.

The center doors are open, but still there are the inspectors who have nabbed the other freeloaders. They are shaking them down, searching them, going through their identity papers.

I can't go forward. I can't go toward the rear. I can't get off.

I could try, I guess, to explain that I didn't understand the procedure.

"You mean you thought the buses were free?" They would laugh because I am so stupid. "Are they free where you come from?"

"No," I would say. "But they ought to be."

That wouldn't work.

Maybe I should pretend not to understand French.

That wouldn't work either.

When they drag me off the bus, maybe I should just run for it as fast as I can and hide.

The men coming from the rear are right beside me. They ask a short man for his ticket. He can't find it. They drag him off and hand him over to the men outside. The men from the front are coming closer.

My heart pounds. Sweat pours from my face and arms. This time it isn't the heat.

The two sets of inspectors are coming together and in an instant they will be right beside me. One man looks at me. Then he looks at the other inspectors. I try to look innocent. I try to look foreign. I stand up tall and try to look American. It works. Something certainly has worked.

Each inspector assumes someone else has already checked my ticket. They all turn at the center doors and get off. The man in the cage is still smiling at me. He has watched and enjoyed it all. The smile I return breaks into uncontrollable laughter, nearly hysteria. I convulse with relief and with disbelief that I would try such a stupid stunt and be so lucky as to escape.

Thirty CFA. Less than one-tenth of a dollar. Not enough at home for a chocolate bar or a cup of coffee.

It is an odd sensation, to feel the helplessness the Africans often feel and yet to escape their fate precisely because I have acted differently. If I was trying hard to belong, my head banging against the top of the bus has reminded me that I do not fit. I am neither one thing nor the other.

My heart is still pounding when I get off the bus at the next stop.

FIVE

THE MISFORTUNE
IN MEN'S EYES ▶▶▶▶▶▶▶▶▶▶▶▶

The Gambia
Guinea-Bissau

Thomas Wolfe said that going home again is like stepping into a river. You cannot step into the same river twice; you cannot go home again. After a very long time away, you will not find the same home you left behind. It will be different, and so will you. It is quite possible that home will not be home at all, meaningless except for its sentimental place in your heart. At best it will point the long way back to where you started, its value lying in how it helped to shape you and in the part of home you have carried away.

Alex Haley went to Africa in the mid-sixties. Somehow he had managed to trace his roots back to a little village called Juffure, upriver from Banjul in the forests of The Gambia. It was the same village from which his ancestors had been stolen and forced into slavery. In some way Haley must have felt he was returning home: a flood of emotions, an awakening of the memories hidden in his genes.

Those were the two extremes between which I was trapped. I could not go home again, yet here I was. Africa was

137

so long ago the land of my ancestors that it held for me only a symbolic significance. Yet there was enough to remind me that what I carry as a human being has come in part from Africa. I did not feel African, but was beginning to feel not wholly American anymore either. I felt like an orphan, a waif without a home.

I was not trying to find the village that had once been home to my people, nor would I stand and talk to people who could claim to be my relatives, as Haley had done. The thought of running into someone who looked like a relative terrified me, for that would have been too concrete, too much proof. My Africanism was abstract and I wanted it to remain so. I did not need to hear the names of my ancient ancestors or know what they looked like. I had seen the ways they loved their children in the love of my father. I would see their faces and their smiles one day in the eyes of my children.

Haley found what he was seeking. I hardly knew what I was looking for, except perhaps to know where home once was, to know how much of me is really me, how much of being black has been carried out of Africa.

I got on another bus and the bus took me to the river. Beside me on the bus sat a Senegalese doctor who looked grim and determined, repeatedly wiping his damp, sweaty brow with a dirty white handkerchief. This bus was a great effort for him. He had been educated in Paris and in Aix-en-Provence, a quiet college town on the southern edge of the French Alps where the weather is always mild. He had been away from home for too long and now he suffered in the heat. He didn't like the dust in his eyes. He was no longer used to it. He would rather have been in France, it seemed, than here.

The bus roared on and the road ahead disappeared around a bend into the bush. Huts, each one with a grass roof, clustered in little villages lining the road. Chickens scurried across the road to avoid being squashed by the bus. Villagers with nothing better to do sat in the shade and watched our passing. The doctor beside me lifted his upper lip in a sneer at the villagers and shook his head.

"How long have you been away?" I asked, for he seemed less acclimated to the heat than I was, and unused to the slow pace and the backwardness.

"It isn't that," he said. "It is simply that one cannot see himself until he has stopped seeing himself. Do you understand?"

I made a long, hesitant sound, encouraging him to go on.

"I shave every morning," he said. "I cannot see the changes in my face because they are so gradual they are not changes at all. I do not know if I looked different last year."

He lifted a finger to his cheek.

"But here is a dark place," he said, pointing to a blemish under his left eye. "If suddenly after two years without seeing my face I notice this thing, I will say to myself, 'That wasn't there before.' And that is how I feel coming home. I see how very little has changed. If we are moving forward at all, we are moving so slowly that in comparison with France and the rest of the world, Africa is moving backwards. Mostly, I think, we are standing still."

On the seat in front of us a mother holds her little two-year-old daughter, who is tiny, much smaller than she ought to be. She wears a dingy little dress and plastic panties. She sucks on her mother's breast only for comfort. For thirst she drinks from a bottle filled with an orange-colored juice. When the juice has run its course, the mother stands the child in the aisle and pulls off the plastic pants. She lets the baby pee on the floor of the bus. Wetness runs down the child's leg and onto the floor in a puddle. When the bus runs up a short hill, the puddle spreads and runs in a long, thin line to the back of the bus and soaks a young man's luggage. He kicks his suitcase out of the path of the little stream and says nothing.

The doctor purses his lips and shakes his head again.

"We are not very advanced," he says. "You wouldn't find this in France."

"Oh, I don't know," I tell him. "I've seen worse in Paris."

He looks at me in disbelief. In defending his native home, however slightly, I have insulted his adoptive home, and he bristles.

"Yes," I say. "I saw a woman stop her car at place de la Madeleine so her little boy could defecate on the curb. Grown men urinate on the street. And there are dogs and cats in every restaurant in Paris. France and Africa are not always so different."

Now he laughs. "Perhaps," he says, "they learned something from us after all." But his mirth doesn't last very long.

The baby, now standing in her mother's lap, peeps around her mother's shoulder at me. Her eyes are big and wide around, like the moon. She coos and grins as any happy baby would. I make faces and she stares at me with those great round eyes. The whites of her eyes are so clear and so bright they seem faintly blue, the black irises so dark I can see myself in them. She smiles and she is beautiful.

The doctor's grim seriousness returns and replaces his smile. "That baby," he says coldly, "will be dead before the year is out."

I let out a little moan.

"Malnutrition," he explains. "Poor hygiene. Dehydration. If she doesn't die this year, she will die next year, or the year after. Chances are that she will never live to be five."

The hammer strikes full force and straight on. All the statistics condense into this one moment, into this one tiny child's bright eyes.

"France and Africa are a little different," he says. "And in many ways it is France's fault."

"I thought you liked France so much."

"I do," he replies. "I love France. I feel more at home there. France is very advanced. And in France there is real freedom. Not like here. In Africa our lives are not our own. There is still slavery here, in Mauritania, in Sudan. There are no freedoms from forced labor or from torture or corporal punishment. And privacy—ha! Privacy is a foreign concept. Our phones are tapped, our mail is read, and we have to carry identity papers to go from one city to the next. This is not freedom. We are only pretending. And Senegal is better than most African countries."

His dark face frowns tightly.

"France is much better with her former colonies than Portugal was, but we are the way we are because of the Europeans. They eroded our culture and left nothing in its place but an envy for theirs. They divided us into countries that make no sense. Some man with a pencil and a map drew our borders according to some European scheme and ignored tribal divisions. We call ourselves Senegalese as if we were one nation, but we are many.

We are Mandigo and Fulani and we do not trust one another. We are poor and our leaders are corrupt and we do not fight back. We don't know how. Instead, we turn them into gods because after so many years of white rulers, any black ruler is better. Or so we think."

It reminds me of home and the crooked black politicians who get into office only because they are black and who stay there. Their black constituents put them there and keep them there. After a while they think they can get away with anything.

The bus stopped at Kaolack, a town halfway between Dakar and the river, and the doctor climbed off. There was time enough to get off the bus and stretch, grab a cold drink, and get something to eat from the crowd of vendors gathered around the bus. I helped the doctor with his bags, and before he left, I asked him why, if he hated this place so much, he had come back.

"I came back because this is my country," he said. "This is where I belong. This is my home and I can help here in ways I never could anywhere else."

He looked at the vendors crowding against the travelers. He looked down the long, dusty road. He looked at the dilapidated bus and he shook his head once more. A broad grin broke out across his face and completely consumed it.

"Hate this place?" he said. "What makes you think I hate this place?" He started to laugh. "This is life. As long as one is living, one is truly alive here." He shook his head again. "I could live in Paris the rest of my days, but always a part of me would be here, in this heat, eating this dust, among these poor people. I love this place."

He took my hand and squeezed it.

"I am of two hearts," he said. "I love Paris, but I don't like to see babies die. One day we will develop and modernize, but I will be sad to see such simple ways of living disappear. If you are not careful, the same thing will happen to you."

"What same thing?"

He grinned even more broadly.

"You will not be the same when you leave. If you leave America behind and get into Africa truly, you will understand my complaints—the suffering and the starvation, the traditions that weigh us down—and you will have a crisis of the heart. When you talk about Africa, people will think you hate this place. That's when you will remember me and you will know then just how much you love this place and these people."

He laughed a hearty, welcoming laugh and finally let go of my hand.

"Be well, my friend," he said. "And have a good journey."

As he walked away, a little pack of children followed like puppies at his heels, trying to sell him a cold drink. He brushed them aside.

I was hungry, and the children sensed it. A swarm of them descended on me and encircled me. They were selling bananas and peanuts, and in little plastic sacks they sold water and juice drinks. I bought peanuts and bananas, but was afraid to drink the water. I shooed the kids away.

A man came to the side of the bus, carrying pieces of hot meat in the bucket dangling at his side. The meat floated in hot water and could have been beef or lamb or goat or someone's dog. It didn't matter. Most of it looked like nothing more than fat and gristle. I didn't want any.

A young man about nineteen years old moved up close and examined the meat floating in the bucket, pointing at various pieces. He had his eye on a particularly large piece and told the vendor to show it to him. The vendor speared it with the sharp end of his knife, but when he held it up, the teenager decided against it. He shook his head and pointed at another piece. The vendor speared it and held it up. This time the young man nodded. The vendor slapped the meat down on a wooden block, then whacked a knife up and down it so quickly that the metal blurred. He sprinkled salt and a spicy red powder on the chunks and laid them on a piece of torn brown wrapping paper. The teenager paid and went back to his seat on the bus. I went back to my seat, too.

On the seat in front of me the woman and her little daughter shared a drink from a plastic bag. When they finished, she tossed the trash out the window and onto the road. I offered her my bunch of bananas. She took two, ate one, and tried to get the little girl to eat the other. She threw the peels out the window.

When I had eaten all the bananas I cared to, I offered the rest to those around me. In exchange they offered me peanuts. The young man who had bought the meat held out the brown paper with the chunks dripping grease on it. I didn't want any, didn't even know quite what it was. But I took a piece anyway.

To go where they go, to eat what they eat, to walk this mile in their shoes: these are the things a traveler must do.

I turned the piece of meat in my hand and the grease ran hot down my arm. I tried to find a bite that was not mostly fat, but there wasn't one. I lost my nerve.

The teenager's name was Peter. He moved up to sit beside me now, waiting to offer me another piece. He grinned and nodded his urging that I hurry and eat the first one. I smiled weakly and popped the thing into my mouth.

The meat was hot and had the texture of coagulated oatmeal. When I bit it, the juice and fat squirted loose and filled my mouth. There was little to chew, only a small bit of meat that was tough and stringy. I thought immediately about spitting it out, but there was no place to spit. I had little choice but to chew and try to swallow. The meat was salty and spicy hot. As I continued to chew, it began to taste quite nice, further arousing my appetite. When he offered me a second piece, I took it and ate that one too.

The road twisted past an old cement factory. The bus clamored and bellowed and coughed out clouds of heavy exhaust. Far ahead the road narrowed, came to a point in the silver haze, and vanished.

Peter sat beside me munching the meat and humming. He had plugged into his ears a tiny pair of headphones connected to a pocket-sized cassette tape player. The music in his head made him bounce in his seat. He tapped his feet on the floor of the bus and swayed back and forth, side to side. His eyes were closed. When he finished eating he tossed the paper out the window and began drumming on the seat in front of him. The little baby had stopped staring at me. She was watching Peter instead. She was captivated by the rhythms he was beating on the seat. The baby bounced up and down, dancing in the arms of her mother, who looked back just as Peter was holding his arms up and reaching for the child. The baby bashfully buried those big round eyes into her mother's shoulder and held tightly to her. Slowly she peeped out again. Peter was still reaching for her. The baby managed a smile. Peter leaned forward and lifted the baby away from her mother. The mother never looked concerned, as if she knew Peter. She didn't, but she trusted him and took a little nap. Peter hugged the baby and they danced to music she could not hear. She hopped around in Peter's lap and laughed and made happy sounds. She never cried or fretted, and only twice turned to make sure Mama was still there.

Something rare and warm was happening. From one moment to the next Africa could be harsh and bitter, then suddenly soft. You never knew what to expect.

And then suddenly the moment passes.

The bus stops, and Mama takes her baby back. The bus has pulled off the road and into a large parking compound. The lot is rutted and brown and red with pebbles and dust. In the very center of the lot there is a flagpole that flies a torn tricolor of green and yellow and red with a green star in the center. It is the Senegalese flag. This is the border station.

There is a mad scramble on the bus to find identity papers. The mother grabs her baby and wraps the child in a long cloth. She ties the cloth around her waist and straps the little girl to her back like a little monkey, facing forward and clinging tight. They get off the bus.

We all climb down, taking our gear with us. One man in the back of the bus, carrying his belongings in two large pillow slips, stuffs the slips under the seat in front of him and jumps off the bus empty-handed.

Soldiers sit in the shade. They wear sunglasses. Their uniforms are olive green and wrinkled, open at the throat. Their boots are covered with the red dust. None of them smiles. They linger as long as they want in the shade, only emerging when they feel like it. They swagger as they walk, purposefully clutching their guns. Now they begin the search through each piece of luggage.

A guard makes a routine walk-through on the bus, then steps down without comment. But a second guard follows him. He searches more thoroughly and discovers the two pillowcases. The man who hid them finally admits they are his, and the soldiers shove him aside. He won't be going anywhere soon. This is more than a matter of simply paying a fine. A group of soldiers encircles him. They tear open the pillowcases, dumping out clothes and food and scattering everything on the ground.

Perhaps they will find what he is trying to smuggle; perhaps they will just have sport with him.

"What are they looking for?" I ask Peter.

"I think some batteries and some clothes he bought in Dakar. He was going to sell them in Banjul. He does it all the time."

"You know him?"

"He is a friend of my brother."

"What will they do to him?"

"They will humiliate him a little, keep his things, and take his money. Then they will let him go."

Peter has seen it a thousand times before. He takes it all casually.

On the other side of a barrier gate we are checked again, this time by Gambian soldiers. And then we come to the river.

The Gambia River spreads out broad and steel gray and raging, tossing waves that are high and frothy, wild as an ocean. The wind storms over the river but never reaches the shore, never stirs the dust. The wind blows and carries with it dark sounds from the forest inland and upriver—animal noises, screeches and grunting sounds, and the heavy wind in the trees and in the scrub bushes sounding like thunder. Seabirds drift in the sky and their shrieks pierce the calm like an alarm. There is no landscape, only water and the faint outline of Banjul on the opposite shore, low on the horizon.

Clouds come together into what might have been thunderheads, but they refuse to rain. The air remains hot and dry and the clouds wisp away into thin feathery streaks that hang on the horizon like a memory. The sun burns down. The ground is parched. The smell of drying peanuts hangs in the air.

Peter leads me down to the wharf, where we slip through the gate at the loading dock. The heavy machinery floods the air with sounds of banging and clanging. Men shout orders and requests. They joke the way men do who lift and labor heavily. They are unloading peanuts from riverboats, preparing them for shipment overland to Dakar. Peanuts litter the ground.

Peter and I sit on the edge of the pier and wait apart from the others, who stand in a big pack of people and their pigs and goats. When the ferry comes, Peter leaps off the wall. I follow him down across the rocks below. We scurry aboard the boat like stowaways. We don't buy tickets.

We sit in the bow of the ferry. The river-spray mists all around us in a cloud that shields us from the heat. Clouds drift in the sky. Schools of thin silvery fish float near the surface of the water. Sea gulls dive down to pick at them. Banjul rises.

Banjul shimmers like an illusion in the rainbow mist of river spray. In the haze of distance the city moves closer and recedes. It pitches on the waves of the river and bobs on the water. When the boat rises on the waves, Banjul sinks just a little.

In Banjul the names of streets and places carry a decidedly British lilt: Wellington Street, Admiralty Wharf, Albert Market. The city itself was called Bathurst until 1973. The police in their khaki-colored shirts and short pants are stiff and crisp with a British air of propriety and duty. But when you ask them directions, they look befuddled and direct you instead to the police station, where maybe someone will be better able to help you.

The Gambia was colonized by Great Britain. Although the country is just a little tongue jutting into the face of Senegal and surrounded by it, and although there was a brief period during which the Gambia and Senegal were linked in a confederation as one country, there is no residual Frenchness. Nothing French has spilled over, not culture, not language. English is the official language in The Gambia.

There are a few two-story buildings in Banjul, but none taller. The streets are not paved. They are almost entirely red laterite crushed to dust, with as many potholes as an exploded minefield. Battered and shabby old cars bounce slowly over the ruts in the road. Taxis honk. Trucks rattle and sputter. The streets are crowded with a confusion of pedestrian traffic. The noise is terrific.

But there is a certain pleasantness. You almost expect to hear the World Service of the BBC coming from a radio on the balcony overhead. However, this is still Africa. Buildings are crumbling down. The water system does not work. Electricity regularly shuts down. Banjul is just another African city on the edge of the world, discarded and forgotten.

The city lies near the mouth of the Gambia River, which is

so wide here that you cannot tell where the river empties in and where the sea begins. Along the beach there are tourist hotels for European travelers. Peter insists that I follow him home and stay the night with his family in his father's compound.

I look up the river from where we stand and I wonder what lies around the next bend. Is there a road into the jungle and out the other side? Haley's Juffure is up there somewhere.

"Come on," Peter urges. "My father's compound is big. There will be very much room, and you will be very comfortable."

I give in and follow him.

Near the market there is a parking lot filled with old, beat-up minibuses. Crowds of people push to get on here. Peter takes me by the hand and pulls me along. The little bus going toward his suburban village is already packed full, but we squeeze in.

The place where Peter lives is a little concrete village of gravel roads and open lots strewn with empty bottles and cans and metal barrels filled with trash. His father's compound is hidden behind a high brick and concrete wall. The gate is made of corrugated tin. It barely hangs on its hinges and never completely closes; it only opens far enough for us to squeeze through sideways. There is no grass in the front yard, just a mound of dirt and small rocks. There is a discarded mattress, stained and dirty. Off to the side of the compound, an old car has been parked for years and left to rust.

This is not what I expected. The big compound doesn't seem so big, certainly not so comfortable.

Out back there is a small grove of bare mango trees. There are also rows plowed in the dirt, but the ground is dry and nothing grows. The rains haven't yet begun.

Peter's father sits on the front porch. He is much older than I imagined, for Peter is only a teenager. Peter's complexion is very dark. His father is much lighter. But the old man has skin like a leather harness, long used and uncared for. He is very bald, wears a long robe, and listens to the afternoon BBC news broadcast. He rises, standing proud and stiff when he looks at me. He frowns in the sun when he offers me his hand.

"Welcome," he shouts. "Be at ease here and come. Sit in the shade."

When he sits, he leans forward as if to hear the radio better.

There is more static than news. I sit back, leaning against a post and fanning flies.

"Are you hot?" the old man asks, still shouting. "Would you like a drink?"

He sends Peter to fetch him a pitcher of water. The water is tempting with its cool wetness, even if the glasses are clouded with stains and very dirty. I want a drink badly, but I force myself to resist.

"Are you sure?" the father asks. He lifts his glass slowly and pours the water into his mouth one swallow at a time, his Adam's apple bobbing like a little heartbeat with each gulp.

Suddenly the air, even in the shade, grows hotter. The old man takes another sip and the air grows hotter still.

I look up to the sky at wispy clouds hanging so tantalizingly high.

"Do you think it will rain soon?" I ask.

His face is dry and crinkled with the same wrinkles that line everyone's face. But it is quick to form an expression of gaiety. The rest of him is slow moving and tired.

"It will rain," he says, "when it rains. Not a moment before."

It is a question of faith.

God fills the air and is as ever-present as the heat.

Their lives are not their own. They sit in the laps of the gods. Destiny and fate are held always in the hands of someone else. They sit and they wait. They wait for rain. They wait for salvation. They wait for God. They have been waiting forever.

Peter and I left the compound to go to a little shop two streets away. He traded a few coins for two paper cones, one of sugar, one of tea. We went back to the compound.

Behind the house we lit a charcoal fire. Peter boiled water and stuffed a small pot full of tea. He dumped in plenty of sugar. We waited for the pot to boil over. Mosquitoes buzzed in the shade. Flies swarmed all around. The metal roof overhanging the concrete patio kept out the sun, but there was no keeping out the heat. It bounced off the dirt and off the walls. It invaded even the shadiest corners. A cold drink would have been nicer.

We settled for the tea. It was sweet and hot. And although tea is very much a West African tradition, it seemed very British.

"Do you know why we always drink three cups of tea?" Peter asked. "And do you know why the first cup is always the sweetest?"

I slurped my tea.

"No, why?"

"The first cup is the love of your mother. The second is the love of your friends. The third is the love of your love."

I laughed.

"It's true," he said. "Ask anybody."

Peter's brother came around the house and interrupted us. I would have asked him about the tradition of the tea but he was in a hurry to take a shower. He wore slip-slops, scuffling his feet when he walked. His shabby black trousers were undone at the waist. A towel hung over his shoulder. He greeted us and knelt to have a glass of tea, but he wasn't very chatty. He only asked if we had eaten yet.

"As soon as we finish the tea," Peter told him. The brother nodded his approval. A second later he went to take a shower.

Two little rooms had been added on to the house. One of them housed the toilet. The other was the shower room. A pump out back fed the shower from pipes that ran above the ground. They lay old and rusty on the concrete floor like a nighttime booby trap, bent in the places where someone had tripped over them in the dark. The water hissed noisily as it ran through these old pipes. It sputtered when it came out in the shower room.

When Peter and I finished our tea, we went into the kitchen to scrounge around for food. Dirty pots and pans were piled high in the sink; glass jars lay overturned on the floor and roaches ran all over everything. Nothing had been washed in ages. Flies were everywhere.

From the ancient little refrigerator Peter pulled out a small pot. He set it on the edge of the sink. When he took the lid off, the stench of old fish escaped in a rush.

"Are you hungry?" he asked.

"No, not very." I lied.

"Good," he said. "There isn't much here. There is only this.

If you would like to take a shower, I will warm this while you wash yourself."

I waited for his brother to come out. Then I went into the shower room to undress. I turned on the water and waited. The pipes sputtered and squirted. The water dribbled barely enough so I could lather the soap. A minute later, the water slowed to a trickle. Then the trickle ran dry. I waited. I turned the spigot off and back on again. I waited for nothing to happen. Nothing did.

Someone called to me.

"The pump is broken. Wait a minute and I will bring you a pail of water."

By the time Peter knocked on the door, the soap had dried to crust caking my body. Peter set the pail down outside the door. The water was rusty brown, and an oily film floated on the surface. I had little choice. I lifted the bucket over my head and poured the water, a little at a time, to rinse away the soap. When I dried off, the towel became black from the dirt.

Peter and his brother were squatted around two pots when I came out. One pot held rice. The other pot held the old, smelly fish. They were mixing the two.

"Come. Sit and eat."

Reluctantly, I did.

Flies buzzed all around. Huge roaches crawled nearby. Peter picked his nose. He wiped his hands on his pants and began to eat. Since the pump had broken, there was no water to wash his hands with. He didn't seem to worry.

The rice was left over from two days ago. Though it had been kept in the refrigerator, the rice was dry and tough to chew. The fish broth moistened it, but not much. The fish, which was old and tasted like sweat, was too small for three people. I tried to eat slowly. I wanted to let Peter and his brother have their fill. I wanted to eat as little as possible. But each time I paused and sat back, the command to eat was hurled at me.

"What's wrong? Don't you like it?"

I made a sound that could have been construed as satisfaction.

"Then eat. Eat!"

So I did.

I chewed slowly, taking my time, trying to make each mouthful last an hour. As I chewed, I took up another handful and kneaded it to make it look as though I were always eating. The slower I chewed, the less I'd have to eat.

Later in the evening, after the sun had gone down, Peter and I argued.

We had taken a walk to meet with some of his friends. They were sitting on a rail outside a shop. As they talked, I went inside the shop to buy cold drinks for everyone. The gravel lot where we sat at the edge of the road was already littered with papers and bottles and cans. When we finished drinking, Peter and his friends tossed their cans to the ground.

"Hey, hey, hey!" I yelled. "Don't throw that trash on the ground."

"Why not?"

"That's why this place looks the way it does," I said.

"What does it matter?" one of the boys said.

"It matters plenty. This is your country. Don't you care how it looks?"

Obviously not. The next man to finish his soda threw his can in the bushes behind.

"Is that better?" he asked. They all laughed.

I might as well have been talking to myself. They ignored me when I gathered up the cans and did not see me when I dropped them into the trash barrel.

As Peter and I left, he said to me, "If they want the place cleaned up, they'll clean it up."

"Who is 'they'?" I said.

"You know. The authorities."

"It's your country too," I said.

It was a new concept for them.

We met Peter's brother outside a bar. Suddenly I was his great new friend. He began ordering beers for all his pals. Without asking me, without even a word, he expected me to pay for them. I resented being taken for granted and was beginning to feel like the owner of a cat. All the cat sees when he looks at you is a can opener.

I felt suddenly empty and very angry, ready to explode.

When Peter and I walked back to the house, he told me

that one day he would travel as I was doing. He would see America and parts of the world that so far lived only in his imagination.

"But first," he said, "I have to wait for the man in the passport bureau to let me have a passport."

"You don't have a passport?"

"No."

"How can you cross the frontier into Senegal?"

"Between The Gambia and Senegal a passport isn't necessary. Only for traveling to other countries. I have applied for one," he said, "but the man in the office will not grant me one."

"Why not?"

"He says because so many people want one. There is a delay. But if I had enough to pay him, I would have one tomorrow."

"You mean the fee? How much is it?"

"Oh, I already paid the fee," he said. "But sometimes you have to pay a little extra. It makes things move a little faster."

"You mean you have to bribe him to get a passport?"

"The same as you have to if you want anything done. But I will get the money. As soon as Allah wills it."

"Allah," I growled. "What has Allah got to do with anything?"

"It is Allah's will. All that happens is Allah's will."

I could feel myself losing control of my anger. I shouted at him.

"Do you think Allah has got nothing better to do than to worry about when you might get a passport? It's got nothing to do with Allah."

"You have no faith," he said. "It has everything to do with Allah."

"Your problem is with some beady-eyed little fat man in the passport office. You'll get a passport when *he* decides, not when God decides."

Peter remained calm.

"You mean Allah," he said.

"Allah. God. It's the same thing."

"Allah created heaven and earth, and everything is done according to his will. Don't you think he has the power to make these things happen?"

"If he did," I said, "why are so many people in Africa starving to death? Why do so many babies die?"

"It is Allah's will," he said.

"God's will? How can you believe in a God like that? If this is God's will, he must be a horrible, horrible thing."

"And what do you think?" he said. "Who do you think is responsible for the good and bad in the world?"

"We are. We alone have the power to make this life better. That's what free will is for. Our lives are our own, and what we make of the world is our fault and our responsibility. Otherwise we're just puppets without any voice in what happens to us. We can't just sit back and let the authorities think for us, clean up our messes for us. We can't let life happen to us as if there's nothing we can do about it. Life is our responsibility. What happens to us is up to us. And it makes no sense to think that one country starves and another country prospers because God makes it so. That's crazy."

"It is a mystery," he said. "Perhaps people suffer because of some evil they have done."

"What about little babies?" I said. I was almost pleading with him. "What crimes have they committed, except to be born in a world where greedy men take and helpless men wait for God to get to work?"

"I will wait," he said. "When Allah wills it, the suffering will end. When Allah wills it, the rains will come. When Allah wills it, I will have my passport."

I nearly screamed.

We walked the rest of the way in silence. By the time we pushed open the broken gate, the compound was completely covered in darkness, but Peter knew where every stumbling block lay. He led me as if I were a blind man.

He lit two candles when we reached the back of the house. I held one as we got ready for sleep. He offered me his bed. It smelled of mildew and sweat. It was covered with dirty clothes and towels and old newspapers, which he took and tossed onto the floor. I insisted that he keep the bed. I could sleep on the floor, I told him, but he refused.

"You are the guest," he said. "Please. Take the bed and be comfortable."

He sat on the floor to take off his shoes and trousers. Then he lit a little green coil that burned like incense. A thin spiraling cloud lifted and fanned out, filling the room with an odd insecticide smell. There was no window to let in air or let out the smoke, and when Peter closed the door, he closed in the heat.

"To keep the mosquitoes out," he said.

He blew out the candles. The room went black. Peter lay on a mat on the concrete floor and went to sleep. He began to snore. I closed my eyes and tried to sleep, but the drone of mosquitoes filled my ears. I lay wide awake for hours slapping at the side of my head, trying to kill what I could not see but could only hear.

The roads across Africa begin and end in big dusty lots. Old cars and small pickup trucks collect there. Crowds of travelers wait there. Not until the car is full of passengers with the same destination will a car move, not even to put in gasoline. There is always this waiting. In this sense there is little difference between The Gambia and Algeria, Mauritania and Morocco.

The minibus pulls into the lot. Vendors selling clothes and fruit weave between the cars. They wander through the crowds of travelers waiting, sitting on the ground, leaning against the cars, lying in the shade, all of them waiting to pack into a car or a small truck. When the vendors pass, the travelers finger the clothes to pass the time. They buy fruit for the journey. They buy sips of water to stave off the heat. Sweet red drinks are sold in little plastic bags, but the water is offered directly from a bucket. The seller dips up a scoop of water in a ladle. The buyer drinks from it.

Cigarettes are very cheap here in The Gambia, but they are still a luxury. Most people can't afford to buy a full pack. So they buy two cigarettes at a time, sometimes three or four.

I buy three packs of an American brand, to have on hand as either gifts or bribes; they are that valuable.

We pack in like olives in a jar. The driver gasses up an old Peugeot and we bump down another long African road to Ziguinchor, where we cross into the slice of Senegal that surrounds The Gambia to the South, and pull into another dirt lot. On one side of the lot, wooden shacks threaten to collapse. On the other side, broken cars have already collapsed and now rest in the shade. Their hoods are all raised. A man half hangs out of the engine compartment of one of them. He bangs at the car with a hammer.

There are promises that some vehicle or other will take the handful of us who want to continue on to Guinea-Bissau, but no one knows which car or which truck. The discussion among the drivers is animated. None of them seems willing to make the short trip.

There are only four of us who want to go to the frontier. The sun is going down. By the time we arrive at the border, there will be no one to bring back, no more money to make, a one-way trip wasted.

Finally a driver volunteers. He isn't a taxi driver, just a man with a truck. He needs the money.

His taxi is an extremely small sort of pickup truck with a hard shell over the truck bed and no rear windows. It is white and rusted all over and there is very little room in the back to fit into. At best it will fit four. Because my legs are long and I would never fit in the back with two others, the driver tells me to sit in the front seat. For a moment it seems almost as if the front seat is a place of privilege and comfort. But the truck has no front windscreen, and the front fender of the truck has rusted through in gaping rips along the side.

As we bounce along the bumpy trail into the jungle, dust and dirt fly up and into my face. Every puddle we splash through sends a spray up my legs. My trousers get wet.

The little truck sits very low to the ground. Every rise in the rutted track scrapes the bottom of the car.

The road is barely two wheel ruts winding through the jungle, past villages and little collections of mud huts. The roofs are made of straw stacked in an upside-down cone. At one village the little truck begins to overheat. The driver stops without shutting off the engine and sends a village boy to hurry and fetch water for him in an old oily plastic bottle. He pours the water into the radiator. When the radiator is filled, he drinks the rest.

The scenery begins to look more like what I imagined Africa to be. Chickens peck about in yards and in the road until the truck rattles by, scattering chickens and goats and children.

They must scatter because the truck never slows down. Our passengers seem to get a kick out of the scampering children. They laugh.

The forest is dense with trees and shrubs, and the villages are laid in clearings cut out of the forest. The road ends abruptly in a sleepy village where a big log has been dropped to bar the way. A little shack stands beside the log. This is the Senegalese border station.

Once formalities are taken care of and my passport has been stamped, I cross into the no-man's-land between border posts. One man from the truck lives in this village, but the others disappear off into the bush. The jungle swallows them up. They speak neither English nor French. Guinea-Bissau is a former Portuguese colony. (It used to be called Portuguese Guinea, but after independence in 1973, *Portuguese* was dropped from the name and *Bissau*, the name of the capital city, was added to distinguish this country from its neighbor, the other Guinea.) The best I can do to communicate is to use a bit of Spanish to ask directions. I ask directions and follow the extended arm pointing the way into the jungle.

A narrow path sparkles beneath the setting sun and I follow it, winding into the densest part of the jungle. The path is no more than a foot and a half wide. When I meet a man coming in the opposite direction, one of us has to step off onto the plowed rows in the fields that border the path. There is a fork in the path. I ask which is the way to Bissau.

This man points in a direction I would not have taken. It doesn't feel right, going more to the west than to the south, but maybe it's the route the locals take who don't have to check in at the border post. It soon runs out at a hedge of bushes where a woman is hoeing the earth. I startle her. She holds the hoe like a weapon and points me back to the way.

There is nothing along this path. It winds through trees and cleared fields, up and down hills and through rice marsh. A little stream flows alongside, and the setting sun reflects orange in the water.

A village lies up ahead. Fields are partitioned off by fences of dried wood and sticks. Tall stalks of thatching for roofs are tied in bundles stacked in the corner of one of the fields. Nothing seems to grow except one skinny mango tree.

The walls of the village huts finally are not concrete here, or mud. They are made of sticks woven together. The roofs are thatched. The grass thatching hangs long and low.

The village women rush out to greet me as I pass. The six bravest ones approach and speak to me in a language I cannot understand and do not even recognize. It is not Portuguese. A young girl of about fourteen carries her baby on her hip. A younger girl totes a bucket of water slung over her shoulder. A beautiful girl stands shyly behind them both. She is biting into a hard mango. Her breasts are bare, youthful, firm. A very old woman staggers beside me and holds out her hands. Her breasts are bare too, but they sag below her waist. She has a huge lump in the middle of her stomach, some kind of hernia where her navel ought to be, and the bones of her chest show through skin stretched tight across her rib cage. She has no teeth but one, and gestures like a drunk woman. Her words slur together. I cannot understand her. She shouts when she talks to me and says something that sounds enough like "tobacco" that I open a box of cigarettes. Her eyes light up. She takes a few and points along the path for me to follow. There, I find the men of the village, all of them helping to construct a small building out of stone and mud bricks. They stop their work. I try to chat in Spanish, but we cannot understand each other. I continue on.

The path rises up a small hill. The jungle stretches endlessly. Palm trees scratch at the sky. In the distance another field has been cleared. The dry stalks of some harvested crop or other litter the earth like stubble on a man's chin. The sun just begins to nick the horizon, formed level and straight by a grove of trees far away, and the air begins to cool. Still, the sweat runs profusely down my brow and my back. I am drenched. My bag becomes heavier with each step. The border post is nowhere in sight. Finally I put the bag down and lie in a cool spot in the shade of a glade of tall trees, where the air smells of the earth and the earth smells of the people who inhabit it. It smells of dirt and mud and green, the smell of moisture and coolness. If not for the mosquitoes, I could sleep here all night.

Another creek snakes lazily across the plain. It smells of stagnant water. When I come to the creek, the sun turns the water to fire with its reflection burning through forest and trees. You could lose yourself here. The imagination conjures a world as it once was, pristine and jungly, not populated by men at all, only elephant and lion and giraffe. A world where the water smelled clean and fresh.

Up ahead, smoke from a village fire spirals against the darkening sky. Footsteps approach me from behind. The man following me passes and turns off the path. He walks up to the little village on the hill. In Spanish I call to him, asking where the border station is. He points across the valley.

His Portuguese is a little clearer. He has understood my Spanish. I must be nearing a town.

The border station, of course, is only a hut. Three soldiers sit on a bench. One sits on the ground. Their uniforms are unbuttoned and dirty. One of the soldiers looks ill. He sits with his elbows on his knees, his head in his hands. The soldier on the ground is asleep. None of them moves as I approach. When I get near I smell the stale odor of strong liquor. The soldiers are drunk.

"Is this the border station?"

The sergeant nods. He looks briefly at my passport, asks me if I'm carrying any weapons, and sends me on with an unsteady wave of his hand.

The sun dips below the horizon. Where the path crosses a bridge over the creek, I stop for a rest. A rickety wooden cart drawn by an old horse wobbles past. The old man driving the thing nods a greeting. The little kid sitting on the back of the wagon swings his legs in slow rhythms to match the gait of the horse. He holds on tightly to the big metal cans that crowd the back of the wagon, keeping them from rattling around.

I can just barely make out the outline of the town sitting on the hill up ahead. The sun has set and darkness is settling like dew all around. Suddenly the night comes alive with screeches and chirping from the jungle. The loud droning of the town's generator begins. A few lights flicker on.

I lift my bag by the shoulder strap. The strap breaks. For a while I carry the bag in my arms, but I have to stop soon and rest again. I am exhausted.

There are footsteps on the path behind me. A young man comes up to me, grabs my bag without a word, and walks off with it. He carries it for me up the hill.

It seems that Africa always has two hands reaching out: one begging, the other giving.

João was a mestizo, a mixture of African and Portuguese blood. I followed him up the hill. He told me there was no hotel in the village. There was a bar, however, with two rooms that the owner sometimes rented out. But when we checked on them, the rooms were filthy.

"You can stay with me and my family," João said.

I followed him around the corner and down the dirt road to his house.

There were two main roads in the town. They ran perpendicularly. Both were dirt, so soft and deep that they were difficult to walk quickly on—like sand, but so much softer. They were wide streets, lined as in any suburban neighborhood with homes and yards. The homes were huts, neatly arranged, separated by yards that were no more than dirt and little plots of growing grain. In the compounds between the huts there were pigs and small goats penned behind fences made of sticks and rope.

There was the bar in town and there was a little shop that was also someone's home. On the front porch a stand had been set up where an old woman sat selling toilet paper and soap and sweets. She doubled as the local black marketeer and changed money.

On the street, children played in the dirt. A dog lay in the middle of the road. Women walked with their babies strapped to their backs. There were no cars.

João's hut was in a small compound. A few pigs rooted around in a small patch of grain stalks that were withering from the lack of rain. The walls of the hut were mud brick. A screen of woven wood ran around a narrow porch for privacy. The roof was a layer of thatch laid over a sheet of corrugated metal.

In back of the hut, hidden behind fences of thatched grass, were the shower and the toilet, nothing but a hole dug deep into the ground. It swarmed with flies. Giant cockroaches crawled in and out. A big rock was used to cover the pit.

João took a shower. When he finished he asked if I wanted one too.

"Do you have other shoes?" he asked.

He lent me his slip-slops and gave me a towel. He said something to a half-naked teenaged woman who then came up behind me with a bucket of water and a plastic cup. That was my shower: dipping the cup into the bucket, pouring the water over head and body, soaping up, and rinsing off. The water was hauled up from the well by the young girl. The well was very deep. The water was very cold. The young girl—dark skinned, bare breasted, very young, and very pretty—was João's wife.

While I showered she cooked for us. We ate on the smooth floor of the hut—João and I, his wife, and the baby—a little bit of rice and two small cubes of meat in a sweet sauce. There was no electricity in the hut. We ate by the light of three candles.

Out in the blackness of the night, the generator droned from far away. It was housed in a shed at the end of a row of small huts and fed tiny bits of electricity to the town. A few lights were turned on—in the bar, and in the Italian logging camp over the ridge. But most of the town swam in total darkness. When João and I walked out in the night we carried flashlights to light the way. So did everyone else. In the huts there was only candlelight.

We went first to the bar. It had been a long and thirsty day. We drank sodas until the last ones in town were gone. Then we switched to beer. The owner of the bar served us small plates of oily spaghetti and goat meat, which we ate greedily, though the meat was dry and tough. But João was still hungry, and I was starving.

We strolled through town, the beams from our flashlights crisscrossing in the darkness. Others were out walking, and it was like a spectacle of fireflies in the night. Every so often one would turn on his flashlight to see or to make a greeting in the dark, then switch it off again to conserve the batteries.

The generator hummed deliberately. The night cooled, bringing on the threat of thunder and the promise of rain. Hints of faint clouds passed like wisps of smoke in front of stars dancing in the sky. Sleepiness descended over the town. The dogs stopped barking. Conversations faded. Men in the street drifted home. João and I stopped for a moment to visit with friends; we sat on the front steps. I could not understand their rapid Portuguese and patois. I leaned against a wooden post and let the soft rhythm of their voices and laughter soothe me like a lullaby. I closed my eyes.

When we reached home, João insisted that I take his bed. He, his wife, and the baby would sleep on the floor. The bed was only a raised wooden plank, not much softer and certainly no more comfortable than the floor, but it was the offer that counted. Symbols are sometimes all we have.

The rains came during the night, soaking through the grass on the roof and tapping lightly against the tin below. Mosquitoes buzzed. João snored. The peaceful African night smelled like wet hay and smoke.

In the morning the hint of rain lingered in the air. The sun had not yet come up strong and full, but the ground was already as dry as ever.

In town, men waited for the bus to the port city of Bissau, but there would be none that day. The bus that did appear was a big green and white disaster covered with rust that must have been thirty or more years old. The side windows were nearly all broken out. There was a massive crack from the front windscreen of the bus right down to the bumper. The headlights were broken out. There was so little air in the tires on the right side that the bus leaned over and nearly scraped the ground. Inside, the seats had no upholstery. People sat on the springs or directly on the metal frames.

When the bus squeaked to a stop, many women carrying bundles on their heads got up and waddled aboard. There was no visible indication of where the bus was bound, no sign stuck in the front window, but I didn't care. A bus like that had to be going someplace interesting. I would take it wherever it was going.

But João stopped me. He had already arranged a ride on the back of a truck loaded with huge sacks of grain and bales of straw. If I wanted to climb aboard and hang on to the person next to me, or cling to a bale of straw, I could go along. The truck wasn't going to Bissau, but where it stopped I could get another ride.

I helped an old woman struggle to climb into the back of the truck, and saw that there were already others up there waiting. I could see it would be every bit as interesting as the bus. I shook hands with João and climbed on.

He waved goodbye and followed the truck a short distance down the road until the dust rose to choke him and cloud his eyes. For a while, he watched with a hand shielding his face, and then the cloud swallowed him up. As quickly as he had appeared along the road the night before, João vanished, and I would never see him again. I would never be back down that road again.

The road out of Ingoré runs straight and level. A few miles out of town the soft dirt becomes hard packed. The road is wide enough for only one vehicle at a time, but we share the road with only one car, a jeep that pulls around us and passes in a raging hurry. It sends up huge plumes of dust that follow it to the end of the road. Apart from the jeep, there is not another car or truck anywhere to be seen.

The old truck speeds over ruts and rises in the road. We in the back hang on tight to the cargo and to one another. A dust cloud kicks up behind us. It takes five minutes to settle.

In the eastern sky, clouds hang heavy and white. Their billowy underbellies are dark as if in a storm, but the tops of the clouds are blindingly bright, big puffy mounds rolling upward to the heavens. They are streaked with yellow from the sun and rimmed with the bright blue of the otherwise clear sky. Straight up into the highest reaches of the heavens the clouds billow ever so slowly until they have built cathedrals of snow ten miles tall, catching the sun and shining brightly, like the heavenly robes of a choir of cherubs.

But there is no rain. The moisture lingering in the air is turned by the heat of the day into a blister of humidity.

And the road runs on and on. Dust flies everywhere, getting into our eyes and in our mouths. We cling to the ropes that tie down the load and we cling to each other as if we were clinging to hope, trying to keep from falling off.

Guinea-Bissau is a small country. The land is lush and wet as marshland. When the rains do come, they will pound the earth. The streams and swamps will overflow.

Mangroves cover the lowlands along the coast, and far in

the distance the faint outline of rain forest scratches the sky. Everything but the dusty road is painted green. The heat is heavy and humid. The air boils rather than bakes. The desert seems years behind.

Hours later we come to the Cacheu River. The jeep that passed us earlier is at the water's edge, trapped and waiting like the rest of us. There is no bridge here. The small ferry that carries traffic from one side to the other is out in the middle of the river, stuck. It moves neither away from us nor toward us. It lists in the water and does not move at all.

There is no shade here; there are no cold drinks for sale. The only water is the river. Babies begin to cry. Their mothers take them down to the river and bathe them. They cup their hands and offer them drinks. And everyone sits on the hot rocks and the dirt and waits. There is not a word of complaint.

Through the small pair of binoculars I carry with me I see the pilot sitting in the wheelhouse of the ferry. Frantically he shouts down instructions to the two men carrying tools. A plume of smoke comes from the engine room. The two mechanics hurry back and forth from the stern to the engine and back again.

On the opposite shore another crowd has collected and is doing what we are, sitting in the dust and waiting.

Three hours later, the ferry arrives. There is only a brief worry that the boat might break down again or even sink. You put the worries out of your mind because this world is without choices.

On the other shore there is a mad scramble to pile into the back of the pickup truck waiting there to carry us the rest of the way to Bissau. There are two benches running lengthwise in the back of the truck. Between them there is a spare tire on the floor. These are the seats. We jam together and manage to squeeze twelve adults and two children into the back of the truck. Luggage and bundles are tied to the top of the truck, and someone has brought along a pig. It gets trussed up too and tied to the top of the truck's cab. The driver hurries us to settle down. There is no bridge at the next river either, and if we hurry we will catch the ferry sooner.

We miss the ferry by two minutes.

More waiting. At least now there is an empty shed to wait in and avoid the relentless sun.

The man with the pig unties it and chains it in the shade. The pig squeals from straining to break the chain, trying to escape.

At the edge of the road a family has set up shop. A little girl totes a bucket full of Coke bottles floating in cool water. I buy one and drink it down so fast there is no time to realize the bottles are not filled with Coca-Cola.

The bottle is very sticky. The drink is just some sweet homemade drink, mostly sugar and water, and there is a very good chance the water came from this river. But at a wickedly hot and thirsty moment like this, who can worry about dysentery or hepatitis or bilharzia?

The water the bottles float in is actually the drink itself. The little girl wipes the sweat from her brow and dries her hand on her dirty dress. She reaches into the bucket of drink and fills the bottle I have just given back to her. When her hand is good and sticky from the sugar, she licks her fingers before reaching in and filling another bottle.

The man beside me buys a drink. The girl gives him the same bottle I just used. When he finishes, I buy another, and she gives the bottle back to me. At this point, what does it matter? As the nurse back home advised, you simply have to relax.

I had taken the recommended precautions. Once a week I took my antimalaria pills—chloroquine. And before I left home I was given a series of shots against diphtheria and tetanus and typhoid, cholera and yellow fever and hepatitis. The shots are mostly pinpricks in the arm, but the gamma globulin—the hepatitis vaccine—is injected into the hip, and the dosage depends on the size and weight of the victim.

"Oh, you're a big one." The nurse was a little too gleeful, enjoyed her work a little too much. "You get a big dose."

She pulled out a needle about the size of an ice pick. She ordered me to drop my trousers and to hold on to the side of her desk. Then she stabbed me.

"This won't hurt much," she said, grunting through gritted teeth. She plunged the needle in viciously, and I yelled as I have never in my life yelled. I thought my eyes would fall out. I tensed every muscle in my body, and the nurse could not push the plunger to get the gamma globulin into me.

"You have to relax or the medicine will never work its way through," she said. "You have to relax."

She was right, of course. You have to relax and surrender.

So I go where the Africans go, eat what they eat, and drink what they drink. Sometimes.

Bissau is an exhausted city sputtering its last breath in the aftermath of colonialism. It will either cough itself back to life, or it will roll over and soon be dead. There is a certain humor in bouncing about in the backs of trucks, a certain romance in the heat and strange food; there is nothing funny here.

Guinea-Bissau doesn't produce much of anything apart from peanuts. It has a one-industry economy, another tragic leftover from the colonial period.

When the Europeans owned the land they forced the Africans to produce crops that would take care of the needs of Europe. They exported crops to pay the cost of administering and defending the colony. The same was true in other countries as well, of course, with other crops: cocoa and coffee, copper and cashews and cobalt. It was like a game, owning the land in order to pay the cost of being there. And all the eggs of each colony were put into one fragile basket.

When the Portuguese abandoned Guinea-Bissau after fourteen years of war, there was only one modern factory in the country. It produced beer for the Portuguese.

Of all the colonial powers in Africa, the Portuguese were arguably the worst. When the Guineans finally won independence and took their country back, all but about three hundred Portuguese fled and took everything with them. They had been here for over three hundred years, and when they fled they left behind barely two hundred miles of paved road. There were only fourteen Africans who had graduated from a university. There was only one doctor. Ninety-seven percent of the Guinean people could not read or write.

Today there are over a million people in Guinea-Bissau. There are fewer than fifty thousand jobs. Most of the jobs are for civil servants and bureaucrats.

When I arrived it was late afternoon. The center of town was nearly deserted. A few dogs foraged for food in the rubble.

An old man sat on the dusty ground in the shade of a leafless and dying tree. All the shops were closed. There was no life anywhere except in the noisy bar on the Praça dos Heróis Nacionais, near the presidential palace. Music poured from the bar's open doors. There were four men inside. Three of them sat at a table and shared a large bottle of beer. The fourth, an Englishman named Michael, stood at the bar.

"Where are you coming from, Yank? And where are you going?"

"From the north," I said. "Going south. Nowhere in particular, just going."

"A little adventuring?"

"I guess. What about you?"

"Me? I'm just staying. Waiting in this fucking hole for somebody to get off his fucking ass and do something."

"Like what?"

"Like get me a fucking permit so I can get to work."

He was a short, squat man with a thin complexion and plenty of freckles. The darkness around his eyes could have been suntan, but more likely it was dirt. He was powerfully built and used to working with his hands. They were crusted with calluses and corns. His arms were thick.

He said he was a miner and an engineer, a surveyor and a driller. He was one of those jacks-of-all-trades who follow the trade winds and the money around the globe. He had worked on the big offshore rigs in the North Sea off the coast of Scotland.

"But I didn't fit in anymore in England," he said. "I was too honest and I lived too hard. The English are getting a bit soft. I had to break out of there."

He came to Africa as an oilman to work first in Nigeria before moving throughout the crumbling remains of the British Empire.

"There's still plenty of money to be made if you know where to go," he said. "South Africa, Australia, Nigeria. No, I'd stay out of fucking Nigeria if I were you. They are the most corrupt bastards you'll ever have the pleasure to piss on. From the fucking top right down to the bastards at the bottom. Every bleeding one of them has his hand out. Every fucking asshole in a uniform is an extortionist, threatening to throw your ass in jail if you don't kick in with a bit of baksheesh—bribery. Every foreign company trying to do business in Nigeria pays bribes. On every budget there is an item labeled 'miscellaneous' that is just money for under-the-fucking-table payments to Nigerian officials. Otherwise your business won't run smooth. It won't run at all."

His face had turned red and I thought he was going to break a blood vessel.

"And the worst fucking thing," he said. "The baksheesh doesn't even go very far. There's always another black bastard waiting to stick you up."

He ran his mitt across his face to wipe away the sweat.

"Don't go to fucking Nigeria," he said. "They'll cut your balls off and give you a fine for bleeding in the street."

He thought this was pretty funny and laughed a little. He looked at me with a rough sideways smile. He wore a thin mustache and three days' stubble on his chin. His shirt was unbuttoned to the waist, his chest was hairy, and his belly was becoming big and round from too much beer and too much waiting around. It protruded through the opening in his shirt. It was not attractive.

"I guess you didn't like Nigeria," I said.

He laughed robustly and said, "No, I didn't like Nigeria. But the money was good. Here the money is better."

"So what happened?"

"You mean, why did I leave Nigeria? Six months in jail is why. And when I got out, all my fucking money was gone. Two years' work, for nothing. And let me tell you, jail in Africa is no fucking picnic."

He had been away from England for twelve years, traveling, working, making his fortune several times and each time spending it—or losing it. He had that weary look about him of those burned-out expatriates who spend their last days sipping gin and tonics, going to seed somewhere along the equator before packing in the adventurer's life and heading home to a row house and a flower garden somewhere in the northwest of England.

"I'm not too good at seeing tomorrow," he said. "If you know what I mean. Maybe that's why I stay in Africa. There's no future here. You'd better live for today because there might not be a tomorrow. So as fast as I earn the money, I spend it."

"And that's what you're doing here?"

"Not this time. This time it's the big one. This time I'm really in and I'm going to score big. And when I do, I'm going to buy me a fucking estate in England and live the good life. I'll get out of fucking Africa once and for all. You can't get any decent beer here."

He slapped his hand on the bar and grinned the sly smirk of a thief with a master plan. He ordered two beers and slid one to me.

He was right. The beer was not very good.

"You know," he said. "Africa is dead. It's the end of the fucking universe. It's a sick pig wallowing in its own shit, waiting to be slaughtered and gutted. Nobody in the real world cares what happens here. And it's a bloody shame. The people here deserve better. They're a good lot. A bit lazy maybe, but then it doesn't pay to be otherwise. The poor peasant bastards bust their asses and still they starve. The presidents and all their bigwig pals line their pockets and live fat. It's ridiculous how fucking corrupt they are."

Michael spoke like a true colonial, in a voice that mixed condescension and selfishness with genuine concern.

"These people could really use a break," he said. "If we find oil, that'll mean jobs. That's something we don't have too much of around here."

"And that's why you're here? Oil?"

"We think there's oil," he said. "And I've got a connection that will get me drilling rights." He whispered like a conspirator. "I married a local woman," he said.

"Is it a secret?"

"No secret, but I don't want everyone to know she's got a connection in the Interior Ministry. As soon as he comes back from wherever the hell he is, he'll be talking to the president about me and then I'm in. That's how it works." He made a sliding motion with his hand. "If you've got the right connections," he said, "you're in."

When I asked his advice, Michael recommended the Hotel 24 Setembro, the expensive luxury hotel in town where the workers all spoke French and the guests were all foreign. The hotel did not accept local currency.

"You can pay in dollars, in francs, in pounds," the lady at the front desk said. "But you cannot pay in pesos."

She made the usual excuse about trying to eliminate black-market transactions, but the real problem was Guinea-Bissau's lack of exports to earn foreign currency with which to buy necessities. This was the state-owned hotel. As for luxury, there was a swimming pool and a bar, but the rooms were very small. And the telephones had been out of order for days.

The rooms were arranged in rows like little apartments, six rooms in each row, each room with a tiny front porch, some with a little grass garden. They were not attached to the main building.

My room was very small, just big enough for the single bed. There was a ceiling fan and a window air-conditioning unit that made a horrible racket when it was switched on. It didn't create very much cool air, and the electricity soon shut down anyway. The toilet seat was missing. The shower head was broken. The promise of hot water was a lie.

I went to the bar to buy two liters of bottled water. I drank them both immediately. I walked out by the pool and suddenly I noticed that the courtyard and the pool area were crawling with Russians—men and their wives, telephone technicians perhaps, or commercial fishermen. I talked to one of the waiters serving them.

He was a middle-aged black man in a white jacket. He was standoffish at first, no doubt thinking I was African. He reserved his friendliness for foreigners.

"Yes, they're Russians," he said. "The Russians supported us when nobody else would. Our countries have remained loyal friends."

The Soviet Union supported and aided Guinea-Bissau during the war for independence from Portugal. As a reward for that support, the Soviets are allowed to fish the rich coastal waters of Guinea-Bissau. The fish that is caught is canned and labeled CAUGHT IN THE SOVIET UNION and then sold back to Guinea-Bissau.

In similar fashion, the Soviet Union is a loyal friend to the many bankrupt African nations it has supplied with arms and Marxist doctrine.

On the rooftop of the main building, overlooking the spot where they dumped the garbage, a flock of vultures was roosting. Dozens of them perched there like some evil omen, hideous, ugly birds waiting for something to die. When they circled in the air, their shadows glided across the ground, more and more swiftly, swooping high and low, crisscrossing back and forth like aerial fighters barely avoiding collision. I watched those hideous buzzards sitting on the roof, and they watched me. Their ugly pink heads were gnarly and deformed, their beady eyes blinking slowly with the mock bravado of cowards, making me shudder. When they flew off the roof they swept low, nearly scraping the ground before banking and struggling into the air. They swooshed past and came very close, their heavy wings beating with an incredible slowness, thumping against the air. Overhead they joined the ones already in flight. They swooped slowly back and forth, their shadows entwining in an eerie aerial ballet, a *danse macabre*. They passed over me once, twice, again and again. Their shadows danced circles around me on the ground. I hurried inside.

On a dusty side street in Bissau there is an old house. Its walls are stucco painted a pale green, chipped and peeling. From the outside, the house is run down and in need of repair, overgrown with low trees and bushes and tall weeds in the small front yard. A low brick wall runs the length of the house, and there is a narrow side porch. An old man trying to look stern and official leans against the wall and blocks the narrow passage to the front door. This house is the embassy for Guinea-Conakry, the next country south. From there I had wanted to go on to Sierra Leone and Liberia and beyond, to the hump in the map where I could begin sliding into the second half of this oddly shaped S-curve and cut across the interior of Africa.

Liberia and Sierra Leone were both already lodged in my imagination. Liberia, of course, was founded by former American slaves returning to Africa in the early 1800s. Sierra Leone I knew from reading Graham Greene. I keenly wanted to see both countries, but as events transpired I would have to find an alternate route. The fat consular official I had come to see at the Guinean embassy would not give me a visa.

Inside the house the dusty hallway was crowded with men

waiting. Three men sat crammed close on an old sofa against the wall opposite the door I entered. Along the adjacent wall three other men were squeezed together on another low sofa. Two others stood in a corner. One man who had been pacing in a small circle went to sit on the arm of one of the sofas. He looked at me with his tired eyes. His expression was sad.

A huge photograph of a stern-looking Guinean president hung on the wall. None of the men in the room spoke, as if the president were watching and listening. But each of them respectfully reached up and held out a hand to shake. Their handshakes were meek and spongy, their greetings mechanical. Each man muttered hello or grunted and nodded. None of them looked me in the eye. In their faces was the tired anguish of helpless waiting, the puffy sadness of uncertainty.

A wooden table blocked the entrance to the inner sanctum, and a man was seated there. He wore an ill-fitting suit that chafed his skin. He hitched his shoulders and fidgeted to scratch himself, but he could never get comfortable. I stood over him. He held out his hand as they all did and weakly shook mine. In rude fashion he asked me what I wanted there, and he never looked up. He continued to read the paper on the table before him, but I never released his hand. I forced him to look up at me. When he did, he knew instantly, in the firmness of my hand, in my refusal to let him brush me aside and ignore me, that I was different.

"Yes," he said timidly. "You are here to see the ambassador?" He did not know if I was friend or dignitary. He was a little nervous.

"I need a visa," I said.

"Yes," he said, now regaining the backbone of his authority. "But you will have to wait." He pointed to the crowd, indicating that I would have to get in line. "The one who decides is not here, and I have not seen him this morning."

"What time does he normally come in?"

He shrugged.

"What nationality are you?" he asked, and when I said American, his eyes brightened. He became nervous once more.

"Oh," he said. "Then he will want to see you first."

Right away he stood, knocking softly on the door behind him. He poked his head inside. He was not fazed in the slightest by his lie that he hadn't seen the consul, or the ambassador, or whoever he was. He didn't hesitate, didn't try to cover the tracks of his lie, didn't make an attempt at subtlety. He poked his head in, came back out, and opened the door wide for me to step inside.

The other men craned their necks to get a glimpse of the man in charge and maybe catch his eye. Then perhaps he would see them, have pity on them, and grant them the interviews they sought. But their pleading glances didn't help. They were just as ignored and insignificant as ever, at the mercy of another man's whim. And the sadness of their expressions deepened, but no one grumbled or said a word.

Through the door I saw the fat man. He sat behind a cluttered desk and glanced up when he was addressed. He looked out to where I stood. He rose, came to me, and was all smiles and warmth. He held out his hammy hand for me to shake. The hand was moist and clammy, a very thick hand, difficult to wrap my fingers around, soft and mushy. With his other hand he grabbed my right elbow and pulled me into his office. He kicked the door closed.

We were not alone in this little office. There was someone else doing business, maybe trying to get a visa, maybe some export license. He wore a suit that was neatly pressed, but his shirt was splotched with tan stains, spilled coffee perhaps. His run-down shoes were covered with dust. He shook my hand. He vacated the chair in front of the desk and took a seat in the corner. The fat man had flashed him some discreet signal to make way for the American.

"Sit," the fat man said. "Sit down."

I had half expected a squeaky voice to come out of him, one of those surprise voices that don't fit the fat men who own them, but his voice rumbled low in pitch, deep and strong.

He was not as tall as I, but twice as wide and twice as heavy. He sat behind his desk and looked out the window. A patch of sky was visible in the upper corner of the window, but the larger view from this window was blocked by the tall bushes overgrowing.

"You want, I am supposing, a visa," he said. His voice rumbled. His accent was spread thick throughout his speech, but he spoke slowly and clearly. And he was shaking his head. "I cannot give you one today."

He turned back from the window to face me now and slumped down, slouching in his chair. He interlocked his thick fingers and lay his heavy hands on his big belly. Very slightly he pushed against the floor with his feet and then relaxed, pushed again and relaxed, as if he were sitting in a rocking chair, but only his head, neck, and shoulders seemed to move. His eyes remained fixed on mine as if he were studying me for reaction. I gave none. I sat placidly, blankly, and disappointed him. I did not protest, refused to grovel, and just nodded. I resisted the urge to be American, to ask to see someone higher in authority or to demand an explanation. He gave me one anyway.

"You Americans," the fat man said, "you are such racists."

He made no distinction between color. It was a cultural racism he referred to.

I looked back at the man now sitting in the corner. He looked sheepishly away, risking nothing that might affect whatever he was seeking from the fat man.

The fat man leaned forward in his seat and crossed his arms on the desk.

"When we apply for a visa to the United States," he said, "you think we are going there never to return home. Europeans can visit there. Asians can visit there. But not Africans. We cannot get visas for your country without first proving that we have a job and a family and a bank account. And then we must find a sponsor who will guarantee to lodge us and feed us, as if we are children and cannot take care of ourselves. And this sponsor must promise that we will not take jobs there and that we will return when we say we will, as if we are children not to be trusted."

"What does this have to do with a visa for me?"

"Everything," he said. "Now we are returning the favor. Before we will grant Americans a visa to visit our country, you must first go to your own embassy and get a letter of recommendation attesting to your character, assuring us first that you will not seek employment there, and second that you will be repatriated if you run out of funds. It is not much, but it is something. It is enough."

The man in the corner crossed his legs and drew patterns with his finger in the dust on his shoe. He did not look at us. He pretended not to be there.

"When you have the letter," the fat man said, "I will be happy to grant for you a visa. Especially for you. You are our brother—even if you are American."

I did not protest. I stood and shook hands, first with the fat man and then with the man in the corner. He got up from his seat and took my place at the fat man's desk. The fat man led me to the door, his broad smile leaving him when he looked out at the other men waiting to see him. He closed the door without a word of acknowledgment to them. The next man who came asking for an audience with the man in charge would probably be told the fat man was not in yet and had not been seen all morning. No one would argue or say otherwise. No one would complain.

So neither, then, would I complain. If I was going to travel like a leaf on a breeze, letting myself be guided by whim and wind and rumor, feeling this helplessness the Africans feel, then I would need to surrender to the caprices of nature and also of authority. My life suddenly was not my own. I found myself sitting in the lap of the gods, the lap of destiny, and the lap of authority.

I ask myself, is it the African character or the colonial presence that defines the way Africa is? The colonials clearly have not left, and Africa asserts its own authority any way it can. And Africans readily submit to authority. They have no tradition of democracy and self-assertion, but of a central authority figure who is leader and father at the same time. Their tradition is devotion to family and tribe. Their tradition is to trust, to surrender to authority, to submit to the will of God, submission to power.

The colonials had the power. Now the demagogues and the despots hold the power. The new colonials are black, and somehow it seems atrocity and indignity at the hands of black men is seen as more acceptable than the same atrocity and indignity at the hands of white men.

Most governments in Africa are military committees, national councils, one-party states. Almost all rely on a kind of cultism, the strength and magnetism of the man in charge, who almost always calls himself president for life. His picture hangs in the banks, in the shops, in every public building and office. In nearly every case he creates an elite class of army officers and government officials—usually from his own tribe. Their loyalty is on the one hand tribal loyalty, and on the other hand bought with money they would not otherwise be able to earn. They willingly keep others in line, committing horrors against other black men who simply have no voice. It is a problem seemingly not limited to South Africa.

Even if they could vote, there are no choices. Even if they had a choice, they probably would not be able to read the names on the ballots, the instructions, the lies. Literacy is not a high priority in Africa. Living is.

But what do human rights mean to governments determined to cling to power? What do human rights mean to people merely trying to cling to another day, find enough to eat, to survive and live to the ripe old age of forty-seven?

In Zaire, Mobutu's soldiers are rumored to have dragged people of other tribes off trains and beaten them to death.

In Burundi and Rwanda, the Hutus and the Tutsis have learned the political expedience of mass slaughter.

The Mauritanians too.

And no one outside of Africa seems to care. And those in Africa care only when it happens to them. By then it is too late.

I did not go to the U.S. embassy to get a letter of recommendation. If the road south along the coast was blocked to me, I would head north and east instead, back to the desert. But now I would need a visa to reenter Senegal. If that too was denied me, if I couldn't go south and couldn't go north, I would be trapped in Guinea-Bissau forever, really forced to become African.

While my visa application was being processed in the Senegalese embassy, I crossed over the Praça dos Heróis and went back to the bar on the corner. The Englishman was not there.

I drank instead with a young Guinean who never told me his name. He was already drunk when I walked in. He came over to me and asked if I wanted a beer. To the bartender he held up two fingers and the bartender put one beer in front of me, one beer in front of my companion.

The young Guinean spoke a bit of English. We chatted the light conversation of a sober man talking to a drunk man. We drank a few more beers together. He got drunker still. Each time I ordered one, he held up two fingers and the bartender put one beer in front of me, one beer in front of my friend. I knew he was my friend because he kept telling me so.

"My friend, if you need a place to sleep," he said, "you will be as welcome in my house as my brother."

Of course.

When the bill for the beers came, my new brother let me pay.

Of course.

He stepped back and removed himself completely from the transaction, as if he had never been there and had nothing whatever to do with the number of beers we had drunk together. His eyelids were heavy, hanging like hoods over eyes barely open. He swayed very slightly and very slowly, back and forth, and he wore the stupid smile of a half-sleeping drunk.

"Are you sure," he said, "you don't want just one more beer?" He held up a crooked, shaking finger.

"I'm sure," I said. We stepped outside.

He walked on unsteady legs and could not keep a straight line. When he stepped off the curb and into the path of an oncoming car, he held up his hand like a traffic cop to stop the car as he staggered across the road. The car did not slow but only swerved to miss him. He hardly noticed at all.

"I know a place where we can get some very good fish, a little rice, and some more beer. Let me invite you, brother."

We crossed over and walked past the presidential palace, down the hill, and onto a dirt path. I followed him to the edge of the city center and to the squalid *barrio*, where thousands of people were joined in poverty and jammed together in a slum of huts and mud and hunger. Little goats and sheep dug in the mud and scavenged for food. Children played in the garbage.

Men and women sat on the porches of houses or leaned against walls or sat on stools in the shade. They were waiting. In their eyes was a forlornness similar to the lifelessness in the eyes of the stray dogs. Their faces and their movements were defined by hunger and by tiredness. Their eyes flickered a life-time of waiting and helplessness. In the eyes of young men there was the look of lost hope and anger wasted.

I followed my friend into a collection of shacks and stooped down to fit beneath the overhanging awnings of cardboard and cloth. Lunch was already over, but my friend convinced the old woman to heat something up for us. I didn't know what it was, but I ate it.

I paid for our lunch of course, thought little of it until he asked to borrow still more, and then I mildly exploded.

"Look," I said loudly, not quite shouting. "Do I look stupid? You're not going to pay me back. Why do you ask to borrow?"

"Because I don't like to beg."

"Why don't you just ask me to give you some money?"

"Okay, okay," he said. "Give me some money."

"No," I said.

I left him standing there and went back to the Senegalese embassy to collect my visa. Then I went back to my hotel to lie down. On the roof a long row of vultures had collected, waiting for the sun to go down, waiting for something to die on the road, some carrion to be picked clean.

I felt empty.

I could have given that poor man some money. Why hadn't I?

Because, I told myself, I was tired of being a can opener. I was tired of being seen as some savior. The African poverty was at last getting to me.

I was trying not to say things to myself like: *How can people live like this?* I was trying merely to see and feel, but what I was feeling wasn't leaving me happy and uplifted, or even grateful to live in the world I come from, for in many ways, the world I come from has created this world. I was becoming angry.

In the morning I found a truck heading north toward the frontier and I got a ride out of town. I sat in the back with first twelve, then thirteen, then fifteen others. We stopped to take on a few drops of gasoline and then drove not more than half a kilometer and stopped. Everyone had to get out to show papers and passports to the Guinean border guards. Then back into the truck and on again, bumping over rutted roads toward the Senegalese border station.

In the back of the truck, someone offered me a little purple piece of something. It was shaped like garlic but looked like a radish. He cut it in half and gave a bit to me, popped the rest in his mouth. I did the same. And oh my God! what a horrid taste. It was like a jolt of lightning, the essence of bitterness. My body shuddered head to toe. We were so crowded in the back of the truck that the man next to me felt the violence of my shuddering and, by the way he looked at me, he must have thought that I was having some kind of seizure. There was no place to spit out this thing I was eating and I had to keep it in my mouth until finally I had chewed it up and swallowed it. I thought to myself: *I've got to stop putting strange things in my mouth. At least until I know what they are.*

"What was that?" I asked.

"You don't know?" asked the astounded man who had given it to me. Perhaps he was astounded that I would eat something without knowing what it was. "It was a cola nut. It gives you energy. It wakes you up."

"It certainly does," I said.

At the frontier, a vendor passed where we waited and a man bought from him two pieces of some green fruit I had never seen before. It was shaped like an avocado. The skin was smooth and cool. The man who bought them offered one to me, and I watched how he ate it. He peeled the green skin off part of the thing and exposed the yellow flesh. Then he bit into it and I did the same with mine. The fruit was hard and stringy, not very sweet. Bits of the pulp got caught in my teeth, and there was a huge pit in the center of the thing. I didn't know what the fruit was, and I didn't like it—at least for now.

Not far away, women sat in the shade by the side of the road. They sat on the ground. They sat in a group and talked. Laid out before them, on blankets or just on the ground, were rows of bananas and those same green fruits I had not liked—mangoes, I discovered.

When a vehicle stopped at the border station, the women would leave their social circle and become instant competitors. They hurried to gather up an armful or a metal dishful of mangoes or bananas and sprinted to the side of the car or truck.

They sold fruit, they sold peanuts, they carried buckets of water and sold drinks. Each one competed with the next and bargained to make the sale, undercutting old friends to sell a commodity that fell as pure profit from the trees. And when the selling frenzy was over, they went back to their huddle, sat in a circle once again, becoming friends again.

They ought to have gotten together and fixed the price. Or at least they could send one group out today to sell; a different team could come out the next day. They could work out some sort of rotation.

But I was thinking from the wrong point of view. Sitting by the side of the road, selling mangoes, selling peanuts, selling drinks: these were more than commerce. They were social hour as well. If the women sold a lot or a little, they didn't seem to care except for the brief spurt of frenzy when a car pulled up and stopped. And if they weren't sitting here, they would be sitting and socializing somewhere else, pounding millet perhaps, or sewing together.

I bought a small bunch of bananas, ate a few, and handed the rest to my traveling companions to share. Together, after buying fruit and cool drinks, we went to the immigration hut and another episode of passport and papers.

I was tired of being a basketball coach, but still worried about being a writer. I told the official I was a doctor. He had found the syringes I carried with me—in case I needed an injection for some reason. I didn't want some African doctor jabbing me with a needle he had used on someone else.

"What are these?" the official asked.

"Syringes," I said.

"What are they for?"

"I'm a doctor," I said, removing suspicions of being a journalist or a drug addict.

"Are you with the Corps de la Paix—the Peace Corps?"

"No, I'm just on holiday."

"Here? On holiday?"

The idea seemed to thrill him. He let me pass. He welcomed me profusely, his severity vanishing like early-morning fog under his bright and sunny smiles.

"We need doctors here," he said. "Do you think you will stay?"

I never suspected anyone would take me quite so seriously. It was just one of those devices you use to make dealing with bureaucrats easier—creative fibbing. To me it was a joke, but it had not been taken lightly. I saw at once what a mistake it was.

I had given the border guard a false sense of hope. I was a liar. But I couldn't recant now. It would have taken more courage than I had. And recanting might have created problems with the border guard that might have hindered my crossing the frontier, or prevented it altogether.

You are not a doctor? Your occupation is liar? We don't allow liars into our country; we have enough here already.

Instead I was greeted as a bit of a hero because I'd said I was a doctor. And I was overheard.

Moustapha was an engineer. He asked where I was going.

"Tonight I'm going to Kolda."

"Will you be there long?"

"Just until tomorrow. I have to be in Tambacounda tomorrow evening to get the train to Mali. It only goes two times a week."

"I know that train. It is not easy to get on it at Tambacounda, and it is a difficult journey, very long and very hot."

"Where are you going?" I asked.

"I am going to Ziguinchor tonight. I have to be in Dakar tomorrow. Do you need a place to stay the night? I have a friend in Kolda who will lodge you. He has not been well lately. Perhaps you could look at him and help him."

"I'm not really prepared," I said. "I'm on vacation and didn't bring anything with me."

"Yes, but you can have a look at him. And then if you miss the train to Mali, you can go back to Kolda and stay with him while you wait for the next one."

Sure, I could have a look, but so could anybody. I could give him an aspirin or a malaria pill or even vitamin C. Or I could just tell the truth. But Moustapha quickly changed the subject. We talked instead about Paris, where he had studied, and about New York, where he longed to visit.

"Have you been to Harlem?" he asked. "How I long to go there and see so many Blackamericans in one place."

"You don't have to go to Harlem to see them. Any big city in the East," I said. "And in the South too."

"No!" he said, astounded. "Everywhere?"

"Not everywhere, not in great numbers, but nearly everywhere."

"What percentage of the population?"

"About twelve percent."

"Of how many?"

"About two hundred fifty million."

"That's twenty-five, thirty million Blackamericans," he said. "Fantastic! I would truly like to see that one day. So many black people prospering. And how is the racism there?"

Racism seems to be the one thing that every black person in the entire world knows about America. It is a little disheartening.

"It exists," I said, "but I think things are slowly getting better. Not like before."

"Fantastic."

When we arrived in Kolda, the word got out immediately that I was a doctor. An American doctor. As if that meant something joyous. For me there was only the guilt and shame of lying, and the fear of being found out. But I felt trapped now, and more than a little scared.

Moustapha found a taxi to drive me to his friend's house and wrote a note of introduction. He couldn't stick around because there was a car leaving right away for Ziguinchor. He gave me a hearty hug and left.

The taxi driver took me down dirt paths to the compound of Moustapha's friend, but the man wasn't home. I gave the note to the man's wife and she welcomed me as if she expected her husband back any minute.

The compound was a dirt yard behind a high concrete wall. There was a huge opening large enough for a car to pass through and park inside the compound. Off to the side there was the wreck of an old, unused automobile, rusted out, hood raised, tires missing.

A large kettle was hanging over an open fire and a young girl was tending to it, making more smoke than either flame or heat.

Asmoa, the wife of Moustapha's friend, walked around the compound with a *pagne* wrapped around her waist and clinging to her narrow hips. She was young and she was very pretty, and though she had already had four children, her naked breasts did not sag from being endlessly pulled on and clung to. They were not as youthful as her daughter's, but they were not like the breasts of most African mothers I had seen. Asmoa told me why—without telling me why. Asmoa and her husband used to live in southern France, in Toulouse.

"I know Toulouse a little," I said, and this seemed to cheer her. We compared notes.

"Did you like it there?" I asked her.

"No," she said. "When you are away from home, home is the place you miss. And I missed Senegal, the warmth of the people here, the ways of doing things. In France I had a refrigerator that worked, I had an abundance of food, there were marvelous things to buy and nice restaurants. But I had no friends. Life is very easy there and very fast. I prefer the life here. Here we can invite strangers into our home. We can only offer them little, but we can offer them all we have."

She lent me her rubber slip-slops and filled a bucket with cold water. There was water heating on an open fire, and she added some to the water in the bucket. She pointed the way to the enclosure that was the shower. When I came out she showed me the place where I would sleep, a small room in the concrete house.

Asmoa fed me plain boiled spaghetti and bits of chopped-up meat. She helped her youngest son feed himself. Her other son and her daughter ate quickly and quietly. We ate together out of a big metal bowl, but we ate with forks.

I worried constantly about her husband's appearance and my exposure as a fraud if he were truly ill, but he never showed, perhaps a very good thing. Perhaps in Moustapha's note were instructions to try to persuade me to stay.

"Do you think you'll ever go to live in France again?" I asked.

"I go where my husband goes," she said. "But I don't think so. France smells of death to me."

She had had another baby, and that baby had been seriously ill. They had flown back to France for treatment in a hospital in Paris. They waited and waited and waited and the doctors never told them what was wrong. In the end, the baby died.

"We left her there. We buried her in a cemetery in Toulouse."

No tears, no quivering voice, no displays of sorrow. As if death were the necessary and expected end of life. But I could see she was crying inside.

We ate in silence after that and sat in the cooling darkness under the stars for a quiet hour before I finally went into my hot concrete box to sweat the night away and fight the mosquitoes.

In the morning there was bread and coffee for breakfast and then I left.

It was Africa. You come and then you are gone. A stranger enters your compound, he says he is a friend of a friend of your husband, and you believe him and you feed him and you shelter him. He says he is a doctor and you come to him for help, the same way he entered your compound looking for help. It is a world of trust. A strange and simple kind of trust.

Asmoa's young son, standing in for his father, carried my bag into the town center, where a massive crowd waited, just hanging around. Many were waiting for the next car to somewhere. Many were just waiting and watching to see who arrived and who left. In my nervousness, I thought the crowd had gathered just for me, just for the doctor. But only two men approached me, one man leading his brother. One of them was blind and suffered from horrible headaches.

The pain started as all headaches do but got worse and worse until finally the man's eyesight just shut off. They wondered if there was anything I could do, any kind of operation I could perform. I had to tell them no. Their disappointment was as deep as any I had ever seen before.

The man's ailment sounded, of course, like a brain tumor, but what did I know? I certainly couldn't suggest anything.

"You need a specialist," I said.

"Aren't you a specialist?"

"Not that kind," I said. I thought hard to find a branch of medicine that would not get me in deeper. I thought: *dentist*. I said: "No, I'm an anesthesiologist."

And it worked, although I had to explain what an anesthesiologist is. The two men went away, and I was left alone feeling vacant and helpless, no longer certain what was the right, the correct thing to do.

I leaned against a car and waited for the long ride to Tambacounda. A thirteen-year-old boy came and stood beside me. He leaned against the car and folded his arms like mine, as a son would imitate his father. After several silent minutes, he spoke.

"You're from America," he said.

"How can you tell?"

"Look at yourself," he said. "And then look at us. It's your clothes, it's your size, it's your eyes. Your body is healthy. We are thin and little. We lack food. We lack vitamins."

"How old are you?" I asked him, rather astonished.

"Thirteen."

Thirteen years old and so aware. How long would he remain so, seeing the world with those fresh eyes unblurred by time, undiminished by despair or by hope deferred, recognizing in the world not only what is but what ought to be, or at least could be?

In time, you know, despair will set in. Hope will vanish. He will spend his time waiting and waiting and waiting, just like everyone else. Of this you are certain, and Cissé more than likely will be forced to surrender his destiny into the hands of fickle gods and cruel fates. Just like everyone else.

You the visitor, you want to help, you want to make some kind of difference. But you're merely a visitor here, only here for a short while. What can you do?

"You could take me with you," he said. "I want to study. I want to stay in school. If you take me with you, I could study in America."

I thought he was joking.

"I'd love to," I said, joking back. "But I don't think your family would like the idea very much."

"But of course they would. They would like me to study too. I would write to them often and when I finish my studies and find work, I would send them money. And one day I would come back to them and help them. They will like this idea. You will see. Just ask them. I beg you. Please."

Cissé nodded his head to a young man across the street. "That's my brother."

"How old is he?"

"He's seventeen."

"Is he still in school?"

"No. He had to leave school and find a job. He drives a taxi."

"Here in Kolda?"

"Well, between Kolda and Ziguinchor. Sometimes he drives to Tambacounda. That's what I will have to do if I can't continue with my studies."

"Drive a taxi?"

"There isn't anything else here."

I looked around. There were many young men, fit and robust but they were all just standing around. Some were helping travelers carry their bags down to the taxi station, but there was no real work to be done, nothing else to do but stand in groups, hope all gone, time passing slowly. It could have been a street corner in Detroit. They pass the days drinking or talking, or else they just wait and wait and wait.

But Cissé wanted something more. Perhaps they all did.

Cissé was a kid, no matter how wise, and when he boasted, his eyes lighted bright. Just like a proud little kid, he was happy with himself.

"I already know how to drive," he said. "And I'm a good driver. Truly. My brother taught me."

His brother came over, this seventeen-year-old half man. He bummed a cigarette from me, lit it, and looked very adult, very serious. He wore dirty old clothes and slip-slops. His feet were dusty and calloused, as if he had paced ruts in the earth from years already of endless and restless waiting. But when the conversation somehow turned to football (soccer), his eyes lighted up bright and young, like a kid's, like his brother's eyes when Cissé was boasting about his driving.

"This is my brother," Cissé said. And to his brother he introduced me as his friend. "He's American," he added.

"Yes, I know," the brother said. "It's evident."

"He's taking me with him," Cissé said.

The brother was very excited for his brother's good fortune.

"You are?" he said with great enthusiasm. "That would be very very good. To live in America." His voice trailed off dreamily.

Suddenly I had adopted a son.

"Maybe I could come visit," the brother said.

"What would your parents say?" I asked. "Wouldn't they miss him if I took your brother off to America?"

"No," said the brother. "It would be hard at first, perhaps, but it would be a good thing for Cissé. If it is true, it will be great and the family will be happy."

"Are you really going to?" Cissé asked.

"I don't really think it's possible. There are so many formalities; and anyway, I'm not going home for several months."

"I will travel with you. I don't mind."

Clearly he didn't.

"I don't think I can," I said. But I wondered if maybe there was some other way to help him. I could send money once a month or something, help the family, which would help Cissé. Maybe he wouldn't have to quit school and go to work if the struggle to feed the family were somehow lessened.

I felt like an idiot. It was stupid even to think it.

"I will write to you," I promised, as if that somehow meant something. "And if you need anything, let me know." I almost added in a very patronizing way, "How does that sound?" Of course I knew how it would have sounded.

But Cissé was ready for me.

"Can you send me a Walkman tape recorder? And some football shorts?"

"Football shorts?"

"And jerseys," the brother said. "With the emblem of the team from Cameroon. Oh, they are fantastic. And Nigeria too. Do you think you can get us shorts and shirts like the ones they wear?"

"And maybe some shoes," Cissé said. "Real shoes."

He was a clever youngster, and I began to wonder just how clever. How much of this encounter was an act?

When I climbed into the taxi going to Tambacounda, Cissé was there to ask me for one last gift.

"Could you give me some money?"

I hesitated, caught between my suspicions and my generous desire to be helpful in some small way. I felt more like a fool.

"How much do you want?"

"Five thousand CFA?"

I laughed a hearty laugh. I knew I was being played, or at least thought so. But can you ever be sure?

And yet five thousand CFA was not much. And it was an answer to my prayers to be able to return in some small way the generosity that so often I had been favored with. And still I failed.

"Here," I said. "Here's fifteen hundred."

"And for my brother?"

"You'll have to share it."

I was jammed tight in the car, thank goodness, and gone.

We stopped for gas, of course, and headed over the dusty red road toward Tambacounda.

SIX

DEATH TRAIN
TO A BROKEN HEART ▶▶▶▶▶▶▶

Mali

A fine mist of red African dust clouds the pale air and fills my nose, stings my eyes. Breathing becomes difficult, swallowing impossible. The African dust settles in the back of my throat with a sour taste. I cough up a ball of phlegm and spit onto the floor. It is a very African thing to do.

More and more I am trying to get used to African ways, trying to live them, trying to understand them, trying to shed the snakeskin of assumptions and expectations and sensibilities of the world I come from. Perhaps for a time now I can put on a coat of African skin, be African for a while and adapt to this strange new place.

I slip a piece of torn paper between the pages to mark my place and close the book I have been reading. My eyes have drifted without focus across pages I have read without really reading. I have not heard the writer's voice. I have not listened to his story. I catch myself in the middle of a passage that seems familiar and realize that I have read this paragraph and this page already four times. I cough up another rust-colored ball and spit again.

I would like to surrender to my fatigue, but sleep is taking no prisoners. The day is too hot. The heat is thick. The air is crowded with dust and sweat and sour smells. There is no way to get comfortable. I am on the death train to Mali, the train from Dakar and Tambacounda to Bamako, the capital of Mali. I cannot breathe, I cannot sleep, I cannot read. I am very hungry but there is nothing to eat, nothing to drink. Like everyone else I am at the mercy of time and the elements. Like everyone else all I can do is sit and endure. Complaining is just not done in Africa. Here one of the things you learn to do is to endure.

The train station at Tambacounda was a redbrick building, ancient and covered with dust. The ground was covered with people already starting to gather, waiting for the train, milling about like restless cattle in a pen. There was nothing tranquil about the mood of the crowd. There was no shouting and no shoving, but the crowd was restless, uncomfortable in the heat and in the uncertainty. These people had come down early to make sure they got a seat. But the station chief was not selling tickets.

"I can't sell tickets," he told me, "until I know how many seats are available."

"And when will that be?"

"When the train gets here."

The train was already late. Rumors were spreading that the train out of Dakar was totally full. The mood shifted. People standing in line at the ticket counter were becoming angrier and more restless.

I pushed deep inside the hot brick building and found the station chief again. He gave the same story and slammed his office door shut. But there was a large crowd camped outside that door and men were pushing to get inside one at a time. Some came out empty-handed. Others were smiling with relief, clutching tickets in their hands. The station chief either was making a little extra money selling tickets at a premium, or he was selling tickets very selectively—to his friends and acquaintances, perhaps. I didn't mind becoming one of his friends, but I would refuse to pay a premium.

As I had done before, I shoved like a madman to the front of the line. Two other men managed to push past me and get inside before I did, but when the next man came out and someone else tried to push past, I pushed in with him. The station chief said he was only dealing with people one at a time. He ordered me to wait outside. I told him no.

"It's too crowded and I'm tired of pushing. I'll wait here," I said.

He frowned and muttered under his breath, but he sold us tickets, gave us reservation numbers, and didn't charge us extra.

When the train finally arrived, it was over four hours late. Nighttime had pushed evening farther west into the dimming glow of the western sky and darkness was advancing from the east. People had begun to cook meals beside the tracks. Open fires pierced bright holes in the night. People were exhausted and lay on the ground. They sprawled across the tracks just to have a place to lie or sit down. Vendors were everywhere hawking all the usual effects: batteries and cold drinks, T-shirts and cigarettes and toothpaste.

When the train came, there was a mad rush to pile on. I took my time. I had a first-class ticket and a seat reservation. But once on board I found there was no seat corresponding to the number on my ticket. No one else seemed to be looking for a specific seat. There *were* no assigned places—the station chief's revenge. As frantically as the others, I leapt into the first seat that was not occupied. I did not want to stand all night.

The first-class carriage was old and filthy. The seats were hard and did not recline. The windows only opened a little. People sprawled everywhere. Some lay on the floor. Some couched in the corners. Some stood at the ends of the car.

I sat next to a man who leaned on me as he slept. In the seat facing mine, a man and his wife huddled close and slept. They sat close enough together that there was a little space for me to put a foot up on the seat beside them. But there wasn't much room between the two seats and our legs tangled together. Our knees banged every time the train rounded a bend and swayed. There was no way to get comfortable.

The train was ancient and had no shock absorbers. It rattled and rocked and bounced. Every clickety-clack in the tracks, every rasp from the wheels, and every creak from the places where the cars coupled together filled the carriage with the terrible sound of steel grating against steel. No sound was absorbed, certainly not the snoring of these people who were all used to such discomfort. I tried to sleep but could not until many hours later. Even then my sleep was fitful. And then my fitful sleep was disturbed.

There were two trains that made the run from Dakar to Bamako and back again: a Senegalese train and a Malian train. I had been warned to take the Senegalese train, which left on Wednesdays. It was Wednesday. This was the Senegalese train?

My God! What must the Malian train be like?

In the night as we approached the border with Mali, a nervous rustling spread through the train. People were preparing to get off. They bundled their things together and pushed toward the end of the carriage. I woke up and followed them into the blackness of the night but left my gear on board.

There was a little hut at the edge of the tracks. A bare light bulb hanging down on the porch cast only a little light. There were soldiers all around, gloomy and menacing in the dark. The passengers formed a long line and marched over to the shack, where we handed over passports and papers, then hung around in a crowd waiting for our names to be called. The soldiers flexed their muscles, filled out forms, and quickly dispensed with the foreigners. With the Africans they took longer.

In the morning as light from the rising sun came into the carriage, I noticed that many of the people who had been on board the night before were not there now. Maybe they had gotten off at stations during the night, but I don't remember the train ever stopping. I hadn't slept so soundly that I would have slept through the train's stopping and the commotion of people crowding the aisles and shoving to get off. But maybe I had. Or maybe they had never gotten back on the train. Maybe they were still at the frontier pleading innocence to some charge of smuggling or espionage, real or made up, or maybe their papers weren't in order. Or maybe I was just being paranoid.

The train stopped often during the morning. Men jumped off at every stop and stood along the side of the tracks to pee. Instead of standing upright to pee, most of them squatted down.

Some were wearing long robes and had to squat in order to protect their privacy. Others wore long pants and squatted anyway.

I jumped off the train every chance I could, mostly just to stretch my legs, but also to pee—standing upright in a most unabashed way—and to buy fruit.

As the train pulled into each station, little children and old women and young girls would hurry to the side of the train and run alongside until the train slowed and stopped. On their heads and in their arms they carried buckets and baskets of fruit, food, cool drinks and bundles of firewood. From them I bought bananas and mounds of mangoes, their juice my only liquid refreshment.

The mangoes were soft inside, not at all fibrous. These were ripe and sweet, not like before. They were so succulent that the first bite sent a torrent of sticky juice through my beard and onto my shirt and trousers. I ate mango after mango and never got enough of them. I was becoming a mango man.

I bought sandwiches whose contents I was not sure of, not even after I ate them. And I bought bits of roasted meat. What meat it was I did not know. But I was hungry enough to have eaten almost anything.

I bought nothing to drink, but from one little girl I bought enough water to wash my face and cool my neck. I soaked a handkerchief and tied it round my neck. It was completely dry again only minutes later.

It was Mali, the desert again, rocky soil and blinding sun and heat that never let up. The journey was impossibly long and just as uncomfortable. The carriage filled with a cloud of dust and smelled of sweat and roasted meat and pee. The toilets had filled and overflowed during the night and the door would not shut. The stench was briefly nauseating, but slowly you got used to it. You couldn't do anything about it anyway. And no one else was complaining.

Soon I noticed a most amazing thing—even in all this discomfort and heat, the babies were not crying. They whimpered a little and wriggled when hungry and grabbed for a breast, but that was the only evidence that what the women carried strapped to their backs was actually alive.

Babies in Africa don't cry very much. They are too secure.

They are strapped to mother all day and breast-fed until they are three, four, five years old. They are given a lot of attention, and they are used to being handled by strangers. When a mother on the train wanted to go to the toilet, she hardly hesitated to ask me to hold her baby for a minute. All she had to do was look at me and smile. I reached out for the baby and took it. The baby snuggled warmly in my arms and looked up into my dirty face. I smiled. She closed her eyes and kicked her tiny legs and her little feet, rocking herself until finally she was still and quiet.

Mother came back and I held up a hand to stop her from taking the baby back. I liked holding her. Neither mother nor baby seemed to mind. The mother took a little nap.

There were wispy clouds in the sky, but they did not suggest rain. The train slowed to a crawl. The windows were barely open and the breeze stilled. The smells increased and the dust inside settled all around. There was no movement, only noise and heat. The baby in my arms left a wet spot on my shirt. It was the only moisture around and for the brief seconds before it dried it left a cool spot on my belly. Then it was gone.

The baby did not move. The mother did not move. No one else on the train moved. The heat beat down like a heavy hammer. There was no air for cooling, hardly any for breathing. The dust settled in my eyes and stung them, entered my nose and clogged my throat. I could not breathe or swallow. And the train chugged on. I squirmed and fidgeted but could not get comfortable. I passed the baby back. The mother smothered the kid in her arms, rolled over, and they slept soundlessly.

Finally and by some miracle, we arrived in Kayes.

It was supposed to have been a twelve-hour journey from Tambacounda to here. It had taken twenty. Now there were only twelve hours more to Bamako.

Kayes wasn't much of a town. Dust and heat and a few old buildings. Everyone had to get off here and report to immigration to do the passport and papers routine again. But immigration had run out of whatever forms they were supposed to make us fill out. They just looked at passports and sent us on, back to the train. No one was sure when it would leave again. I tried to read but couldn't concentrate. Finally I closed the book and put it away.

The man across from me was picking his nose. His finger was buried deep, hidden almost to the second joint. He was rooting around shamelessly, excavating with his finger rotating slowly in his wide nostril. When he pulled it out, he rolled the moist little ball of mucus and dust between his thumb and forefinger, and when the little ball was a little less sticky, he flung it across the carriage.

And I, now lacking shame, did the same, digging around in my nose to clear out the dust and dirt. It was a very African thing to do.

I was dying of thirst. The man across from me and I were the only ones left on the train. I got off and stepped down onto a horde of people lying in the minimal shade of the platform. They must have known something I didn't. I found the station chief and asked him when the train would leave. He didn't know.

"Maybe this evening at seven o'clock," he said. "But be here at four, just in case."

I wandered through the dusty town, and through the market, but there was no place to eat. I tried to phone home, but the lines were not working today. And when I asked if there was some other way to get to Bamako, I was told to take the train.

"But the train won't leave for hours yet."

"That is the only way."

"No taxis or buses?"

"There is no road between here and Bamako."

But there was a little hotel with a kind of restaurant serving rice and some kind of meat tougher than shoes. Happily there were a few sodas left.

The Senegal River passes through Kayes. Down a high hill men were bathing in the river. Women were doing the laundry, rubbing clothes with soap and beating them against the rocks, then rinsing the clothes in the current. I wanted to go down to the river and fall in to cool myself, but the hill was steep and the river was far away—thank goodness, for I had been warned to stay out of African rivers. Just swimming in them could leave you with bilharzia, blood flukes.

Back to the train to find some shade, even if it was not cool, and some sleep. The only way to battle the heat was to sleep, but it's a fitful sleep. You wake up hotter still and covered with sweat. Your face feels grimy, your body is filthy. You scratch your hair and grease coats your hand. Grime cakes black beneath your fingernails.

The train journey to Bamako lasted another night and half-day of death, another night of hell.

Picking his nose, spitting on the floor do not make a man African. Nor is it enough to eat what the Africans eat and go where they go, to travel the death train into Mali. This is a world where all the sights and sounds and smells are as foreign as another language. At first you want to translate every sentence word for word until finally you are so overwhelmed by the effort that you resign yourself to capturing only the sense of what you hear. After a time you learn to absorb the nuances of what you hear. Eventually, you find yourself speaking the language.

I stepped off the train and into the station at Bamako. The big hall was dense with people pushing and shouting, some trying to squeeze out, others trying to squeeze in. The travelers were so loaded down with their possessions, it seemed as if they had packed up all their belongings and carried everything with them—in case a coup was in progress or the borders were closed, no doubt, and they never made it home again. Big suitcases, cardboard boxes splitting open, bundles tied with twine.

Waiting to help them were porters pushing drays into the crowd. They pushed them the same way that drivers in Africa drive: without regard to who or what might be in the way.

Someone grabbed my bag and carried it for me. He was stooped at the waist. When he walked he shuffled under the weight of the bag, but he wore a huge grin.

"How far are you going, boss?"

"I don't know. I guess I want to find a hotel."

"I'll take you there."

"If you want to," I said, "but I'm not going to pay you."

He kept the grin glued tight to his face. He showed all of his teeth, but the sparkle faded from his eyes. He was not sure whether to believe me. His mouth was a rigid smile but not a very warm one, and his eyes were a frown of shock.

"What do you mean to say?" he asked.

"I mean I'm not going to pay you."

His grin left.

"I didn't ask you to carry my bag," I said. "You just came along and grabbed it."

"Yes," he said. "I am doing you a service."

"Why should I pay for a service I never asked for? I'm not weak or ill. I can carry my own bag. If I couldn't or didn't want to, then I would have asked you. But you should have waited. I'm not going to pay you."

He never put the bag down. He was still going to do me this service, and in case he thought I was pretending, I insisted to him that I would not pay him. He accepted my edict as if he had been responsible for the blunder, and as if the blunder were irreversible. Instead of dropping the bag, he carried it dutifully, as he would have carried his penance.

"I know a good hotel," he said, "and I know a bad hotel. Which one do you want?"

"Even though I am not going to pay you," I said, "you will still carry my bag?"

"Yes," he said. "Why not?"

He was guileless. His easy grin returned. He would make no money today, but so what. There would be other days. There had been plenty already when he had earned none. *The world has many mornings.*

He mumbled something in a tribal language.

"What was that?" I asked.

"That was Bambara," he said. "It is the true language of my people."

"And what did you say?"

"What I said means 'It is God who provides.' It comes through you, or it comes through another, but it is God who provides. I have no quarrel with you."

"Then your quarrel must be with God," I said.

"Why with God?"

"Because if it is God who provides," I said, "then it is also God who denies. Look around you. This is what God has provided."

I had never seen anything like it.

We passed the American Cultural Center and turned the corner. Sitting along the street was a row of beggars who looked as dazed and emaciated as if they had just been liberated from a Nazi death camp. One man's left leg was as thin as the bone beneath his skin. His thigh was no bigger than my wrist. He had no right leg.

Another man had no legs at all. He scooted himself on bleeding knuckles across the red dust of the street to hold out a beggar's bloody hand to anyone who passed.

People walked in the crowded streets and never looked twice. The lame hobbled along after them. A car passed and never slowed down, barely missing a blind beggar stumbling in the road. The driver screamed and honked his horn.

Bamako was noisy. People shouted. Cars honked continually. They drove swiftly, clanging and rattling noisily over the rutted dirt roads, doors hanging loosely on rusted and broken hinges, filling the air with their banging, old engines roaring like thunder. Big black clouds of diesel exhaust floated just behind each one. The cars obviously didn't speed fast enough to kill, just fast enough to maim and mutilate. There was plenty of evidence.

On one corner was the American embassy. Across the street was a bar and café called Ali Baba's with a few tables and chairs on the small terrace. This was where the Europeans and the Americans sat for lunch. They chatted breezily and laughed, eating merrily, without looking once toward the street. They seemed oblivious to the beggars and to the poverty that surrounded them. They were embassy officials and aid workers from the United States, from Canada, from France, who had been here long enough to get used to what I saw as purest agony, the bitterest suffering. Maybe to survive here you would have to be a little blind, care a little less.

No conversation stopped when I passed. No one noticed in my walk or in the way I dressed that I was any different from the rest of the black mass on the street. No one greeted me as a new arrival to the community of Americans living there. I was not one of them.

But the Africans knew. They didn't know where I was from, but they knew I was a stranger in Mali. They stopped and stared, greeted me first with smiles, nods of their heads and little waves, and then with begging hands held out to me. By the time we reached the Hotel Djallo, I was like the Pied Piper leading a small crowd of beggars and young boys selling candy and T-shirts and toothpaste.

"This is the place?" I asked.

"Yes," he said, and he handed me my bag.

I gave him some money.

"This is not for carrying my bag," I assured him. "I'm giving you this for helping me find a hotel."

"You see?" he said. "It is not a question of why you give, only that you give. It is God who provides."

He leered at me smugly, as if he had known all along that I would give him something. And as if he were reading my thoughts even now, he clutched the coins tightly in his fist and jammed his hand in his pocket.

"Thank you very much," he said. "God will smile on you and on your children. You are a generous man. You may not know it, but you are not so hard as you pretend."

The frozen grin thawed on his face and became a real smile. He turned away, still stooped at the waist, and hobbled up the street. It wasn't the weight of the bag after all that had bowed him.

A car screamed at him. The little man hobbled as fast as he could.

The entry to the hotel was guarded by a door of hanging beads. A short, skinny fellow sat sleeping in the long, dark corridor. He slept among the many trinkets and souvenirs he sold, but there had been no buyers this morning. I sneaked past him, but he awakened when the woman at the table greeted me. He came to me with a wood carving in each hand and asked with his eyes if I was interested.

"Not now," I said. "Maybe later."

"Come. Just have a look," he said. "You don't have to buy anything."

"Later," I said firmly. I didn't want to be bothered. I gave my attention back to the woman behind the table.

She only had one room left, she said. She led me up the narrow stairs and showed it to me. It was a huge circular room, very dim, with a bed in the very center. The bed was shrouded with a mosquito net hanging from a ceiling fan. There was a wooden table against the wall, and there was nothing else in the room. She showed me how to work the ceiling fan, showed me where the shower was.

"Is there hot water?" I asked.

"Yes," she said, and lied.

Finally she introduced me to the bartender who sat on a stool at the small bar in the corner.

"If there is anything at all you want," she said, "he can help you find it."

The bartender shook my hand and smiled a slow, sneaky grin.

The bar was a tall wicker stand with two stools in front of it. There was beer and soda, but nothing else. Several men were strewn about the room, either sleeping on the floor or propped up in chairs. Perhaps they were left over from last night's revelry; perhaps they were guests who could afford to sleep on the floor but not in a room. There were lots of empty beer bottles all around.

"Will you take the room?"

"Yes," I said. "But can I pay you later? I'm running out of money."

Her face twisted and she shook her head very slowly. "I really don't think so," she said.

I fished out of my pocket all the money I had left and gave it to her. It was just enough.

"Where can I change dollars?" I asked.

"If you hurry you can change money at the bank. But they close today at eleven."

It was Friday. Everything shut down early on Fridays. By the time I got to the bank, it was already too late.

As I crossed the street, two cars nearly ran me over. I walked slowly, daring them. The drivers honked and hurled profanities at me. As I wandered further and crossed Avenue Kasse Keita, a presidential motorcade screamed by. I would have challenged them too, but a soldier on the corner shouted at me to get off the street. His hand slid up the barrel of the machine gun hanging from his shoulder.

First the jeeps sped past with machine gunners standing in the back. They were clearing the road, threatening to shoot anyone who got in the way of the motorcade, vigilant against any possibility of assassination. When the road was cleared, the six black limos carrying the president and his entourage raced through the narrow streets. They were preceded and followed by a motorcycle escort. They did not slow at intersections and would not have slowed for any stragglers caught in the road. But the streets had emptied and everyone driving or walking had stopped dead in his tracks to watch. When the motorcade had flown past and all was normal again, the motorists resumed their crazy honking and driving. It all trickles from the top down: the presidential motorcade had been their example.

The president was Moussa Traoré. His picture hung in every bank and government office, in most unofficial offices too. His photo was plastered everywhere—a dignified likeness in semimilitary uniform, his official sash draped over one shoulder and cutting boldly across his chest. He stood not quite full face and not quite in profile, his big round face looking noble and concerned. But he could not hide his girth. He was a fat man, well rounded from a lot of good eating, a lot of good living. Maybe he wanted to show it. Rumor was that he was at once one of Africa's richest men and the president of one of Africa's poorest nations.

Traoré, like most African leaders, seemed to think of himself as a hero to his people, almost a god. But behind his back his people called him *le grand bouffeur*—the big cheater—a nickname earned by his blatant corruption and thievery. The money he stole and routed to numbered bank accounts in Switzerland for his personal use came from foreign economic and development aid. Grain donated by the United States and France and others to avert hunger and starvation in his country reportedly ended up for sale in the markets. It was Louis XIV taken one step further. *C'est moi, l'état.* The state is me; what's yours is mine.

There was a story making the rounds. Schoolteachers in Mali had not been paid for a very long time. They had been asked to be patient a little longer, always just a little longer. They would soon be paid, they were promised—no doubt out of the latest installment of economic aid from Paris; it was already in the pipeline.

At this same time, Moussa Traoré's son had a serious accident and was in Paris for medical treatment. To pay the hospital bills, Traoré supposedly appropriated a huge portion of French aid money, but in fact designated only a small amount to pay for his son's treatment. The rest he intended to deposit into a numbered Swiss bank account.

The man in charge of overseeing the transaction was Traoré's ambassador to France. He did indeed help Traoré divert the aid money, but it was never used to pay hospital bills. Nor did it make its way into Traoré's bank accounts.

Initially, the ambassador later claimed, he had intended to use the money to pay the teachers, but of course once the money entered Mali, Traoré would get his hands on it. So the former ambassador decided simply to keep it. He asked France for political asylum and is now something of a folk hero in Mali.

Rumor said that Moussa Traoré's wife had a heart attack when she heard the news that her money had been stolen. Because of her lavish life-style and wicked ways, she was very possibly the most hated individual in Mali. The former ambassador became a hero partly because he caused this hated woman to grieve, but mostly because he had succeeded in cheating the big cheater.

The money had been intended for the Malian people, and they were the ones who were really cheated, but that mattered little. They cheered the results because they were no worse off. They wouldn't have seen the money anyway. And any Malian in the former ambassador's place would have wanted to do the same.

The man who told me that story feared greatly when he told it. There is no political opposition or activism in Mali, there are no voices of dissent, no voices of ridicule. There is only fear. Fear of disappearance, fear of death, fear of Malian prisons, which can be worse than death. The man who told the story had been there.

Just as there is no dissent, there is no easy communication. There is no decent telephone service, there are no open roads. Roadblocks and checkpoints impede the way. Papers are checked. Reasons for traveling are doubted. Mail is intercepted. People disappear. Rumors abound.

Once a French aid worker wrote a letter in Spanish and sent it to a friend in Spain. The writer had a few critical things to say about Madame Traoré, the president's wife. The letter was intercepted, opened, and read. The French volunteer found himself in jail one morning. It took the direct intervention of France, so the rumor goes, and the threat of an end to French aid money—half of Mali's GNP—to get him released.

Malians hate Traoré. He has a huge presidential palace high on a hill overlooking the city. But he spends most nights—another rumor perhaps—with his soldiers in the army barracks. It seems he lives in fear too. He stays near his men to keep an eye on them, to guard against plots to overthrow him. He is not the beloved leader he pretends to be.

But for the moment he is his country's president, and until the next coup, his people will feign respect when his motorcade screams past. They will hurry out of the way. They will even salute and wave. And they will do the same for the next dictator's motorcade. (I did not know it then, but the next coup would come in March 1991, and Traoré would die.)

There are only a few paved streets in Bamako. The rest are hard-packed dirt. When it rains, the roads turn to red mud and the potholes fill with water. Cars bumping along those bad roads splash water and mud everywhere. Pedestrians too slow to avoid them get wet and muddied. They never curse. They accept it.

It was raining one Friday afternoon when I hurried into the American embassy to see if someone there could help me change money. They assumed I was with the Peace Corps and sent me across the street to the embassy services office. The man in the window was Malian and when he asked if I was with the Peace Corps, I said yes. He asked to see my ID. I said I was new, had just arrived, and hadn't been given one yet. He told me to wait while he went to check with his boss.

In the back office, I told his American boss the truth. It was Friday, the banks were closed, and I was broke.

"How much do you need to change?"

"How much can I?"

"Not very much. This is a service for Americans in some sort of government service. We're not really equipped to take care of tourists, but I could let them cash a hundred fifty dollars for you. Would that help?"

"Greatly," I said. The exchange rate there was much better than any bank would give.

Monday morning I finally made it to the bank. I wanted to change more money, to have enough on hand to last more than a few days. Inside the bank there was an incredible crowd of people jammed from one wall to the other. I pushed to the front and asked if they changed dollars.

"Not here. Try the bank down the street."

There was an incredible crowd in the second bank too, as if people came inside just to escape the heat. But the bank changed dollars and gave a fairly good rate.

I handed over my passport and the man behind the counter filled out forms. He stamped everything twice and then handed the forms and the passport to the man who sat behind him. That second man first had to finish what he had already started. When he was done with that, he checked all the figures and checked all the entries on the forms. He looked at the passport. He looked up at me. Then he signed his name to the back of the forms, handed the forms and the passport to someone else. That man also was busy. He was talking to someone and had to finish his conversation first. Then he too ran all the figures through his old adding machine. He punched buttons like a madman and pulled the mechanical lever. He checked the entries on the forms, looked up at me, then looked in the passport to make sure it was really me. He signed his name to the back and handed everything back to the first man. That man laid everything on the shelf of a glass booth where the cashier was supposed to sit, but she wasn't there. The man at the counter, the first man, held up his hand. The cashier would be there in just a few minutes. No initiative. No one wanting to accept responsibility. No one in authority wanting to give it up. The entire procedure took one hour and forty minutes.

Outside the bank the beggars were waiting for me. They knew why I had gone in. Their hands were already out-stretched. They pulled at my arm, at my fingers, at the hems of my trousers. Two of them were blind. One man with no legs and only stubs for arms had the most heart-wrenching way of pro-pelling himself. He wriggled on his stomach like a worm and scooted himself along by shoving against the ground with his chin. I couldn't watch.

And yet, when I discovered there was a leper colony near Bamako, I went there. I don't know why. I guess I just wanted to see what there was to see. A pickup truck taxied me there and I walked around. It was meant to be a hospital, but they didn't provide much relief. They merely kept the lepers isolated, though many of them had left the colony to beg on the streets of Bamako. The lepers I saw were without fingers and feet, without noses and teeth. They were twisted into inhuman shapes and did not smile. They had no lips. Their eyes haunted my nights and tormented my every meal. Every time I tasted meat I could not recognize, I tasted human flesh and I gnawed human bone.

I ate dinner that night back in Bamako with a toothless little man who wanted to be my guide. I had asked him where the market was, and instead of telling me, he had walked me there. He was proud that I had asked him, that I had bothered to talk to him, and he was prouder still of his name, which was Pierre.

"It is a Christian name," he said. "Are you Christian?"

"Yes," I said.

"Then you know it is a Christian name. What do you want at the market? I know many people. I can get you the right prices."

"I'm not looking for anything special," I said. "I just want to see what's there."

He showed it to me.

But this wasn't an ordinary market. Away from the stalls selling mangoes and bananas, away from the colorful pagnes, there was a row of stalls selling shrunken animal heads, dogs' teeth, fur from camels and goats, the limbs of cats and monkeys.

"What is all this stuff?"

The man on the ground was beating himself with a fly whisk. He was rocking back and forth. His eyes were closed and he chanted softly to himself. He looked up at me and said, "These are the things that will heal your body. These are the things to make potions from. These are the things that will keep away evil spirits."

Pierre whispered to me, "He's not a Christian."

"No," the animist said. "That is the white man's religion. It is powerless here. It brings with it only evil. These . . . ," he said, sweeping his hand before him to indicate the bits of dead animals on the ground, "these are the things we need. Only these can fight the evil spirits brought on us by the outsiders. Are you one of them, or are you one of us?"

Pierre pulled at me to leave. I wanted to stay.

"How does it work?" I asked the animist.

"You have to believe," he said. "You have to be taught the secrets. Even I do not know how it all works, only that it works."

I tried to toy with him, but he was ready.

"Can it mend a broken leg?"

"And a broken heart," he said. "When your eyes water and you sneeze all day. When there is pain in your back and when your head aches so much you cannot see. All these things can be fixed, and you can keep away evil spirits. Believe me."

And I think I did. I bought a little metal box from him, empty but for the magic inside.

"You are wise," he said.

"Those ways are the old ways," Pierre told me. "They don't work anymore."

I looked around at the results of the new ways; they didn't seem to be working much either.

Being in Africa is a little like being on the far side of the moon. Its gravity is a different gravity, its laws and logics are different laws and logics. It is a world where belief in witch doctors does not seem unreasonable, a place where men submit to authority and are forever at the mercy of heat and dust and dry winds that never cool but only stir the heat and throw dust into men's eyes and into their throats. Africa is a place where men sit in the shadows of outside influences stranger than themselves—the way they sit in the shade of the baobab tree waiting for a ride. They feel powerless in the face of tradition and the vagueness of time. The waiting is endless waiting, the uncertainty is harsh. Nature and the random whimsy of authority. Witch doctors and bureaucrats and God. Capricious and arbitrary. Always powerful, always lording over them.

Africa is a place where it is important to carry a gris-gris, to have something to believe in.

There was a young American, very gentle and soft-spoken, who refused to conform. He once entered a dry and dusty village in the outer reaches of Mali and there he was met by the village witch doctor, who greeted him and approached him, and they passed the time of day. It was a remote village. Nevertheless the witch doctor knew much about Americans and he believed the rumor that all Americans are rich. He demanded ten thousand

CFA from the young man in exchange for protection against evil spirits and spells. But the American believed neither in witch doctors nor in ghosts, and certainly not in extortion. He had not managed yet to shed the snakeskin of *his* world, where right was right and wrong was clearly wrong and things made sense in ways that were familiar to him. Scientific in background and pragmatic in nature, the American refused to pay. He told the witch doctor to piss up a rope. He further told him into which of his body's dark orifices to shove his spells and evil spirits. Then he made an impolite gesture.

The witch doctor was insulted. Had no one been there to see, he might have let the injury pass, but by now a crowd of villagers had gathered and the witch doctor was shamed as well. He hurled his own abuse at the arrogant American, cursed him, and threw a hex upon him. Then he went away muttering to himself. The American merely laughed.

Not very long afterwards, a scorpion stung the American in his leg. Although scorpion stings are rarely fatal, the thing hurt like hell and the American worried greatly.

A little later still, another ugly bug attacked the American. It crawled into the hammock where he slept in the night and bit him in the same leg, which swelled huge, like an overinflated balloon about to explode. The American was scared witless. Eventually the swelling went down.

Then of course the American was bitten by a snake that no one ever saw, not even the American. It was not known if the snake was cobra or viper, poisonous or not, and no one knew which antivenom to inject. The American was put into a *taxi-brousse*—a bush taxi—and shipped down to Mopti, where there should have been a doctor, but the doctor wasn't there.

The snake turned out to be a poisonous one, its venom a horrible anticoagulant. By the time the American arrived in Bamako, where he went next to find a doctor, he was bleeding from his pores and from his eyes and from every sore he had ever had. He fell into a coma and was flown to Paris in a jet-ambulance. He was wrapped from head to toe in compresses and spent many months lying like a mummy in a special ward in a French hospital.

One of his friends back in Mali finally got the message and found another witch doctor, a friendlier witch doctor, to make a gris-gris for the young American, a little charm that, while it couldn't break the initial spell, could at least mitigate its effects.

The American pulled through. He still refuses to believe in witch doctors, but when he is in Africa he is never without his gris-gris.

To understand this place, these peoples and their ways, it would be better to have been born here, to have been raised here. Your genes would carry the memories of generations past, the rhythms of this world, the dark cloud of its collective unconscious. Perhaps then this submission to authority would not seem so mindless, the strange harshness of life and death and mutilation not so senseless and devoid of justice, the belief in witch doctors not so bizarre.

A year here is not enough. A traveler cannot possibly see all there is to see and know all there is to know. Not in one year, nor in ten. It would, perhaps, be better to live and travel like the tortoise who spends the 150 years of its life moving slowly, learning intimately every inch of ground it covers. Going so far and so fast, as I was doing, a traveler sees the world rush by like streaks of rain on the windscreen of a speeding car. In the blur there are slashes of color, little bites of life. The best I could hope for was to stand back from the tableau and absorb it, to let the myriad impressions come together and offer an image.

I went to buy a mango and the little toothless man was right there with me. I bought him one too. We ate them by the drainage ditch that runs the length of the market. It was swarming with flies and mosquitoes. They seemed to breed there. The water was stagnant sludge, some of it raw sewage, some of it mango skins and banana peels tossed in because it was the handiest place to throw them. Nearby was a water spigot. Hesitantly I rinsed the mango juice off my hands.

I bought a cold drink. Pierre wanted one too. I walked through the dusty streets and through the tired crowds. Pierre never left my side. He led me to the post office, where I could phone home. He waited for me outside. And when it was time for dinner, Pierre went with me and showed me the best place to eat.

I followed him through the darkness. We crossed rue Keita

and went down to the ravine, another sewage ditch, that ran under the road. An old woman was bent over a charcoal fire there in the dark where the glowing coals were her only light. They blazed in her eyes and lighted the fat cheeks of her face. She did not smile, not even once. Pierre knew her. He greeted her happily. She merely grunted. He was happy to be getting a meal.

Three men were already sitting at her bench. We waited until they finished eating and left. We took their places and ordered spaghetti. Spaghetti was all she had.

"With meat?" she asked.

"Of course," Pierre said. He was really living.

The woman swished a big ladle around in a huge metal pot and dished up two small plates of mushy spaghetti. There was not enough food on both plates combined to make a decent appetizer for me. When I finished a second helping I asked Pierre if he wanted more.

"No thank you. I've had enough." And he patted his tummy as if he had eaten at a lavish banquet.

Hunger is a way of life. A little is a lot.

Waiting for me in the little bar of my hotel that night was a beautiful woman from Nigeria. The bartender, she said, had told her an American man was staying in the hotel. She was there to meet me.

"I was here last night too," she said.

"I know. I saw you."

"Why didn't you say hello and come talk to me? I was waiting for you."

"I didn't know," I said.

We sat on stools pushed very close together. Our knees touched.

"Will you buy me a beer?" she asked.

"Certainly," I said.

"Will you sleep with me tonight?" she asked.

"I don't think so," I said.

The light in the bar came from a few candles and from a bare bulb hanging in the hallway behind us. Her face was dimly lit, half of it hidden in shadow. She leaned closer so I could see her better.

"Please," she said.

Her eyes were shaped like cat's eyes, pointed at the corners and accentuated by a thick dark line of mascara. Her nose was flat and very broad, her cheeks very round, her hair pressed straight. She wore a soft cotton dress that opened at her throat and when she leaned forward, her breasts spilled halfway out. I could not tell how old she was, but she said she was only twenty-one years old.

Her father had married his third wife and there were too many people living in the house. There was little to eat, too many brothers and sisters, too many wives. She left Nigeria two years ago, first to Ouagadougou and then to Bamako. She would keep working until she could make her way to Europe.

"This is how I earn my money," she told me. "Won't you help me?"

"No," I said.

"Don't you like the way I look?"

"You're very pretty."

"Then what is it?" She grabbed between my legs. "Doesn't this work? Don't you like women?"

I got up to leave. She began to beg.

"You can pay me anything you like. We'll go to bed first, and you can pay me in the morning—whatever you think I'm worth. I'm very good. You'll see," she said. "And you'll be glad you did."

"Not tonight."

"Anything you want to give. One thousand CFA. Five hundred. Three hundred."

She was down to a dollar and would have given herself to me for cab fare home.

"I don't think I can afford even that," I said.

They are elusive, these emotions of mine, so ephemeral that I can barely put a name to them, so tangible that I become physically ill. The dirt and the squalor are everywhere here: little children begging, lepers and cripples dragging themselves piece by piece across the road, clawing at the ground with their gnarled hands and bleeding fingers. The misery in Mali is appalling, the shock to the observer electrifying. I have become too soft. I cannot take the suffering.

I stayed in Mali nearly a month.

▲

South of Bamako, in a little mud hut village, a man was sitting in the shade of a leafy tree. His leg was propped up on a bench. He held a thin stick above his leg, very delicately turning the stick like a spit between his fingers. Something was coming out of his leg and the man was wrapping it like twine around the stick, very carefully so as to keep the thing from breaking off. It was a worm, and if he tore it in two, he feared he might never get the thing out of his leg.

He cursed himself, as if he had been to blame.

"I cannot understand what I did to make this happen," he said.

I did not know what he meant, except perhaps that he was trying to remember what he had drunk that gave him the worms.

These Guinea worms, as they're called, enter the human body as larvae and live beneath the skin. The larvae, ingested by fleas that swim in the streams and ponds, emerge when the infested water is drunk. The fleas die in the stomach of the human host, but not so the Guinea worm larvae. They mature and mate. The males die, and the females migrate from the stomach to other parts of the body. After a year's incubation, when the female worm is about three feet long, she moves to the surface of the skin and secretes a poison that causes the skin to burn and itch. Blisters form and when they burst, the worm pops through the skin, wriggling free, debilitating the victim with pain and severe itching. It may take each worm three full weeks to emerge completely. The man I met was helping the process along by trying to pull the worm out. But there were probably other worms living inside him, waiting their turn to break the surface of his skin and dangle loose. A story goes that one man had thirty-five worms coming out of his legs and feet at the same time.

New larvae hatch, make their way back to the water, and the whole process starts all over again.

Parasites are a way of life in this part of Africa.

Farther south, in another village along the Bani River, half the population is blind. The black flies that breed in the fast-moving waters of the nearby river carry parasitic worms. When the flies bite their human victims to suck a meal of blood, they deposit the worm larvae into the human body. They grow quickly into long, thin worms that can live under the skin for twelve years, not thirty-five or forty at one time, as in the case of the Guinean worms, but two hundred million of the parasitic microworms. In time, they migrate through the skin and the itching is severe. The skin of the victim decays and loses color, stretches and becomes scaly. Lesions form in the eyes. Sometimes the tiny worms crawl through the eyes and dangle from the socket, or from a tear duct. In time the victim will be blind.

Before they are old, all the men and women in the village expect to be blind.

A young boy led one of the village elders through the maze of mud huts. The old man held the young boy by the shoulder and followed. His skin was splotched, his eyes opaque and milky. His head was tossed back. He hardly ever blinked. He lifted his face toward heaven and told me his blindness was payment for his sins.

"If not my sins," he said, "then for the sins of my father."

Could it possibly be true, that these torments are some colossal practical joke inspired by God? If Africa is Eden, isn't it also Original Sin as well? And perhaps the disaster that is Africa somehow is a penance for man's greatest sin, not just slavery but the willing participation in it, the selling of one's brothers and tribesmen.

The slavery hasn't ended. Not when you think about the Traorés and the Mobutus and their ilk, the self-proclaimed presidents for life, the ones who call themselves "number one peasant," "the wise old man," "the all-powerful warrior who leaves fire in his wake." What they have done and continue to do carries on a practical joke even greater than God's, the one started by the colonial Europeans that perpetuates black self-disdain and self-hatred. It is subconscious and subtle. But it is there. Anything white has got to be better. How could it be otherwise when to look out at the world is to see prosperity and progress, to look in at the black world is to see crooks and corruption and starvation, nothing working the way it should, no roads, no work, nothing but misery?

In Bamako, as in other African cities, women buy and use skin bleach to lighten their skin.

The Malians are quick to tell me how much they hate their noses.

"They are so wide and flat," one man said. "It is a very ugly nose."

My nose, he said, was different. He could tell I was American by the shape of my nose.

Another man could tell by the color of my skin, another by the texture of my skin.

"My skin?" I said in wild disbelief. I held out my arm and he extended his. They looked the same to me.

He touched mine and he touched his.

"They are not the same," he said. "They do not feel the same, and they are not the same color. Your skin is better."

He, of course, saw what I could not see. Just as the Eskimos have a plethora of words for snow, so too the Africans can tell the subtlest gradations in skin color, as if color were so important.

"But it is," he said. "As is everything."

And he pointed out to me men of different tribes. To him they were different peoples, and he could tell them apart by the color of their skin, by the markings on their faces, by the way they held themselves, the way they walked.

What did they see, then, when they saw me? They never failed, in some wretched way, to tell me that I was not one of them.

Along the road to Ségou and Mopti, hitchhiking toward Timbuktu, I could not get a ride. No car would stop for me. But the white aid workers from abroad had no trouble.

I sat one morning by the side of the road with a Peace Corps worker named Steve. When we were together, no car stopped. The moment I went to sit in the shade, the next car that passed stopped for Steve. There was room for only one of us.

"You take it," Steve told me. "It might be a little easier for me than for you."

It was true, of course. Steve was aware of it too, and the thought killed me.

The colonial conquest of Africa didn't begin when the Europeans first arrived and didn't end when finally they granted emancipation and left. Fact is, they never really went away. They only moved aside and never left Africa alone, never allowed Africa to be what it was, what it could have been, what it ought to be.

"The Arab empires were first," Keita said. He was a man I met as I had met all the others. He came to me on the street, took me by the hand and walked with me. He wanted me to know who he was and how he thought. "They brought their religion, which taught us to give to the poor, which is good; but it also taught us to beg, which is bad. It taught us to have many wives and many, many children, which only perpetuates our poverty."

And then the Europeans came.

"What they left us with," he said, "perpetuates our poverty also. What they have done and continue to do, and the Americans too, makes beggars of us all and does nothing to ease our poverty."

Aid money and grain, he said, gets dumped like loads of sand.

"Your government doesn't really care where it goes," he said, "and doesn't watch where it ends up. You send us aid not to help us develop, but to appease your conscience, and the aid gets corrupted. The money finds its way into Swiss banks. Everyone knows it. And you send us aid workers, but they only keep us reliant. They do water projects and they show us a few things, but they don't really teach us anything useful. They give us tractors but no spare parts. It is good will, but not much more. And always we are forced to look up to white men who seem to know more about everything than we do. It is another form of imperialism."

And when he said "they," he meant me too.

In the market in Mopti, large burlap sacks of grain are stacked up. They are on sale, even though they are stamped in large black letters: US AID. NOT FOR RESALE. No one was giving away anything.

The Peace Corps volunteers I met in Ségou were kind to me and very friendly. They were young and purposeful and all of them were white, brimming with ideals of hope and charity, saving the world in the name of humanity, for God and country. But ultimately I came to see them in a light no less ambivalent than the light that fell upon Africa itself and affected my eyesight.

In any other time or any other place we might have become good friends. But they threatened to break the spell of Africa for me, and I resented their being here.

I refused to see Africa as my homeland, and yet I was suddenly very possessive, as if I, like Keita, wanted the foreigners to go home. They did not see this place as I saw it, did not feel the pain that was shattering my heart. They (as if I weren't) were on some kind of holiday adventure, no matter what their stated purposes and goals. Many of them were directionless and looking to find themselves, taking a two-year time-out to decide which paths to pursue, a two-year paid holiday at summer camp.

Certainly I could not begrudge them that. Not I. But they did not seem aware of the damage they were doing, not aware of what footprints they would leave behind when they returned home. They saw only the good in their being here and had grown used to the suffering that surrounded them. They had been here longer than I and had inured themselves in ways that I refused.

The volunteers lived comfortably in little villages where African women cleaned for them, cooked for them. In Bamako, I spent many days behind the high walls of the compound of an American diplomat. She worked for a U.S. government aid agency and she lived in comfort. Her home was air-conditioned and equipped with an emergency generator for those times when electricity in the city went dead. She had guards and servants and real food to eat. She had a swimming pool. And I lounged there sipping gin and tonics in the afternoon, floating in her pool to rinse away the heat of the day, and eating what nearby Africans, even the servants who worked in this house, could never afford to eat.

Not far from her home, the paved roads ended and the Africans lived in squalor. Their homes were shacks, dirt and mud and cardboard. Many people slept in the streets. The beggars and the lepers and the lame walked past the diplomatic compounds with hardly a second glance. If they complained, they did so in private and quietly endured what I, had I lived there, would have been too proud and too angry to endure.

▲

An American Peace Corps volunteer named Karen DeMoss pointed out to me that this was the third world. If I expected comfort, she said, I should have stayed home.

We had ridden from Ségou to Bamako together in the back of a truck that belonged to a Canadian aid worker. Beside Karen was a woman carrying an infant to a doctor in Bamako. The child was very frail, abnormally tiny, suffering from diarrhea and dehydration.

"This is Africa," Karen pointed out to me. "Things are different here. Customs are different. Ways of seeing the world are different. Everything is different."

"And you think that excuses anything?"

"It does," she said, and made a good defense for not leaving footprints too wide and too deep, as colonials are wont to do.

"I am not here to change them," she said. "Their customs are just as valid as ours. We have no right to try and make them into us."

Later, we talked as we walked along a shady street in the evening, looking for a place to eat. There was no one around to hear my tirade, and I went crazy, ranting in the middle of the street like some madman.

"And if you see a man beating his wife," I said, "what do you do? Because it is someone's custom doesn't make it excusable and certainly doesn't make it right. Do you think it's right that African women have their clitorises lopped off when they're fourteen years old?"

"I think it serves a purpose, yes."

"Sure it serves a purpose. It takes away sexual pleasure so a woman is less likely to sleep with someone other than her husband. It's done purely for the man's sake."

"Then why," she said, "in this ever-changing world is it mothers themselves who insist on having it done to their daughters?"

"It's like hazing at private schools for boys and at fraternities. It was done to you, and now it's your turn to do it to someone else. It's idiotic ritual."

"It's ritual, yes," she said. "And socialization. It is a way for women to follow a path toward belonging."

"And so it's okay?" I shouted. "Would you let it happen to your daughter?"

"I'm not African."

"And what about infibulation?"

"What's that?" she asked.

I calmed down to explain.

"In Sudan," I said, "when a woman is very young—I don't know how old—her vagina is sewn up. Just a little opening is left for her to pee through. If the opening isn't right, of course, there will be a lot of infection, but that's something else. Over the years, as the young girl gets older, her vagina grows closed, ensuring her virginity and staying that way until her wedding night. When wedding night comes, a sword is placed on the bridal bed, symbolic, I think, of two things: her wedding night deflowering and the husband's lifelong mastery of his wife.

"On the wedding night, after the celebration, the husband takes his bride and lays her on the bed. If he cannot break her open with his penis, ripping her to pieces in the process, it is his duty as a man to cut open her vagina with the sword. Either way it is a painful and bloody affair, and if there is no blood on the bed the morning after, or—these days—if a doctor is called, the husband's manhood is questioned."

The images were sickening. Karen was holding her stomach. And I was holding mine.

"That is tradition," I said. "It doesn't mean it's right."

"But just because it's wrong from my point of view," she said, "doesn't give me the right to object. That's a cultural kind of colonialism."

"You're right," I said. "But aren't there some absolutes in life that have nothing to do with cultures and only with humanity? Poverty. Dignity. Equality. How can anybody not respond? How could anybody not see the suffering that takes place here day after day and year after year and not rebel against it or go crazy? I guess I'm just not that strong."

I felt a little as Jesus must have felt, surrounded by misery, approached at every turn by lepers wanting a miracle from me, beggars after a meal, jobless men wanting to go to America. I came close to losing my mind. One too many beggars. One too many sardine sandwiches bought and eaten on the street, one too many globs of gristle substituting for meat. I had lost over twenty pounds. My chest was shrinking and my arms had lost any bulk they ever had. I wanted to eat. I hadn't seen a fresh vegetable in what seemed like an age, and I had been getting more calories from beer than from food. More nutrients too.

At Ali Baba's on the corner across from the American embassy, I saw carrots on the menu. A luxury item, no doubt, for the Americans who ate there. And listed on the menu were other delicacies to make a homesick American drool: hamburgers and cheeseburgers and club sandwiches. *And don't hesitate any longer to try our milk shakes.* I hadn't tasted milk in a long time.

I ordered the carrots and a cheeseburger. My stomach howled in thanksgiving. Then the food came. It tasted of the metal cans it had been packed in—at best. Or maybe of axle grease. Colorless, tasteless, valueless, it only served to remind me of what I lacked. I wanted to shout.

I took a long walk in the darkness up avenue van Vollenhoven. Beside the entrance to a small gasoline station, a family was sitting in the shadows. In the dark by the edge of the road, a small boy slept sprawled on a cardboard mat. Who in the world would have seen him there? If a driver had misjudged the distance to the gas station, or swerved to avoid a pothole—the boy would have been a mangled memory. Dead, or worse: one more mutilated beggar lining the side of the dusty road.

Human beings aren't supposed to live like this.

Another beggar approached. She saw me and emerged from the shadows. Her hand was already out. I wanted to punch her, knock her down. I hated her for begging, for her poverty. I was sick of seeing it. I was tired of this constant assault on my senses.

She wasn't very old, couldn't have been much older than I was. The light from the passing cars revealed a dirty face of a woman tired of begging, tired of living, slowly dying. The way she looked, I thought she might prefer it if I knocked her down, beat her senseless, and threw her in the path of speeding traffic. I would be ending the misery for her.

But she carried a baby strapped to her back. Her appeal was not anonymous. It was to me. Direct. Her eyes pleaded. She touched my sleeve.

I haven't much trouble saying no to anonymous begging, to people who hold out a hand or a cup or sit on chalked pavement squares with a message written there: *I have lost my plane ticket and have nothing to eat; please feed me and my dog.*

You find them in Paris, often running a scam. In some cities people make a small fortune panhandling and begging on the streets. But not here. Not this woman.

She had singled me out and asked me directly for help. Her appeal was personal. Her need and her baby's were so much right in front of me, so close now, I could smell it on her breath. How could I possibly refuse her?

She stood beside me, her eyes watery and sad, her face filthy. She breathed on me and her breath was foul. But I gave. I had no choice. I dug in my pockets, and took her hand and pressed money into her palm. And now there was a little gratitude in her eyes. But when she looked at the amount I had given her, when she unwadded the bank note and looked at it, she looked up at me with shocked disbelief and her thank-you was such a sad and pleading sound that I wanted to crawl away somewhere and die. I was ashamed of my own good fortune.

She hurried off back into the shadows and I watched her fade into the darkness.

I ran away myself then, bought a whole roasted chicken from a little shack at the side of the road, not a very good chicken, an African chicken, old and tough and stringy, not much taste and very difficult to chew. I ran with it under my arm and went to hide in a secret place somewhere in the dark. Sitting on a fallen tree and sobbing, I devoured that chicken as if I hadn't seen meat in thirty years. Dogs would growl curses at me for how little I left behind on the bones.

The next day I went to the Air Afrique office to buy a plane ticket. In the airline office there was a poster of a small boy smiling. The caption at the top read: *What does he want to be when he grows up?* At the bottom was the reply: ALIVE!

That afternoon I flew to the Ivory Coast, to Abidjan, where I debauched like a madman and went crazy. Ouagadougou would have to wait.

SEVEN

JUNGLES OF
LOVE AND LUNACY ▶▶▶▶▶▶▶▶▶▶

Ivory Coast
Liberia

A hot wind blows slowly across the land and moisture hangs heavy in the air. The desert has come at last to an end, the sand giving way first to hard red laterite, then to rocky soil and scrub bushes, and finally now to the dark loamy soil of the rain forest. The colors of one landscape have collided with those of another. The land from there to here and beyond has gone in broad stripes from gold to red and orange, to the dark rich brown of the earth, and finally now to the blaze of green that burns in the trees.

There is only green and the cold blue of the sea. Here where forest and sea come together Abidjan teeters, a modern city on the edge of a shelf of antiques, a city where cardboard shacks lie in the shadow of skyscrapers, glass and steel, fifty stories tall.

The canopy of jungle surrenders suddenly to asphalt and concrete. Instead of trees tall buildings sprout, the glass of one tinted pink, the glass of another reflecting the bright blue of the sky, sparkling in the sunlight. Clouds drifting overhead appear

twice—once in the sky, once in the outer walls of these buildings, which are like mirrors, reflections of heaven. Skyscrapers
on the horizon stand like beacons in the distance, beacons of the
modern world, beacons of prosperity.

Two blocks away stands a market that is like all other
markets in Africa, a cramped collection of shaky wooden stalls
with cardboard for walls and roofs. This is where the African
peasants shop. They stop to touch and smell and talk prices.
They carry armloads of fruits and meats and cloths, and count
their money carefully. Money spent is money not easily earned.
The prosperity of the city does not trickle down, and most of the
shoppers and sellers are gaunt and shoeless and in ragged
clothes.

Children in tow tote little baskets and are given treats for
being so helpful, small candies to chew. Babies are strapped
tight to their mothers. The pace seems somehow leisurely, as if
despite the noise and the activity, nothing is really happening
here. But hidden beneath the tedium there is a certain frenzy—
just as beneath the frenzy there is tedium.

A woman selling bananas sits all day at her stall. She waits
patiently for someone to pass and inspect and buy. She rocks
herself gently and hums with her eyes half-closed. She is on the
edge of sleeping. She does little. She sits. She waits. But already
the day has been a long one. No one sees her when she awakens
at four o'clock in the morning, long before light glows on the
horizon. No one sees her plodding along the road to buy the fruit
she sells. No one is with her when she hauls it down to market.
No one helps her set up for the day's sitting, the day's waiting—
no one but the young child she must bring with her each day.
She and the child will not leave here until the sun goes down or
she has sold all she has to sell. This waiting, which the child will
learn, is as important to her as the rushing about that the businessmen do who pass this market with hardly a glance. They are
in a hurry, have many pressing matters of their own to attend
to, have letters to mail and fees to pay. They live and work in
an Abidjan that is a world away.

Not far from the old market there are shops that sell pens
costing hundreds of dollars, thousand-dollar watches, hand-
made clothing imported from Europe for the many Europeans
who live here and work here and shop here in this *quartier* that

is more white than black, more French than African. There are travel agencies and bookshops and boutiques nearly as fancy as anything on rue Saint-Honoré in Paris. And everywhere there is glass, the glass of the buildings, the glass windows of the shop displays, the glass windows of the cafés where people sit to see and be seen. Somewhere two glasses tinkle in a toast before the wine is drunk. A spoon stirring sugar clinks against a coffee cup.

It is a bit like France, this conscious effort to enjoy life, these exhibitionist-voyeurs, everything and everyone on parade, and everyone aware of it. The windows of the shop displays are shiny enough to be mirrors. People stop to admire themselves and preen, comb hair, straighten ties, dust dandruff off a collar.

The African peasants who pass don't usually look in the windows. They feel out of place in this *quartier*. They walk with their heads down, their eyes averted. They hurry past. They do not interact with the Europeans or the black bureaucrats and bankers.

But there is one African man, as dark from dirt as from the sun, who wanders through the crowds of Europeans strolling on the street. He crosses from one side of the pavement to the other and back again, drifting aimlessly, pestering the Europeans with his very presence. Even when he has not directly addressed them in whatever language it is that he speaks, he invades their world and insults their sensibilities. Perhaps he makes them feel more vulnerable, less insulated, more aware. He makes them see the difference.

His hair is long and matted together, filthy and full of spider eggs and lice. It has never seen a comb, has not been washed in a year. It is so dirty it has ceased to be black except in patches. Mostly his hair is the reddish brown color of dust. He has no shirt. He wears no shoes. His pants are shreds, one leg ripped ragged just below the knee, the other leg torn off so short that it barely covers the left cheek of his flat buttock. There is no roundness to his buttocks. He has no flesh there. He is very thin and his legs are like twigs. He stares wild-eyed and dazed. When he talks, he mostly talks to himself. What he must be thinking, if he thinks at all, I cannot imagine. He wanders on alone, down the hill, toward the sea.

Abidjan sits on an inlet arm of the Atlantic. On soft sandy beaches not far away, Europeans lie nearly naked in the sun.

Theirs is a different kind of idleness, a different kind of nothing to do. Their skin is oiled for protection against the sun. The men have paunches of prosperity. Women display breasts that are firm and young, sometimes full and heavy, but always they are more than just sacks of milk for nursing babies. They are sources of self-esteem and image, sexual attractants, decorative ornaments.

The bare breasts of African women in the market sag to the waist and are stretched beyond recognition by so many children sucking endlessly there. The elasticity is all but gone. The breasts are nothing but skin and stretch marks and a dark, shriveled nipple on the end, conduits for milk, comfort for babies and young children, nothing more. Like an arm or a leg, a breast is another body part, a tool with a practical function, nothing more than that. Hips are for tying things to, for carrying. Legs are for standing. Other luxuries don't exist here.

In Abidjan the two worlds are poised side by side, like crippled legs of uneven lengths belonging to a lame man. When he walks there is pain and discomfort. He manages to hobble, but not without a great deal of effort.

In African terms, the Ivory Coast is prosperous. Its literacy rate is nearly 60 percent. Per capita income is nearly eight hundred dollars. The agriculture sector is fairly diverse and fairly productive: the country is a major exporter of coffee and sugar and cocoa, bananas and pineapples and palm oil.

Since independence from France in 1960, the Ivory Coast has emphasized agriculture, not industrialization. While other African nations were trying to industrialize, President Félix Houphouët-Boigny, the only president the Ivory Coast has known, led the country down a different road toward modernization, developing agriculture first before turning the country's attention and resources to good roads, electrical power plants, and communications networks. Perhaps because the emphasis on technology was delayed, telephones in the Ivory Coast actually work.

Agriculture continues to head the list. Each night as the television stations sign off, the last transmitted images are of agricultural prosperity. Ivorian farms and fields are shown lush and fertile, crops in bloom and plentiful, blowing in a gentle breeze, floating beneath Houphouët-Boigny's superimposed silhouette. A choir sings the national anthem. The voice of the president reminds his people that the road to independence and prosperity runs through these Ivorian farms and fields. You cannot be free if you cannot feed yourself.

On the road to industrialization, Houphouët-Boigny did what other African leaders did not do. He resisted the fierce nationalism that was sweeping the continent and invited foreigners to come. He made sure the laws that regulate the movement of money and profits were not so restrictive that foreigners would be afraid to come to the Ivory Coast and invest. As a result there are more French in the Ivory Coast now than there were before independence. French investment has helped the Ivory Coast to succeed where other African countries have not. The importance of France is profound and evident.

While agriculture is firmly in the control of Ivorians, investment in industry is 40 percent French. Nearly 80 percent of the jobs that require education are performed by the French. Elsewhere in Africa foreigners are not allowed to hold jobs that Africans are capable of doing, but in the Ivory Coast there are French waiters and vendors, shopkeepers and clerks. French civil servants play key roles at every level in the Ivorian government, and French soldiers even shore up the army.

But what of the young Ivorians who cannot find jobs? Colonialism has changed its name, but not its stripes. The Ivory Coast remains in the control of the French, and still at their mercy. The next generation has not been trained for what comes next. They will not be ready for the future.

Nor has Houphouët-Boigny chosen his successor, as if he, like the other presidents for life, plans to live forever. Or perhaps he thinks naming a successor will invite coups and power grabbing, which is perhaps what will happen upon his death: a power vacuum, perhaps even a civil war.

The French will be there to pick up the pieces, of course, and to profit if profit is to be found in the chaos of a former colony's collapse.

In Abidjan there are outdoor cafés where a man can sit and eat hot croissants in the morning and drink thick hot chocolates while he reads the daily newspaper. In the afternoon there are hot dogs with melted cheese, croque-monsieur and salade niçoise. Always there are French pastries and tea, and Kronenbourg beer. If eating well can be called debauchery, in Abidjan I debauched like a condemned prisoner. I ate rabbit sautéed with plum wine and onions. I ate steak au poivre vert. I ate stale pastries. I drank decent wines from the Rhône Valley. It was not the best wine or the best food, but it sufficed. And then I grew tired of it.

It was not Paris. Neither was it Africa.

On the corner where avenue Chardy crosses the boulevard de la République, I met Gabeu Briébia. He recognized me as a stranger and called me over.

He told me his name but asked me to call him Denis because, he said, it sounded more French. He loved France and his great dream was the dream of many: to leave this place and live one day in France.

"It is just a dream I have," he said. "To live there for a little while. To see the other side of life. I think I would prefer the United States, but your embassy will not give me a visa."

Denis wore a thin mustache neatly trimmed above his lips. The mustache twitched when he talked. His eyes swam merrily. He was middle-aged and prosperous, tall and lean and handsome. His hair was mostly gray. His face was creased from the hard work and the worry that creates good fortune. And the good fortune made him quick to smile and be generous. When he smiled, the lines stretched thin across his face and vanished. But they always returned.

"I am not looking for a way to escape," he said. "Not like many other men. This country is my home. My family is here. The ghosts of my ancestors are here. I eat. I have a home. I have this business. So far I haven't done badly."

Laughing, he said he was not sure if the French were saviors or Satans, but he was glad they were there. He had managed to profit from their presence. He sold them souvenirs.

Across the boulevard, high-rise buildings rose against the sky and cast the shadows we sat in. Down avenue Chardy were the fine shops, owned probably by someone French, catering more to Europeans than to Africans. On our side of the street was a long row of souvenir booths, wooden stalls.

"They come over here to buy from us," Denis said, "but we can't go over there. It's strange."

On this grass and cement island lying between two large boulevards, the two worlds came together from time to time. The Europeans would come over to buy trinkets and souvenirs. Then they would go back. Poor Africans from other parts of Abidjan would often come here to visit with their friends who owned or worked the stands and sold the souvenirs. Their paths would cross, but nothing more.

Denis was not complaining. He had done well.

"If others could do what I have done," Denis said, "all of Africa would not be headed for such a disaster. It takes only a little hard work and initiative, you see. But we have become a lazy people. We have forgotten how to work. When the French owned us, they did everything, and we learned to rely on them. Now we wait for someone else to do what we could do for ourselves. I've done it; I've survived and become successful in my modest way. Why can't everyone else?"

It was the argument of the fortunate few who often forget that good fortune is blown by a very capricious wind, that circumstances and opportunities are not always the same, even for two brothers standing side by side.

He was not complaining, but he could not hide his hostility. He clenched his teeth. The muscles in his jaws quivered.

"If we don't wake up to our laziness and stupidity," he said, "the time will come when we will bring disaster to ourselves. No one can see it. No one does anything to stop it. No one really cares what happens to us. If you go to Yamoussoukro you will see what I mean."

"What's in Yamoussoukro?" I asked.

"Go there and you will see the folly of Africa," he said. "You will see what fools we have allowed ourselves to become while we stand idly by."

His eyes squinted in the harsh light. The lines on his face deepened with growing concern. He struggled to keep his passions in check, but once he got started, they wanted to run wild.

"One day we will wake up," he said. "One day we will learn to fight. When that day comes, we will harm most of all those of our own who have allowed these things to be done to us. You will see."

He looked at me with hot, accusing eyes. I wanted to raise my hands in protection and say, "I didn't do it," but he was not looking at me. He stared past me, looking forward in time, as if he could see the day in the not so distant future when anger would erupt, when crowds would demonstrate in the streets of Abidjan and turn violent, clashing with soldiers and police.

"It's coming," he said. "Then the shops of both sides of this street will be ours. And maybe one day our brothers from across the sea will come home to us and help us build this place. I will come home too. That is, if I ever get to leave. By the grace of God I will keep what I have earned, and my family will never go hungry."

That, he said, was why he wanted to go to France or to America: to find work, to save money, and come home a rich man.

"I suppose that is the dream of every man," he said. "To go away from home and return rich, like a hero."

He closed his eyes to savor the dream.

"Then I too will be able to travel," he said. "But I would not stay in five-star hotels. I would rather stay in the neighborhoods, with the people. I would get tired of too much comfort. Don't you?"

"Tired of comfort? Not me."

"Comfort," he said, "can give you such a false impression of life. You need to see what is real."

He was inviting me to his home.

Of course I knew he was pulling my strings, seducing me with his hospitality, leading me to the moment when he would ask me to help him with the American embassy, agree to be his sponsor so he could get a visa. By then, of course, I wouldn't be able to say no.

"Come meet my family," he said. "You will see Abidjan away from all this." He pointed to the traffic and the tall buildings. "You will be welcomed in my home."

When I had collected my gear and checked out of my hotel, Denis and I crossed the lagoon on a ferry that rattled and billowed smoke. He carried my bag part of the way, but it was too heavy. He handed it back. I followed him through a *quartier* that was more village than city, that was no longer the same Abidjan, where all the roads except the main road were dirt and rutted and many of them sloped steeply down toward the lagoon. In the open fields there were heaps of garbage and mounds of human excrement. In one of the fields a group of boys played football. They were careful to stay away from the heaps.

On the other side of the lagoon Abidjan glittered in the sun, rising like an emerald city behind a range of trees. Every poor boy playing in this field was haunted by the lure of the clean brightness, the beacon of prosperity that the city from a distance seemed. When there was no work in the village, no more land to farm, the city was always there, pulling like a magnet.

Denis lived in a compound completely paved with concrete. There was a little common area surrounded by three small buildings. In each building, a family lived. As we passed through a narrow gangway, Denis transformed before my eyes. He stood taller. His chest puffed and he drew in more air. He took on a sheen of pride and authority. He patted the buildings as he pointed each one out to me.

"This is where you shower," he said. "And here is the toilet. Other families live here too, you know, but this is mine." He said it with a sweep of his hand. "I own all of this. These people pay me rent." He thumped his chest with a forefinger.

"This one over here," he said, "is my home."

His family greeted him at the door, his wife and his three children, a boy of seventeen, a daughter of eleven, and the youngest child—a little girl of five. They were courteous and polite, shook my hand and quickly went back to a television program they had been watching. His wife went back to the kitchen. She never said more than hello to me.

The floor and the walls of the house were concrete. The television was in the corner. The children sat on the floor. There were only three wooden chairs to sit on.

Lunch was set up on a little table placed in front of my chair. A big bowl of rice and a chunky stew of very tough meat. We ate with spoons.

"Do you like escargots?" Denis asked.

"Very much," I said, but the snails I imagined, soft and tender, dripping with butter and garlic, were not the snails I got. The snails we ate were the huge slugs found in someone's garden—very hard and not delicate at all. They crunched when I bit down. They tasted rancid.

Luckily, someone came to the door with a crisis and ended our feast. Denis signaled to me that we would have to go.

"Did you get enough to eat?"

"Oh yes," I said. "I'm fine."

But as we walked and passed a man roasting ears of corn over a fire in a barrel, I stopped to buy one.

"Are you still hungry?"

"Not really," I lied. "It's just that I've been seeing these all over and have never eaten one. I just wondered how they would taste."

He paid the man for two, gave me one, ate one himself.

I protested. "Let me pay." But it was already done, one more inducement to secure my sponsorship of his request for a visa to the United States.

The crisis we were called to that afternoon concerned the son of his friend. According to some tradition, it was Denis's duty to help mediate.

"What happens between a young boy and a young girl has happened to the son of my friend," Denis said, delicately telling me his friend's son was going to be a father. The pregnancy had not been planned. The two young people were not married or even engaged. Honor was involved. Some sort of settlement would be required to appease the father of the pregnant girl, to soothe the shame, to take care of the responsibility.

"Someone will have to feed the child," Denis said.

There was no question of abortion, no mention of marriage—only of honor and pride and shame.

We went first to the home of the girl, another concrete compound of several homes sharing a yard. The yard was a large square of dirt and the women who lived in the compound sat around discussing what had happened. The father wasn't there.

The daughter was bathing. While we waited for her we talked to the mother, who said the girl was definitely pregnant. She had missed two monthly bleedings.

When the girl appeared, she and the mother and Denis talked. Denis told me later that the girl had taken, as many young women in Africa were doing, a morning-after pill, medication taken after intercourse to prevent pregnancy. The pill hadn't worked.

"Or else," Denis said, "the stupid girl forgot to take it. Or she took it too late."

The neighbor women seemed more concerned with the affair than did the mother and the daughter. The mother bent over and resumed her sweeping, stirring the dust, moving a pile of twigs and straw from one side of the yard to another. The daughter dried her hair with a towel that had once been white. A small child played in the dust at the base of a tree.

We tracked down the father, and an enormous meeting was held in the front room of a house. The women were sent away, but they lingered on the front porch and listened. This was village or tribal business the way it was handled long before modern ideas of judges and courts. Men only. Three friends of the girl's father faced off against three friends of the boy's father. They argued and explained and remonstrated with great gestures. They talked about the old days, about honor, about what ought to be done. It was up to them to decide the fate of the young people involved. The father of the girl sat like a fierce statue of granite. He never moved, never said a word until his turn. Each man spoke his piece. Each one stood in the center of the room and addressed the assembly. The meeting lasted several hours and they didn't speak French. From time to time Denis would whisper translations to me.

The heat and the boredom finally wore me down. I sneaked out to get a drink. The young father-to-be was out on the porch. He walked with me and I bought him a soda.

"It's no big thing," he said, so young and so old. "I already have three other sons. My father doesn't even know about them." It was a matter of pride.

"I hope to have a hundred," he boasted.

When Denis was finished inside the house, he came out. He was shaking his head.

"What's the news?"

"Nothing," he said. "There is more talking to be done, but we'll do it later."

"It's very tiring, isn't it?" I said.

"Very," he replied. "But it is the way we have done things for a long time. It is how we solve our problems and stay together. It is how we touch the past. It is how we know who we are and where we are."

When he looked up, stars were beginning to dance overhead. In the sky above the bright lights rising from the city, there was nothing. The lights had erased the stars from the sky. There was nothing but a ghostly gray dome glowing over the tall buildings in the distance.

Denis asked if I was hungry and took me to the home of a woman making stew. He was tired and so was I. It had been a very long day. We would rest awhile and have something to eat with her before going home.

We sat outside and drank millet beer, frothy and sweet. Then we ate this woman's strange stew. Denis watched me carefully—too carefully, it seemed.

"What's the matter?" I asked.

I thought I knew what it was, of course, that Denis was thinking about escaping, thinking about getting away to America or to Europe, leaving behind all these worrisome ways and living his own life with none of the responsibilities of friendship and village. He was waiting for the right moment to ask for my help.

"Nothing," he said. "How do you like the stew?"

"It's different," I said. "But it's good."

He was playful again.

"Did you ever eat a rat before?"

I kept eating. Nothing surprised me anymore.

"Don't worry," he said. "It's not like a rat in the sewer. It's more like a field rat."

"Oh, I wasn't worried," I said, glad he had explained the difference.

The stew was vaguely sweet, pungent, a new taste.

We drank more millet beer and the evening began to glow. Denis smiled. He became for me then all that was right about Africa, the warmth, the generosity, the laughter.

But away from Africa Denis would be trapped, as I was here, in the margins. If he left Africa he would never be all the new thing, and he would soon cease to be all the old thing. Here at home he could feel the warm wind of tradition and loyalty and pride. He could be counted on when his village, his people, called on him. It was this way for his father, as it had been for his grandfather before that. If he was lucky, he thought, it would be that way for his children as well.

He never did ask me about sponsoring him for the visa, never said a word about it.

The road to Yamoussoukro is wide and smooth, a shiny black carpet of undulating asphalt that connects the old capital, Abidjan, with this new one. Yamoussoukro is the place where President Houphouët-Boigny was born, eighty-five years ago.

He may not hide behind tribal trappings of power the way other African leaders do—Mobutu in his leopard-skin hat, Kamuzu Banda with his fly whisk—but like other African heads of state, Houphouët-Boigny could not resist the temptation to deify himself. He is as guilty as the others of extravagances and excesses his country can hardly afford.

The Ivory Coast miracle is over. World market prices for coffee and cocoa have fallen. Unemployment is rampant. The government talks of austerity measures. There are overwhelming health problems. There are people who eat rats in their stew. But at least now they will have a source of pride. A new capital city. A new road that leads there. A great and monumental church, big and beautiful and lasting.

Mobutu in Zaire builds palaces and an airport runway extension for supersonic planes to land in the town of his birth, Gbadolite. Bongo in Gabon builds a $3 billion railroad from the capital city to Franceville, the city of his birth. Félix Houphouët-Boigny builds a massive Catholic basilica in the jungle of a nation of people the vast majority of whom are animists.

When it is finished, this monstrosity, this gigantic basilica, will be the largest Christian church in the world, larger even than Saint Peter's Basilica in Rome. Houphouët-Boigny says the church is being built with family money.

Constructed of marble imported from a quarry somewhere in Italy, the church will be called Our Lady of Peace. It has taken three years of round-the-clock labor to build and so far has cost over $250 million. Construction is nearly finished. The final touches are being added. When all is said and done, there will be two acres of stained glass for windows. There are 272 columns supporting the thing. From the ground to the tip of the cross at the top of the dome, the building will be 489 feet tall.

The dome alone is 380 feet high. There will be space enough for more than ten thousand faithful, but only one Ivorian in five is a Christian. The church will be air-conditioned. It will be a great place for a funeral.

Houphouët-Boigny says it is a monument to his people. But it is his monument to himself.

Africa.

The basilica rises into view over the distant trees of the rain forest. It quivers like a hulking ghost riding on crests of jungle heat shimmering in the distance, eerily out of place in a landscape of peasants walking barefoot, baskets on their heads, babies strapped to their backs.

Not far from the basilica there is a mosque. It is a simple, boxy little building with minarets. It sits in the middle of a walled courtyard. The stones of the square and the stones of the mosque are fitted together like a mosaic of beautiful little tiles sparkling in the late-afternoon sun as if they are streaked with gold and have flecks of diamonds crushed in. On the shady side the mosque is very cool to the touch. The air is very cool too. The sun is on the other side of a grove of trees. The courtyard is half in shadow. The mosque isn't very big, but there is a steady stream of men going in to pray and coming out again.

At the basilica no one even dares to approach. No one is allowed. Not to walk, not to pray, not to take pictures or even look around.

A taxi driver took me up for a closer look, and as we drew near, the church that had looked so impressive from a distance now only looked big, monstrous, like the carcass of an elephant rotting on the savanna. One day the church will sit on a huge esplanade of bright green grass, but the grass hadn't been planted yet. The basilica sat instead on a field of dirt at the end of a long and dusty road worn unsmooth by heavy trucks carrying marble to the construction site.

A little shed for a guardpost blocked the entrance to the site. Three soldiers stood guard there. One was talking to his girlfriend, who had sauntered by. The other two were talking quietly one with the other. They stopped their conversation to watch me as I walked up the incline to where they stood. My taxi driver hadn't dared park any closer, nor come with me. He waited by the car.

I walked up the slight hill, nodded a very friendly hello to the soldiers, and walked on past them. As if they were stunned and couldn't believe what I had done, they let me go about thirty feet before one of them yelled for me to halt.

"Where do you think you're going?"

"I just want to look at the basilica."

"You can't go in there without asking first. You have to have permission."

So I asked permission.

"You have to ask him." He pointed to the soldier talking to his girlfriend. "He's the one in charge."

So I walked over to him and quite pleasantly asked him. But he acted as if I had disturbed him from some important task. He cocked his head to one side and squinted. He put on a pair of dark sunglasses and looked me up and down. Without uttering a word he shook his head—no. He turned away from me immediately and started talking to the girl again. The two other soldiers laughed out loud.

"Why not?" I asked. Perhaps he thought I was a journalist. Perhaps he had orders not to let journalists in, for fear that they would write about this crazy basilica in the jungle and expose the folly.

He turned to me and leaned back, tilting to look down his nose at me. But he had to look up to do it.

"Because I am in charge," he said. "And because I say so."

He sounded like a six-year-old.

"And why is that? So you can impress your little friend there? Won't she think you're a man if you don't order people around?"

He straightened up then and snapped angrily at me.

"Who do you think you are? You aren't in charge of anything here. I can have you detained."

"For what?" I was just as angry as he was.

"For being too close to a sensitive area. You might be a spy. So if you don't want any trouble, get back in your taxi and go back where you've come from."

He scowled and I scowled back. Finally I turned and walked away.

The taxi driver met me halfway to the car. He pulled on my sleeve and told me, "That is not how things are done here. You have to be timid. You have to grovel at the feet of men like this. Come. I'll go with you, but you have to ask nicely. Bow to him. Beg a little."

"You must be crazy too," I said. "Why should I have to beg?"

"It is the way things are done here."

I walked with him back to the guardpost, but I simply could not bring myself to grovel. I stood for many long seconds there in silence until finally the soldier in charge felt my presence and looked over. I hated the way he glowered at me. I hated him and his whole family, the other soldiers too.

"What do you want now?" he said.

My hands were clenched in fists. I shoved them into my pockets to hide.

"I want to go up to the basilica, please. Is there anything I can do so you will let me go there?"

"No." He turned back to the girl. She giggled.

Very exaggeratedly I spat on the ground in their direction. The soldier snarled. I turned and walked away.

"Wait, wait, wait," the taxi driver pleaded, but I was too angry to listen.

"I'm not going to beg," I told him. "Where I come from, if a man says no, it means no. You don't have to beg and plead."

"Oh, please," he said, as if somehow he were being injured if I didn't get a picture of the basilica. "Let me try," he said. "I'm good at it."

He went to the three soldiers and began talking in a low voice. His head was bent as if he were sorry, and he held his hands in prayerful point in front of his heart. The soldier still shook his head.

"Come on," I shouted impatiently. "Let's go. We don't have to plead with these idiots. If I can't get a photo from here, I'll take one from the road."

"Don't you do it," the soldier ordered. "If you take so much as one picture I'll have you arrested."

"Fine," I yelled back. "Come follow us."

Quickly I walked down the hill and the taxi driver ran after me.

"You have angered them," he said.

"Good. They need to be angered. They need to know that we have no respect for them."

"They don't want our respect," he said. "They know their place, and we know ours. They have power, and we don't."

"They only have power if you let them have it," I told him. We drove back to the main road.

When I told the driver to stop the car so I could take a photo, he panicked.

"No, no, no," he said. "They'll be watching."

"Good," I said. "Let them."

"No, not good," he said. "But wait."

He went to the end of the road and turned the car around, driving very slowly as we came back alongside the basilica.

"Now," he said. "Take your photo."

I did. But when I realized the cowardice of shooting from a moving car, I became even angrier.

"Wait a minute," I said. "This is stupid."

I ordered him to stop.

"Let me out," I said. "I'll walk from here. I'm going to take more photos, as many photos as I like, and I don't want to cause trouble for you."

"I wish you would stay in the car."

"No. You go on. I'll catch you later."

I got out of the car and waited for it to disappear. Hoping the soldiers could see me, I waved my arms and took more photos than I wanted, but I wanted them to see what contempt I had for them. I wanted to see what might happen.

Nothing did.

I did not want to get shot or thrown in jail. There was no great issue at stake worth dying for. But it was more than just wanting a photograph. It was a question of common civil decency, a desire to be treated humanly.

On a grander scale, perhaps it was all about human rights. This idiot basilica itself was about human rights, human dignity, all about squandering wealth for one man's personal glorification. Traoré, Mobutu, Houphouët-Boigny.

I could eat what the Africans eat and I could try to do what they do, but that would not make me one of them. I had grown up differently. I could not grovel because of a uniform and a gun. I had to take those photos.

A traveler ought to be sensitive to the other cultures and customs he encounters, for they are often very fragile, but for the sake of *nothing* ought a man abandon his humanness. After all, you are who you are most of all when no one is looking. And maybe, that can make a difference.

Large fleecy clouds formed and rolled across the sky. They hovered over the city and over the basilica. The sky threw shadows on the ground and everything cooled. It was going to rain.

A large lake ran along one side of the basilica. It ran the length of the road and bent left into the trees. Beyond the trees the road bent too, and along that road there were fabulous houses with rose gardens and courtyards and lush lawns glittering like carpets of emeralds. On one side of the trees a dusty African village was being turned into the new capital city. There was a lot of noise and new construction and frenzied chaos. On the other side was a suburban street, calm and quiet and pretty. It was another world, too serene to be Africa. I calmed down. The gardens and the roses had a quieting effect.

Quite suddenly an Italian restaurant appeared before me, there in the middle of this suburban, residential neighborhood. There were no other shops, only houses and gardens on the one side of the street, a narrow grove of palm trees and the lake on the other. The restaurant was like a mirage. White tablecloths and sparkling silverware were laid neatly on the tables. Of course I went inside.

"*Buongiorno,*" I said.

"*Bonsoir,*" came the reply from the woman behind the bar.

"Can I get something to eat?"

"Not right away. We are not open."

"What time do you start serving?"

She called out to the cook. An old black man came from the back of the restaurant. He was the Italian chef. They had a few words.

"If you would like to wait, we will be ready soon."

I grabbed a beer from the bar and went to sit at one of the tables outside. I ordered lasagna for dinner and a half bottle of wine. A storm was forming. I watched it come closer.

It was the strangest thing. Those big puffy clouds looked so peaceful, but soon they were conspiring. All of a sudden they were swirling together, covering the sun, blotting out all the light that was in the sky. The rains came lightly down over the basilica, then built into a heavy downpour. The wind swept in from the north and brought heavier rains. It was the strangest storm I had ever seen.

I was sitting in Africa on the terrace of an Italian restaurant overlooking the lake just across the street. A massive Catholic basilica beyond the lake was reflected in the water, bouncing up and down on waves created by wind and beating rain.

On my side of the street, the wind blew violently and the palm trees bent almost double. But it did not rain. I have seen it rain on one side of the street while the sun shone on the other, but only on delicate days, never in a violent storm. The devil, as we said in childhood, must really have been beating his wife.

I waited out the storm with a half bottle of wine and a plate of lasagna, creamy and cheesy and dignified, freshly made and hot. For some odd reason, it reminded me of a Florence I had visited fifteen years before and the lasagne I had eaten there. All too quickly, I was sliding back into a world where food was more than a means to survive—a recreation, an art.

I love how the mouth waters at the sight and smell of something wonderful to eat. The loaded fork is on its way to your mouth and just before you open wide, you become suddenly aware of how the mouth has watered in anticipation. You never think of it until it happens, and then it's almost too late to appreciate. Almost. You need only a moment's awareness.

I heard there was a bus that would take me through Daloa to Man and over a bad road right to the Liberian border. I wanted to go there, but the bus never came.

Liberia was founded as a country by former American slaves freed from the plantation and eager to return home to Africa. Forty-five thousand freed slaves went back to West Africa beginning in 1822. They were searching for freedom, but they were not necessarily looking to share it. They dominated the local population, turned them into lower-class masses, and declared a new country in 1847. Liberia. Foster child of the USA.

Along the side of the road across from the big lot that was used as a bus depot, there was a row of shacks where soft drinks and snacks were sold. Other shacks sold records and cassette tapes. From big speakers nailed to the walls loud music flooded the street and filled in the edges of the night. There was much activity, much noise, and many people traveling. Every half hour, a bus from Abidjan stopped to let off a load of people. There was no sign on the front of any bus that passed, no way to know where the bus was going. Each time I asked, I was told it was not the right bus for me. Perhaps I was asking the wrong question.

"Is this bus going toward Liberia?"

"No. That bus will be here later."

But how much later?

The shed that handled tickets for buses back to Abidjan was closing. They knew only that the next bus to Abidjan was due shortly. They knew nothing about going to Liberia.

The rains came. I sat on a bench beneath a tin roof and tried to stay dry. When the wind blew, the rain slanted and came in. Six others were waiting for a bus to somewhere. They huddled under a tarp. Maybe they weren't traveling at all. Maybe they lived there.

The rains stopped. The loud tapping on the metal roof ended. I tried to catch a little sleep.

All of a sudden there was a young man standing beside me. How long he had been standing there I couldn't tell, but he was waiting for me to awaken.

"Are you waiting for a bus?" he asked. "Where are you going?"

"To Liberia."

"It's easier to get a bus to Ouagadougou," he said. He picked up my bag and waved for me to follow. "But come," he said. "We will find the bus to Liberia."

We crossed the road, back to the shacks, the noise, and the music. Many young men were loitering about. They were porters waiting for buses to arrive. They carried the bags and belongings of travelers to and from the buses.

"Wait here. I will see what I can find out."

While he was gone, two other men came to help me, but they didn't know anything about a bus going to Liberia. So we stood around talking and dancing in the street.

I asked why there were so many of them.

"It is our job, man. We come here to work, to help people get on the buses, to listen to music, and to dance in the streets."

"And you sleep all day?"

The one fellow nodded.

"Sleep all day," he said. "Work and dance all night."

"Not me," the other fellow said. "In the day I drive a taxi."

"When do you sleep?"

"Only a little in the early morning."

The first young man returned. He said there was no bus to where I was going.

"If you want to go to Liberia," he said, "you will have to find a different way." He went away again.

We stood around in the middle of the street, in the middle of the night. The music from the shacks came up louder. The two young men I had been talking with began to move slowly to the rhythms.

One of them finally asked me, "Why are you going to Liberia?"

"I thought it might be interesting."

"Not Liberia," he said. "You ought to stay here."

"What for? I've already seen the basilica. Just thinking about it makes me angry."

"Angry? Why?"

"Because it's such a waste of money. The Ivory Coast can't afford such stupidity."

"It's our money," he said. "We can do what we want with it."

"That's true," I said. "And it's too bad you're so stupid you want to build a church instead of doing something useful."

"What's wrong with a church?"

"It's nice to look at, but in the end all you have is something to look at. It's money that could be used for something else. Like a factory. Like jobs. Like a hospital."

He got angry then.

"You're just like the Europeans," he said. "You don't want

us to have anything of beauty. You've got big monuments. Why shouldn't we? You get to spend your money any way you want. Why shouldn't we? No. You have some image of how you want us to live and you don't want us to change. You like to think of us in huts made of sticks, rags for clothes, baskets on our heads. You don't want us to move forward. You don't want us to have what you have."

The second fellow stopped dancing and got in the argument. He agreed with me.

"My friend," he said. "The American is right. If we didn't spend money so foolishly, maybe I could go to school and wouldn't have to do this work."

"What's wrong with this work?"

"You see?" he said. "It's you who wants things to stay as they always were. Me? I don't want to stay up all night to earn money to feed my brothers and my sisters. I never even get to see them. We don't need churches. We need education and jobs."

"We have jobs," the other one said. "We have more jobs than anybody. People from Burkina Faso come to the Ivory Coast to work. They come to build this church. People from Ghana and people from Liberia."

"Fantastic," the first one said. "Our government wastes money so foreign men can come and work, and we have to work in the streets at night. Does this make sense to you?"

"I like this work."

"Yes, but if no one travels and passes through Yamoussoukro, we starve. It doesn't matter how hard we work. We are at the mercy of other people."

I stood silent. The two young men argued.

Over the tops of the trees, the tip of the basilica's dome appeared. It was lighted and reached into the night sky.

The man who had awakened me came back.

"I found your bus," he said. "I think it's that one over there. Let me take you."

We stood outside the bus until the driver came out of nowhere and confirmed the route to Daloa and then Man and on to the Liberian border. The man who was helping me handed me my bag.

"Have a good voyage and be careful in Liberia," he said. "And remember us. Maybe one day you will come back."

The old bus rumbled and rattled its age. Its engine bellowed in defiance and made a horrible, thunderous roar. I thought I would never get to sleep. It was my last thought that night. I did not awaken until the mist was rising over the road, hanging like little clouds in the tangle of branches and trees in the jungle.

The sun rises. The mist burns off. The sky clears and brightens to cobalt blue. The morning is warm.

We have come to a town that isn't on the map. I still have no idea where we are. People are speaking such a strange mixture of French and thick English that I cannot understand without effort. It is heavily accented and twisted with African syllables. It sounds like the unintelligible language of a dream, but it is Liberian English. We must be somewhere near the frontier.

"You are going to Liberia?"

"Yes."

"Quickly. Get into that truck."

It is already crowded, of course, but one more won't hurt. Nor will two or three more. We all squeeze in and then we wait until the driver can be found.

A mother in the back of the little pickup truck butters the breakfast bread. The three children with her look on greedily. One beautiful little girl is so thrilled by the prospect of eating that she beams bright eyes at me as if in conspiracy. I smile back and she looks bashfully away, sneaking glances at me now and again. For the other two children, the eating of the bread isn't nearly so thrilling as the expectation. They gobble the bread down quickly, as if they had been starving. They ask for more, but there is no more. The two children grow sullen and quiet.

For the other little girl, the eating is a party. She dances as she sits and chews, her feet tapping, her little body bouncing and swaying. She continues to steal glances at me from time to time and she smiles often. When she is done eating she sits quietly smearing her greasy fingers across the windows of the truck's front cabin.

Without a word the driver climbs in. The brake is released

and the truck rolls down the hill, gathering more and more speed until finally the clutch is engaged, grabs loosely and slips, grabs again, and the truck coughs itself to life. We drive deeper into the jungle until the road becomes two dirt tracks and the dirt tracks become no more than worn places where the brush is bent.

The way narrows. The worn places turn into ruts of soft earth and mud. The men climb down, lightening the load, and the truck goes on with only the women and the children. The men walk. I walk last of all, taking photos of the jungle that surrounds us. We have been swallowed by the forest. We have disappeared from the face of the earth. Anything could happen to us here, and not a soul would know or be able to find us.

The last stretch of the path in the jungle ends at the river. There is no bridge across, only a rope. As ferry there is a pirogue. The ferryman stands in the canoe, pulling on the rope until the boat reaches the opposite shore. The river is not very wide but it is very swift. The current drags us downstream. The rope stretches and stretches—any more and it would break. But it holds fast. The ferryman carries us across five at a time.

We climb up the steep bank to the clearing, where we stand waiting at the border station. The group that crossed the river first has passed through customs and gone on. They have walked around the bend in the path and disappeared into the trees. Only the woman with the three children goes slow enough that I can still see her. She drags her children along after her. From time to time she glances back as if to see what has happened to me. Then she too is gone. I walk to the border station all alone.

There is at every border crossing an increased anxiety. The heart beats a little faster, bangs a little louder. There is a little more sweat on the palms.

There is always a sense of arbitrariness in dealings with police, with soldiers, with anyone who carries a gun for a living. They wield more than just the authority of a position. They wield power. They evoke fear. It is their job to scare people, and in those situations where they earn no respect they can certainly demand it. To them very often fear looks and acts like respect.

Perhaps I wasn't respectful enough at the border station into Liberia. Certainly I wasn't fearful enough. By now I had crossed too many frontiers. By now too many border guards had

welcomed me heartfully. I could not be nervous now. Perhaps
I should have been.

When the border guards were searching through my bag,
I wasn't even concerned enough to watch them. When they
asked me if I had any weapons, I laughed.

"Why do you laugh?" they asked.

"Because it's such a silly question. If I were going to carry
guns, would I cross at a border post, knowing you'd search me
and find them?"

They went back to their search. They whispered. I casually
looked around.

The compound looked more like a military outpost than the
usual border station. There were a few wooden buildings laid
out in a rough horseshoe shape, and in the center was a little
patch of dirt half surrounded by a wooden hitching rail. In the
middle of the dirt clearing the Liberian flag was flying from a
wooden pole not very tall. The Liberian flag. Copied from the
U.S. flag. Red and white stripes, a blue field, one big white star
in the center of the field. From a distance and at first glance you
would think that the flags were the same. But they are not.

"Are you sure you don't have any weapons?"

"Yes, I'm sure."

"What is this?"

"That's a camera."

"And what is this?"

"A tripod for the camera."

"And in this bag?"

"Film."

"How many films?"

"I don't know. About fifty. You can count them if you like."

"That is not necessary, but why do you need so much film?"

"I take a lot of pictures."

"And what is this?"

"Binoculars."

"Why do you need binoculars?"

"I'm going to Kenya. I want to see the animals."

"And what are these?"

"A wide-angle lens and a telephoto. Different lenses for
different situations."

"And what is this?"

He had found my miniature tape recorder, and I told him what it was.

"Why is it so small?"

"I don't know. I didn't make it. It's easier to carry than a big one."

"All right. You may close your bag."

"Great. Am I done?"

"No. I think you had better wait and talk with the chief of security."

He kept my passport.

The interrogation continued in a little log cabin not far away. I waited on the wooden porch, sitting on a bench made from a log split in two. A soldier asked me a few questions. Then a man not in uniform came along and asked me to step inside the door marked CUSTOMS. The orange letters on the crude wooden plank had been printed by an unsteady hand.

This new man went through the same routine. He had me dump all my gear onto the floor.

"This stuff has already been searched," I said. "Why do you need to make me do this again?"

"I have to see for myself."

He asked me the same set of questions. And then he found my map. "What is your mission here?" he asked sinisterly.

"What do you mean, mission? I have no mission."

"Who sent you?" he asked. "What is your mission?"

"I am just a tourist."

It must have been a foreign concept for him.

"A tourist," he said. "Why?"

"I just want to see Africa."

"Why? Have you nothing better to do than go around the world taking photographs?"

"Traveling," I replied, "is a way to see how other parts of the world live. It is a way to broaden your mind. . . ." I couldn't resist. "If you have one," I said. "If you traveled, maybe you would understand more than you do."

He looked up sharply.

"Are you calling me stupid?"

I ignored the question and gave him an overly sweet smile.

"Sometimes," I said, "traveling makes you appreciate home a whole lot more."

Now he did the ignoring.

"Are you sure you have no weapons?"

"You've looked through all I have," I said angrily. "Can't you see for yourself?"

"Yes, I can see for myself," he answered just as angrily. "But I want to hear it from you."

"No, I have no weapons."

"Then why do you have this map?"

It was exasperating. I got a grip on myself and tried to calm down.

"So I will know where I am," I said.

"This is highly strange," he said.

He gave me back my passport.

"But we are keeping these," he said.

"No you aren't," I said.

He had put the camera, the film, the lenses, the map, and the tape recorder on the edge of his desk. I thought then that this whole procedure was some scam to steal my belongings.

"You're not keeping any of that," I said.

"Then we will not be able to release you," he said.

"I guess you'll have to put me in jail," I said, sounding much braver than I actually felt. "I'm not afraid of you. I'm not going to let you steal anything from me. So you find somebody who's in charge, and we'll see what he has to say about what you're trying to do."

He called for something he could put my things into. He shouted angrily.

A tall, very thin, not very young sergeant brought in a pillowcase—of all things. Everything was put into the case.

Then the customs man told me to go with the sergeant.

"Where are we going?"

"You are under arrest," the customs man said. "The sergeant will take you to the barracks. You will be dealt with there."

The barracks were in another town.

The Liberian army is not very well equipped. It has no transportation. The sergeant and I walked to the next village to wait for a ride. In one hand he carried the pillowcase with my equipment. In his other hand he carried an old bolt-action rifle.

We walked down a dirt path in the forest and came to a little village sitting in a clearing. The houses were concrete. The shacks were wooden. The waiting was the same as it always was. We sat and waited along with everyone else for a truck to come, waited for the sun to cross the sky, waited for the sun to go down.

Time in Africa is a curious thing. Long days contract into nothing, and the shortest moment seems sometimes to take forever. It could not have been later than nine o'clock in the morning when I crossed the frontier into Liberia. By the time the truck came to take us all to the next town, it was late afternoon. By the time we finally arrived there, it was night. By then the sergeant was very drunk and I had a new girlfriend.

While we waited, we sat in little groups. I sat beside the woman with the three children who had feasted on the breakfast bread earlier that morning in the back of the pickup. The sergeant disappeared. Periodically he would return to make sure I was still there. He swaggered proudly in his uniform, under the weight of his official duty. He made sure everyone saw the rifle. Always he carried the rifle in one hand, the pillowcase in the other. Each time he returned, he was a little drunker.

It would have been easy to snatch the rifle out of his hands. I could have bashed him in the face with the rifle butt and put him in a coma for a week. I could then have gone back to the border station and with one clip of ammo I could have shot up the place and gained my freedom.

But there was no need. If the rest of the Liberian army was as inept, I would not be in custody for long. And I could escape almost anytime.

Besides, I had a new friend.

The children had played themselves out. They were exhausted from the waiting. The little girl who had been so energetic back on the pickup now was a spent dervish lying in the dust at her mother's feet. She stared at me as if there remained in her no energy even to close her eyes. The other two children slept quietly in the shade.

The mother and I talked. She was speaking English, but her accent was thick and she spoke quickly. I had difficulty understanding all that she said, but not all that she meant. She sat close beside me and pressed her thigh against mine. She touched my hand. Her shoulder brushed against me. When she leaned forward, her shirt parted just above her top button.

She wore a cotton shirt tucked into her pagne. She wore no shoes and her feet were covered with dust. Her lips were thick and dry. She licked them often. Her hair was very short and knotted tightly in little coiled braids that framed her triangular face. Her eyes were bright. She smiled easily and laughed heartily when I said anything even remotely funny.

We rode in the truck together when it finally came. The sergeant, in his position of authority, sat in the front seat next to the driver and slept, his rifle held between his knees.

Sixteen people squeezed into the back of the truck, a mass of people locked together, trying to find a way to fit. It was very uncomfortable.

My new friend sat beside me. Our legs entwined. I wrapped one arm around her shoulders. She leaned across my knees and I slumped over her back. She slept and I tried to. She had taken my hand and was caressing it as she dozed, and every bump in the road was an excuse for her to wedge nearer to me, to pull my hand closer and hold it tighter. Night slid down around us and no one could see. There was no light except the dim light from the truck's weak headlamps. She snuggled closer to me, held my hand against her chest, warm and moist with perspiration. After the next bump we hit, my hand was inside her shirt, and her breast fell into my hand. She was rocking pleasantly against me. It was a good thing I was under arrest.

There were many bumps in the road that night. We got a flat tire. Everyone climbed down so the driver could get to the spare tire. Someone held a flashlight. The good tire was just as bald as the old tire, no tread, a few gashes in the rubber. There was no second spare. And there was no jack. The men had to help hold the truck steady while the new tire was bolted on.

When we finally arrived in town my new girlfriend invited me to come with her and spend the night.

"There aren't many other places to sleep," she said.

"I can't right now," I said. "I'm under arrest."

"How long will they keep you?"

"Who knows? Maybe tonight, maybe tomorrow. Will you be around tomorrow?"

"Yes," she said. "I'll look for you in the market."
But it wasn't to be.

The army barracks were a long way out of town. After the crowd had climbed down from the back of the truck and one by one had scattered into the darkness, the drunken sergeant ordered the driver to take us there. The driver protested. He wanted to go home. The sergeant held up the rifle. The driver grumbled but got back behind the wheel. The sergeant ordered me to climb in and we drove off.

There was no fence and no gate barring the entrance to the barracks. In the darkness there was no way of knowing what this place was. Only the small building housing headquarters could be seen. A bare light bulb hung over the closed door. The light was on.

The sergeant knocked and knocked. For the longest time there was no reply. Finally, the duty officer awakened and came out to yell at the sergeant for disturbing his sleep.

"What do you want, man?"

"I have a prisoner, sir." He clapped his heels lazily together and stood at attention, saluting. In his drunken condition, he swayed like a sapling caught in a breeze. His salute was never returned, and he stood there swaying and waiting.

"What did he do?"

"We don't know, sir. He was arrested at Grio border. I was told to bring him here." He handed over the pillowcase.

"Okay, you've brought him. Go."

The sergeant continued to wait for his salute. It was never acknowledged.

"Thanks, man," I said. "Catch you later."

I was laughing.

The sergeant staggered off into the darkness, back down the road we had come up. He had, perhaps, expected a place to sleep for the night, but no such offer was made. He was on his own and wandered back toward town.

"Are you American?"

"Yes."

"Got a passport?"

I showed it to him.

"Come on in," he said. "Make yourself comfortable."

I followed him inside and sat on a bench. He asked me what it was all about. I explained what I could and he shrugged.

Another soldier was sleeping with his head down on a desk. He woke up, pretending to listen. His only real interest was in getting back to sleep. He folded his arms on the desk and laid his head back down.

The duty officer sat again at his own desk, leaned back in a chair, and put his feet up.

"Sleep," he said. "We'll take care of this in the morning."

I tried first to sleep on the bench, but it was too short. I was too long. The bench didn't curve where I needed it to. The floor wasn't much better. It was concrete and cold, very hard. The room was abuzz with mosquitoes. I spent the first fifteen minutes slapping myself. I took my raincoat and draped it over me like a blanket to keep the mosquitoes from biting. But parts of me were still exposed. And the mosquitoes droned constantly in my ears. The assault never ended. I slapped noisily at the hateful things.

The duty officer came and knelt beside me. He put something on the floor near my head and lit a match.

"This might help a little," he said in a kindly voice.

It was a coil of mosquito repellent. He lit it. It flared up briefly before the flame went out. The tip of the coil glowed red and a spiral of smoke rose and billowed out. Suddenly the mosquitoes were gone.

"It's only good while it burns," he said. "But it will help you get to sleep, and then you won't notice."

When light broke into the room the next morning, I was stiff and sore and itchy from the mosquitoes that had feasted on me. And I was alone. I got up, stretched, and went outside.

The army post was a scattering of about eight one-story buildings that housed the soldiers. There was a big field with a flagpole in the middle; dirt paths went from the headquarters down to the barracks.

A group of soldiers were hanging around waiting for the bugle to blow and the flag to be raised. They were scattered about, peeing in the bushes, against the side of the building, on the road.

The bugle blew an off-key reveille. The soldiers stood at a loose kind of attention and saluted. The flag slowly went up.

A sergeant came to ask who I was. I explained the situation to him. Then he went away. A captain appeared. He asked what I was doing there. I told him. No one seemed to care a great deal. They sat around and we talked. Everything was fairly pleasant.

"Do you need to wash?"

The toilet inside the building was broken. I peed outside like everyone else. The water in the sink did not run. Someone brought me a bucket of water.

"Would you like coffee? Something to eat?"

I was given a piece of bread. It wasn't much, but it was no less than anyone else was eating. They were trying to be kind and friendly, trying to help, but no one was doing anything about my being there.

"Who's in charge here?" I finally asked.

"He'll be here soon. Relax and don't worry."

You could tell when the officer in charge arrived. Suddenly everyone started lacing shoes and buttoning uniforms. The questioning of the prisoner was about to begin.

"What is your mission here?"

"Who sent you?"

"Where are you going?"

"Why did you cross the border there?"

The first to get his hands on me was some major whose name I never learned. When he finished he passed me to Lieutenant Colonel Toe, who passed me on to Colonel Jahalo, base commander. Each one asked me the same questions. Each one didn't know what to make of it all. Each one passed me on to someone else.

Africa!

Later in the day Captain Gayeyou pulled two chairs and a small table to the space where I had slept. We sat opposite each other. He took two sheets of paper and sandwiched them around a piece of carbon paper that had been used several times. There was no typewriter. He wrote everything by hand, pressing very hard onto the carbon. He asked the same questions over again, wrote down everything I said, and asked me to sign my name. They thought I was a spy.

"I'm a tourist," I said.

"You're a spy. Why won't you tell us what your mission is?"

"I have no mission."

"Why did you cross at Grio border?"

"I was on a bus from Yamoussoukro. I was following people coming to Liberia. They went that way, so I did too."

"That is not the place for foreigners to cross."

"Then why the hell didn't your people turn me back? We wouldn't be in this mess if those idiots at the frontier had told me I couldn't cross there."

"But that is not a regular border crossing. That is only for Liberians and people from the Ivory Coast who cross over to work. Weren't you concerned when you saw there was no bridge over the river?"

"Are you crazy?" I shouted. "This is Africa!"

"And weren't you concerned that you were the only tourist, as you say?"

"No," I said. "What tourist is stupid enough to come to Liberia? He'd just get arrested. It's no wonder you people don't know what a tourist is."

"Yes," he said. "And what is your mission here?"

"I have no mission."

"And what about AIDS?"

"What about it?"

He had put the pencil down.

"Do you believe in it?"

"What does that mean?"

"Do you believe it really exists?"

"Don't you?"

"Ten years ago you never heard of it before, right?"

"So what?"

"So ten years ago it didn't exist. There is no AIDS," he said. "It is an invention to keep Africans from having sex."

"Right," I said. "And what does this have to do with my being under arrest?"

"Nothing. I just wanted to know."

Captain Gayeyou went and conferred with the colonel.

Colonel Jahalo invited me into his office. He asked if I wanted a beer. He sent out for two, one gigantic bottle for each of us. When the beers arrived, the colonel was once again asking me the same questions. The favorite question seemed to be: "What is your mission here?"

"Look," I shouted. "I've told you twelve times already. I have no mission here. I'm a tourist. I've been traveling Africa for many months and this is the first time anyone has arrested me for being a spy. I'm not a spy. I don't work for the CIA, if that's what you think. I only wanted to see Africa, for what idiotic reasons I don't know now. I wish I had stayed home. I certainly wish I had never come to this godforsaken place."

I banged my fist on his desk in anger and frustration.

"You people are so inept and so stupid," I shouted. "I can't believe this is happening."

I started pacing in the small office.

"I thought Liberia and the U.S. were on such good terms," I said.

"We are," Colonel Jahalo said.

"Don't you use U.S. dollars as your currency?"

"Yes," he said. "We are close, our two countries."

"Then why would I be spying for them?"

"I don't know. You tell me."

"I'm not spying for them," I yelled. "Why can't you call someone in Monrovia? Call the American embassy. They'll tell you."

"We have no phones here."

I wanted to scream. I thought I was going to cry. Tears were welling up in my eyes and a sob was forming in my voice. I fought hard to control them.

"Shall I open your beer?"

"No," I said. "I don't want to drink with you."

I was trying hard to be hateful.

"I have to pay for that beer," he said. "If you didn't want it, why did you ask for it?"

"I wanted it when I asked for it, but I don't want it now. I hate this place. I hate you and I hate all these stupid people."

"It's not our fault," he said. "This is simply the way things are. I'm sorry."

"Right," I said, and went out to sit on a bench.

I was angry and hurt. Not just for me, but the poor souls who have to live in this fear and poverty of spirit perpetually. If they get arrested, they would certainly be too scared to shout back and hammer on desks. They have no voice. They have no recourse. And they have no way out.

Outside it began to rain.

A witch doctor dressed in fur and the mask of a lion's face had come onto the army base. He jingled when he walked. No one had tried to stop him. Perhaps everyone was afraid of him. He carried a long staff. Bells were strapped to his ankles. A little boy walked in front of him beating a drum. The witch doctor danced in small circles in front of the barracks headquarters.

Several soldiers offered him money—paying to see him perform? buying protection against evil spirits? He chanted and he danced and he shook a rattle all around. I went to the colonel.

"Come," I said.

The colonel followed me to the porch.

"You see?" I said. "This is why I carry the camera. These are the memories I want to take home with me. This is what I want to remember. This is what you are stealing from me."

We went back into his office. He sat at his desk and looked out the window. He pursed his lips and looked sorry. I opened the beers and we drank together.

It wasn't his fault. He was as trapped as I was, almost as much victim as the victim. Almost.

They weren't evil people. It would have been easier to understand them if they had been—easier to hate them, too.

Lunchtime came. Colonel Jahalo sent me with one of his captains, who took me into his home—quarters in the barracks where he lived with his wife, but his home nonetheless. They fed me fish and rice and some green vegetable boiled up soft and mushy until it looked like spinach. They were manioc leaves, spicy hot and very good.

"Would you like a cold drink?"

He sent a private to fetch a Coke for me.

It was hospitality warm and friendly, made odd by the circumstances.

Outside the rain came down in sheets. The wind blew a gale. The red, white, and blue flag snapped in the storm and billowed back and forth.

▲

Each day there was rough edged and ugly, lingering like a scab that would not fall off. I sulked the mornings away, slept in the afternoons. I sat and waited. There was nothing else to do. No one else knew what to do either, and so nothing was done. There were no phones, no way to get permission to set me free or to shoot me. I did not know if I would be a prisoner for three days or thirty. The uncertainty was killing.

There was a torn and broken couch in the major's office. I slept on it in the afternoons. At night I slept on the floor and fought mosquitoes. They chewed me up. There was the risk of malaria, but I couldn't think past the itching and the aggravation.

Each day was spent like the one in front of it. I slept, I waited, I walked up to the barracks to buy cold drinks. Then finally Captain Gayeyou took me into town with a private who was going to escort me to the capital. Someone had decided they should get rid of me and let Monrovia deal with this problem.

Of course there was no military vehicle to transport us. We went into town to sit with everyone else waiting for a car that was going to Monrovia. Captain Gayeyou bought rice and sauce for me to eat. He gave Private Josiah Gaye money and orders and a pass written on crumpled paper. He had two days to get me there. We sat in the front seat beside the driver.

Away from the capital, all the roads are bad, nothing but dirt and ruts through the jungle. At every bend in the route, a roadblock and a checkpoint. The threat of a coup was always in the air. That was how the current head of state got his job, and no doubt how he expected to lose it. He was paranoid. And he was right. By September of 1990 he would be dead, assassinated.

Back in April of 1980 Samuel Doe was a twenty-eight-year-old sergeant in the army. President William Tolbert was sixty-seven. He had served as vice-president for twenty years and had become president when his predecessor, William Tubman, died in 1971. In an amazing first such event in all of black Africa, power was transferred to Tolbert peacefully and in accordance with the constitution. Liberia had known over a hundred years of dictatorial stability, not a single coup in all that time.

But that tradition of stability and transferring of power ended late in the night of April 12, 1980. The economy was falling apart, and the indigenous African population had come more and more to resent the way they were treated by the former American slaves who held all the power. Tolbert himself was the grandson of a former American slave. The native masses were treated as little more than slaves themselves, at best as little more than second-class citizens.

Changes were being made, but not fast enough for some. Sergeant Samuel Doe was one of them. The opportunity was there, and he seized it.

Tolbert had spent the evening at a diplomatic reception. He returned home around midnight and went to bed. Sergeant Doe and a small band of rebels in the presidential guard, no more than twenty men, stormed the president's mansion and killed the soldiers who remained loyal to the president. They cut the phone lines so that the army could not be summoned. They found Tolbert, cut out his eye, shot him three times, and split him open. His body and the bodies of his dead guards were disposed of without ceremony, bulldozed into an unmarked grave. A new era of terror had begun in Liberia.

Soldiers who had so recently been loyal to Tolbert spat on his grave. They switched allegiance without missing stride. President Doe, of course, doubled their salaries immediately. He needed them to hold the power he had stolen. His army then went on a looting and shooting spree. They vandalized shops and hotels, and finally rounded up Mr. Tolbert's governmental ministers, former associates, friends. Thirteen men were put on trial at the Barclay Training Center, publicly humiliated, and executed.

Private Gaye and I were on our way to the same Barclay Training Center.

We stopped in Gbarnga. Private Gaye and I stepped through a screen door and into a dingy restaurant. We ate rice and chicken with groundnut sauce. Gaye ate twice. He was spending someone else's money.

"Give the prisoner something to drink," he said. He carried his rifle conspicuously. He was only twenty-two years old.

From Gbarnga there was finally a decent road to Monrovia. But there were many roadblocks. At the final checkpoint before we entered the city, I was pulled aside by the soldiers and taken to an office. Once again I was asked those crazy questions. This time, there was more than a glance at Gaye's orders. This time, I was interrogated and asked to write a statement. I signed it. We were closer to the capital. The paranoia of the army increased.

Nothing had changed after Doe seized power. He had made himself general, of course, and rode through Monrovia behind a motorcycle escort. The gap between rich and poor grew, political stability was gone, the economy did not improve. Doe's tribe, which had been among those oppressed, became the privileged class. Doe's friends and cronies became the elite.

For the U.S. government, more concerned about an anti-Communist ally and about listening stations than about liberty and legitimate governments, it was business as usual. Economic grants and military aid continued. American soldiers maintained their presence in the capital. They called themselves advisers.

Meanwhile Doe, who could barely read let alone govern effectively, carefully eliminated his opposition. Disappearances were frequent. Trials were secret. But executions were always public. Fear became a way of life.

Private Gaye had been given two days to get me to Monrovia. We arrived very late the day we left and went to visit his friends. He had to let them see the importance of his mission. He kept calling me "the prisoner."

He wasn't a bad fellow. He bought beers with the last of his expense money, and we drank deep into the night until Gaye got drunk. Once again I could easily have escaped.

The next day, I did escape.

We were taking a taxi to Barclay Training Center and went through the center of town. The taxi got caught in a long line of traffic. The light was red. I opened the car door and leapt out. Gaye panicked, fumbled with his rifle, but he was too slow. I closed the door and told him to sit tight.

"I'll be right back," I said.

I had run out of money. There was an American Express office around the corner.

"Tell the driver to turn up there and wait for me."

"Wait, wait. You can't go." But I was gone.

Private Gaye fell out of the car. He dropped the rifle in the street. I dashed around the corner, went to American Express, and cashed a personal check. Unfortunately, they wouldn't cash much. They were short on traveler's checks.

When I came out I found Private Gaye searching frantically for me. He was crazed.

"I told you not to go," he said.

"I told you I'd be right back," I said calmly.

He was yelling. A small crowd gathered.

"You're my prisoner," he shouted. "I decide where you go and what you do. You're not supposed to run away from me like that. I could shoot you."

"Yeah, yeah, yeah," I said. "Come on. Let's go."

Then he pushed me.

"Hey!" I shouted. "Don't push me."

When I turned, he was pointing the rifle at me. I stepped quickly against him, and when he took a step back I grabbed the rifle and twisted it out of his hands. I held it like a club.

"Don't you ever point this thing at me again," I yelled. "And don't you ever push me. Do you understand? I'm not afraid of you. Remember that. You only *think* you're the boss around here. And if you push me again I'll hurt you. Then we'll both be sorry."

I gave him back his gun and we got back in the taxi. I don't think he felt so much in charge anymore.

At Barclay Training Center, Private Gaye handed me over to men who ignored him now. He was dismissed. No one asked about his getting back to his post. No one asked him anything at all. He was free to leave but had no money for the return journey. He asked if I could let him have a few dollars to get back.

The air was completely out of his bubble now. He no longer had a mission, no longer had any importance. He took the clip of ammunition out of his rifle and walked off the army base.

Several hours later I was still sitting there answering questions, waiting for someone to make a decision either to let me go or shoot me. Finally I was taken to the Defense Ministry to talk to General Craig.

General Craig was a cheerful man who had spent several

months doing advanced training at a U.S. base somewhere in
Texas. His round face was handsome. He looked like my father.
It took about five minutes to explain everything to him, and he
saw at once the whole affair had been a series of mistakes. He
apologized to me.

"I'm really very sorry," he said. "But I'm afraid this is how
things are here."

"Yeah," I said. "I know."

He sent one of his aides to pick up hamburgers and Cokes
for us and we ate them in his office. I thought everything was
going to be fine. Of course, it wasn't.

My passport had not been stamped with an entry permit.
By now I had a pretty good idea what would happen when I
tried to leave.

"They'll want to know how I crossed the frontier without
getting the passport stamped," I said. "I'll be in another mess."

"I'll give you a letter," General Craig said. "Take it over to
the commissioner of immigration. He'll take care of it for you."

But the high commissioner of immigration, a short, dark,
brooding man, would do no such thing. The statement I had
signed at the last checkpoint coming into the city had reached
his desk. He already knew about me.

"You Americans," he said. He sneered when he spoke.
Leaning back in his swivel chair, he picked up the phone and
dialed. The call did not go through on the first try. He had to dial
again.

He called the American embassy to let them know I was
being detained. When he hung up, the commissioner started his
tirade. First against America in general, then against Blackamericans. He said we were worse than white Americans. He
couldn't understand why we didn't come to Africa to help build
it up.

"Are you crazy?" I said. "I could no more live here than I
could live on the moon. Nothing works the way it's supposed to.
The phones don't work. There are no roads. There's no freedom. There's only fear. You can't cross the street without some
goon pointing a gun at you and asking to see your papers. What
kind of idiot would choose to live like that?"

It wasn't what he wanted to hear. He had wanted me to

join him in deploring America and vilifying white men. When I wouldn't, he claimed I had been brainwashed.

"You could come here and be a citizen," he said. "Our constitution welcomes you. Our constitution invites all black men and gives them the rights of citizenship. But you Blackamericans have been brainwashed. We are your brothers; not white men. You should come to help us. Instead you come here trying to overthrow our governments."

I found out later that some months before I arrived, some sort of coup attempt *had* taken place. A small band had crossed the frontier at Grio border and shot up the place. Apparently the vice-president had been killed. The leader of the band had been either a Blackamerican, as the commissioner claimed, or a Liberian educated in America, as I heard from someone else. He had been tried, and as a humanitarian gesture, he had been released. The Liberians with him had been executed.

"We are going to make an example of you and keep you here," the commissioner said. "We need to investigate this further."

He sent me then to be interrogated by Colonel Bantoe, chief of internal security. By then, of course, I was sick of all the nonsense. When he asked me what I was doing at Grio border, I shouted at him.

"I made a mistake, all right?"

Then he shouted at me.

"What gives you the right to come here and tell us how to run our country?"

"If you ran your country right, I wouldn't have to tell you how to run it."

"I could have you shot."

"No. You're a coward," I shouted. "You're afraid of what would happen."

"Get out of here before I . . . before I . . ." His voice trailed off. "Get out of here."

Of course I spent the next nights in jail.

It was degrading and inhuman, and I cried. It was worse than Michael, the Briton in Guinea-Bissau, had warned. There was only one cell. There were no beds in it. There was no water for washing or drinking. There was no toilet. Instead, there were metal pans on the concrete floor to pee in and defecate in. The place reeked. I sat on a bench outside the cell and cried, not for myself but for these others.

The cell was crowded with six other prisoners picked up for being in Liberia illegally. So much for the commissioner's promise of citizenship for all black men. (I eventually bought a copy of Liberia's constitution. It makes no such promise.) So much for Liberia's motto, plastered all over town: "The love of liberty brought us here." There was no liberty except for Doe and his cronies.

Who knew how long these other men had been locked up or how long they would remain. It was not clear what would happen to them, but they were starving. Prisons in Africa don't feed the prisoners. If you don't have family to bring food or the money to buy it, you simply do not eat. These men hadn't eaten in a long time. They were thin and dirty, their clothes were shreds, their hair matted and filthy, their eyes flooded with tears and despair.

I, of course, was a privileged prisoner. I was never put into the cell, but was allowed to sleep on the concrete floor in the security office. The guards let me send out for cold drinks and food. They let me use the toilet—which was broken. And I had a voice. The American embassy knew I was there. If they couldn't get me released, they could at least keep an eye on me and make sure I hadn't been shot and wasn't being abused.

Not so these poor others. No one was concerned with their welfare. No one cared whether they lived or died. No one cared if they even ate.

They reached through the bars of the cell and pleaded with me. I thought they were just begging for coins. They were begging to be fed.

When I sent out for food for myself, I sent out for food for them. When I was finally released, I left them money so they could eat for a few more days, but what good would that do? The money would run out. They would be forgotten and ignored, and soon starving again.

I cried. I hated this place.

▲

They eventually released me. I was too much bother and not enough afraid. I shouted and ranted and exasperated them. And I played them the tapes I had made of my journey so far. I played them the sounds, the voices, and the songs, my notes and my impressions. My captors listened and nodded at what they heard, as if they understood why I had come. They finally let me go.

The corner of Center and Ashmun streets is a block away from the jail. On that corner is Providence Baptist Church. Early Sunday morning I was drawn to the steps of the church by the music and singing, so uplifting and glorious. An American, a white man from somewhere in the South, was the guest preacher that day. I sat on the steps outside the church and listened to him banging on his Bible and firing out the lessons of the Gospels, the teachings of Christ. He was ablaze with his ardor, exhorting these people to look kindly on their fellow men. They responded the way black Baptists in America do, yelling back *amens* in response. For an hour, anyway, they were great believers in love and justice.

Down the street in the jail men languished and were starving to death.

I could not understand the horrible treatment of those poor souls in the jail down the street. They were hanging out the window. They pleaded with their arms through the bars for some attention, for someone to notice and help them. Just to send them food would have been miracle enough. They pleaded with gestures but their voices were silent.

When I passed they waved down to me. A sinking feeling hit my stomach. It was Sunday. All the shops and restaurants were closed. I could do nothing for them today. I lifted my arms to show my helplessness, but they raised their arms in greeting just the same. They waved and their silence ended. They weren't begging from me this time. They were shouting down little cheers of gratitude.

In Africa you learn what the Africans have learned: how to endure.

Long ago I was told that the best thing a writer can do is to write his heart out and then burn what he has written. Or leave it behind on the subway. Or have it stolen. And then start all over. He will be left with only a vague sense of what he has written, a skeleton of his work, the way an artist drawing a human figure begins first with the skeleton in his mind and then layers on muscle and tendons before flesh and features. The brilliant ideas and phrases will remain. I hoped that was so.

Some Liberian security slime stole my little cassette recorder and all my cassettes, my notes and all that I had written. I didn't notice until I was long gone.

I didn't mind the recorder, but the notes and the tapes. I had recorded a Senegalese woman singing on a street corner one evening, and another woman singing outside my hotel room window early one morning in Mali. I had the early-evening sounds of the jungle captured there. I had stolen the voices of men greeting on the road. I had captured a little boy's laughter. Now someone had stolen these from me.

Will whoever stole them ever listen to those tapes? Will he hear what I would have heard and remembered? I would rather have given up the camera if I could have kept the film. Why do villains always seem to know our most vulnerable spots?

I felt truly helpless, powerless. I felt what the Africans themselves must feel, at the mercy of the weather and the land and the elements, victims of the powers above.

Africa had made me wish for the first time in my life that I were someone else, made me wish I were shorter so I could squeeze in the backs of trucks better, made me wish I were richer so I could help more or hide more, insulate myself better, made me wish I were poorer so I would not be so affected by the poverty.

But it was why I had come: to walk the same earth, choke on the same dust, and feel what they feel. I was feeling it. And I was hating what I felt.

EIGHT

AT THE MERCY
OF GODS AND MEN ▶▶▶▶▶▶▶▶▶▶

Burkina Faso
Togo
Benin
Nigeria
Cameroon

Fever hit on the road to Ouagadougou. I thought only that it was heat and fatigue. But suddenly I was more tired than I had ever been, sweating more than I had ever sweated. A large wet spot stained the front of my shirt and never left, not even when I thought I was cooling off in an evening breeze. My face dripped sweat. The legs of my trousers were moist. I ached.

The night was clear. The smell of rain drifted in and out of the cool evening air. Nine of us were packed uncomfortably in the back of a Peugeot, and we rode through a tunnel of darkness toward the north and east. Far ahead of us, flashes of diffused light radiated in the night. As we drew nearer, the soft light brightened and exploded. Lightning ripped through the darkness and crackled like the spiny fingers of skeleton hands. Thunder boomed and shook the earth, rows and rows of it resonating across the sky like endless sonic booms dragged by a squadron of fighter jets. I counted the seconds, as a child would, between the lightning and the thunder to see how fast the storm was approaching. It was yet a long way off. There was no rain. And the night was still clear.

I counted the stars until a flurry of flashing light erased them from the sky, a dark blue velvet night into which the lightning punched periodic holes. Soon it was the opposite. Series after series of lightning flashes brightened the sky like day and was only momentarily dimmed by the darkness of night.

Rain tapped lightly on the roof of the old Peugeot and we stopped somewhere in the night to wait out the storm and the evening curfew in Burkina Faso. Soon the storm was heavily upon us and we would go no farther.

Some slept in the car, others inside the shed. I lay on the porch beneath a tin roof that sang with the falling rain. When I awoke, the porch was strewn with dozens of men sleeping, the parking lot full of cars. Snoring scratched the night.

And there was another sound coming toward us, a buzzing like a great swarm of flies, millions of them, or African killer bees hovering on the breeze, searching for us, moving from right to left with the wind. I tried to sleep again, but only drifted in and out. The night air became suddenly cold and the place where I slept was hard and uncomfortable. Deep in the night, when the cold and the discomfort had awakened me fully, the sound came again, distinct and clear this time, crowding out the snoring and filling the night. There was no wind now, and I finally recognized the sound. It was the night croaking of frogs singing their thanks to the rain.

By morning all was dry again. We drove through the bush and into arid land again, stopped for coffee and milk and customs. There was a sign demanding proof of vaccination against cholera and warning that if such proof was not available, immediate inoculation was obligatory. There was already a long line of men standing to get an injection. Someone said something about not having enough needles to go around. I searched for the yellow card I carried. It was falling apart and faded. Some of the vaccinations were about to expire, but no one checked dates. Luckily, the card was enough.

For those who had no proof, there was the long line and the wait. And while they waited, I sat on a bench. The table in front of me was a cracked plank laid across two metal barrels. An old woman poured an inch and a half of thick condensed milk from an opened can into the bottom of a tall plastic cup. She added coffee and sugar and gave it to me. I drank it and felt miserable and hot. When I finished, she refilled the cup and gave it to someone else.

I didn't think I was really sick. I just felt a little weak. Maybe it was something I ate, maybe the rat in the stew. Whatever it was, I was sure it would pass.

Then the headache began. It resisted the handfuls of aspirin I ate one after another. It was no ordinary headache.

The fever turned to chills. I got the shakes. I ached all over. It was, of course, malaria. The road to Ouagadougou was a blur of pain and confusion.

We sped along in the old Peugeot, bouncing over ruts and holes in the pavement, honking as we passed through small villages to clear the road of men and their families. They were old men bent double with loads of sticks and wood slats bundled on their backs. They were children playing. They were women walking with baskets on their heads. We did not slow for any of them.

We slowed a little for chickens crossing the road, running in crazy zigzags trying to escape. We slowed a little more for goats and sheep—but not enough.

The driver slammed on the brakes. The back end of the car skidded sideways and we slid on bald tires. The thud of contact ripped through the car and we came to an abrupt stop, throwing everyone forward.

In the road behind us an old ewe stood on wobbly legs. She stared at the car, not able to understand what had happened. She was dazed, in pain, and confused. She wanted to move but couldn't. She wanted the burning in her belly to end, but it wouldn't. She wanted to die. Finally she hobbled off into the open field and fell down. The driver cursed.

There was a hut at the far end of a field. A woman and two young girls sat there. As the driver walked to the hut, one of the girls ran to find her father. When he arrived, father and driver engaged in a great, animated discussion. The two men walked to where the sheep lay sputtering the last of its life. They nodded in deep seriousness. The driver now owned the sheep and would pay this man the next time he passed by here.

Together they lifted the sheep and set it down so that its

head faced east. The driver slit the sheep's throat and split its carcass to let the blood drain out. The rest of us got out of the car to watch. The man beside me explained: "You cannot eat a sheep that has been improperly killed," he said. Now it had been done properly.

Ferkéssédougou, Bobo-Dioulasso, Ouagadougou. There is magic in the African place-names, but there is none in the air. There is nothing magical anymore in the rutted roads and the dying sheep or the dust in the eyes and throat. The railroad tracks crisscrossing vacant lots are rusted. They don't glitter in the sun. The wooden shacks and stalls are dilapidated. Men sell cigarettes and pencils and carved wood, shirts and toothpaste and soap. They sit in the dust and wait. Women sell mangoes by the side of the road. Meat roasts over open fires. The women cut the meat into chunks and stab them onto thin strips of wood. Smoke billows in dark clouds, mixing with the obnoxious odor of diesel exhaust, such a foul combination of smells. There is beer to wash the dust away, and there is Coca-Cola. Of course there is Coca-Cola.

Was it the fever or was it that I had gotten too close to Africa? I once had warned myself not to get too close. When you get too close to a thing, it loses its magic. The pyramids turn into nothing more than a big pile of neatly arranged rocks. When you come too close to the edge of mystery, you risk falling in. Africa is an abyss of mystery. Come too close to the edge and the mystery swallows you. You try to claw your way out. You chip at it piece by piece until you think the mystery is no more. You think you have finally figured it out. All at once the sparkling object that captured you with its colored lights grows dull. The mystery and magic that lured you in the first place become no more than grains of sand, translated into your own terms, terms you think you understand.

Africa is slavery and slaughter, river blindness and poverty. The folly and fear rob a man of his dignity and his strength. They steal his authority until he is utterly defenseless and voiceless and accepting. Basilicas in the jungle, roadblocks everywhere, bank accounts in Switzerland.

But somehow they endure, as if they truly believe the proverbs. *The world has many mornings.* Their faith in the gods of Islam and Christianity, their faith in trees and rivers and rocks, is a mighty weapon in their war for survival and endurance. Job, the man of nearly limitless patience, must have been an African.

I sat beside a soldier and ate a dinner of rice and sauce. He was an officer in the army. People bowed greetings as they passed, but there had been no smiles on their faces as they approached. As soon as they passed, their smiles vanished.

We sat on the porch of a small restaurant. I drank a beer. He ate peanuts from a plate in front of him, throwing the soft shells on the floor. He offered me a handful. They were soft and unroasted, a little moist. He pulled his chair closer to mine. He was well on the way to being drunk.

"It is a sad thing," he said, "that men should bow to the uniform but not the man. It is a sad thing that men should be so afraid."

"Then why do you do it?" I asked him. It was what he wanted me to ask. And I was too tired to be diplomatic. "It is you who make them this way," I said.

"And I do it," he said, "because I also am very afraid. I am afraid to die of hunger, afraid for my family. Like all men, I love my family. I want my children to grow up and grow old and I do what I must. It is so difficult to survive here; there is so little work. This is my job."

"That's everybody's great excuse," I said. "Just doing my job, just following orders. That doesn't make it right, you know."

"I know," he said.

"Wherever there is this kind of repression, the soldiers are always the people who get paid first."

"Yes," he said. "So I am a soldier, and I get paid first, and I wait for the next coup, just as I waited through the last one. It is the way we have learned to live. It is very sad."

His uniform was olive green and dusty. His beret was folded and clipped in place under an epaulet on his left shoulder. He was not heavy but not thin either. You could tell neither position nor poverty by looking at him. At his temples there was a sprinkling of gray hairs that might have been dust reflecting the light. I could not tell how old he was. There were a few lines in his face, lines of sadness and concern. His eyes were sad and watery, a little bloodshot. His lids were heavy.

A man passed. He was not a soldier but he saluted the officer. His head was bent, his eyes averted. He lifted them only to salute. Then he looked away.

The soldier said, "This is what we have become. We learned this from the Europeans, that we are inferior people, sometimes even less than people. We hate the way we look and we hate the way we act. And we try so desperately to be like them, to have what they have."

He sipped his beer and talked into his bottle.

"We should be prouder of ourselves," he continued. "Prouder of who we are and what we come from. But our heritage was stolen from us by the Europeans and now we are left without a history, except their history. We have forgotten who we are. And we have forgotten how to be human."

The roads of Ouagadougou were rutted dirt packed hard by traffic and pounding rain. The houses were shacks. The automobiles that passed were rattling heaps of junk.

"There were great empires in Africa," he said. "Great roads and fine houses. We were weavers of the very finest cloth. We cast iron and bronze. Our civilizations were vast and they were magnificent and they came to an end at the hands of other Africans. It is what we do to ourselves that gives me this crisis of the heart."

"Why does it happen? Why don't you do something about it?"

"What can I do?" he said. "We know no other way. We had no written languages. Our history and our skills were passed from one generation to the next, from a father to his son, in our stories, in our traditions. When the Europeans came, they destroyed all that. They separated tribes and made new political boundaries. They gave us their traditions. We have formed new traditions of our own but they are the ugly mixed-breed children of an unnatural copulation. We try our hands at democracy but we aren't ready for it. Some captain always stages a coup."

He lowered his voice and leaned closer.

"Here in Burkina we had democracy," he said. "But our president became like a dictator. He ran the affairs of government badly. He ruined the economy. There was a coup. Four years later, another try at democracy. Another coup. And then another. This becomes our tradition."

The soldier stared into his plate of peanuts as if they were tea leaves telling the future. There was nothing to be read there. I ate the rice and the sauce, I drank my beer.

I talked to a young man in the market. He kept calling me brother. I offered him a cigarette. He took the pack and kept it. I had to argue with him to get him to share the pack with his friends who had gathered around. It was every man for himself.

The malaria was getting worse. The headache was constant and centered just behind my left eye. The eye would no longer open. A huge spike was being driven into that eye, hammered into my head and nailing me to some imaginary wall. I was fiercely hot and shivering at the same time. I was soaked with sweat. I could not see. I could not walk. I wanted to vomit. The countryside was a blur. I saw no more jungle, no lakes, no color.

I made it to Lomé, Togo, and checked into an expensive five-star hotel. I called room service. They sent up a sandwich, french fries, and a cold drink. It sat on the table in the room for three days. I opened the curtains. The light blinded me and I fell to the floor. The curtains stayed closed for three days. I crawled to the toilet and threw up. I didn't have strength enough to flush. I crawled back to bed and got under the covers without taking off my clothes. My shirt was covered with sweat still. My pants were filthy. My boots were covered with sand. Now there was sand all over the bed.

There was nothing I could do about it, about any of it. I was too weak. The pain in my head was constant. I heaved involuntarily. Somehow I managed to pass out.

I had a book that recommended massive doses of chloroquine, the same stuff I had been taking each week to prevent malaria from attacking me. I didn't remember missing a week, but at the time I couldn't remember much more than my name.

I took six hundred milligrams as soon as I was able to stand and turn on the tap in the bathroom. I took three hundred milligrams six hours later. Three hundred milligrams the next day; and the next, three hundred more just to be sure.

Suddenly malaria was, if not fun, very interesting.

Chloroquine in large doses has a startling side effect. Hallucinations. Chloroquine dreams. In the cocoon of my room, night and day came together and lost themselves in the darkness behind the heavy curtains. Visions came to me of strange birds I had never seen before, birds of bright colors and fluffy feathers flying toward my eyes and pecking at them, plucking them out, gnawing on them, swallowing the shredded pieces.

A band of naked hunters stalked prey in the nighttime jungle. They were following a wounded animal that bled red and green and dark dark blue. A profuse trail of spilled blood and entrails led them. They came upon the suffering beast and tortured it endlessly, tortured it until it could not resist, could not move, making it cry out its anguish to the four winds, to the desert and the river and the jungle. But it would not die.

The fever slowly broke. I found strength to get up and eat the three-day-old sandwich and the cold, stiff french fries. I showered and dressed and went to the American embassy, hoping someone there would help me find a doctor. But the woman in the office was more concerned with registering me so that the State Department would know where I was and where I planned to go next. She didn't seem to mind that I sweated profusely, was so weak that I had to lean on the counter to fill out her forms, or that I might vomit at any moment. But finally, she gave me the name of a doctor and his address.

"How do I get there?" I asked.

"Well," she said, "I think it will be easier if you take a taxi. Just give the driver this address and he will take you there."

But the first driver had no idea where it was, and by the time I had flagged down a second car I was too weak to bother. I had him take me back to the hotel and I went back to bed, back to another session of vivid colors shimmering in my imagination, back to my chloroquine dreams. I did not care if I lived or died. I would have preferred to die.

Malaria is an ailment Africa lives with constantly. In the markets, antimalaria pills are sold, but they often are too weak, often are too old. And they are not cheap, so they are not used as prophylaxis, but instead as cure. Africans have learned to live with the disease as they have learned to live with everything else. They suffer the fevers and the chills and the violent stomachs. And then the malaria runs its course and is gone—until it decides again to occur.

Either my malaria ran its course or the chloroquine did its job. I awakened from my dreams burning not with fever this time but with hunger and hardly knowing where I was or how many days had passed since my last encounter with reality. I bathed and sent my clothes to the hotel laundry. I went down to the restaurant and ate a steak.

In the morning I walked the streets of Lomé. I had not cared if I lived or died, but now I was thankful to be still breathing. A quiet peace settled on me, the peace of surviving. I bought souvenirs from a man selling from a stall on the beach. I bought brightly colored shirts from a stall on the edge of the grand marché. As I was walking away, an old man pleaded with me to buy ivory carved into the shape of elephants.

"It's ivory? Are you sure?"

He said he was absolutely sure.

"Then I don't want it," I said.

All along the avenue de la Libération there were many shops selling objets d'art carved from ivory. The shops were bright and shiny clean, catering to tourists without regard to the elephant herds disappearing from the bush.

I went to the grand marché to change CFA into Nigerian naira on the black market. Among the stalls and the sellers of fruit and clothes, amid all the noise, men stood in a long row offering black-market prices for naira, for dollars, for francs. They sold gold watches and they sold marijuana. I was interested only in the Nigerian money. I got a good price. They too called me brother, but there was some fast sleight of hand. When it was all over and I had walked away, a man who had been watching came to me and said I had been cheated. He told me to count the money. I did, but I had forgotten how much I had changed, how much I had started with, and I didn't much care at that point. But he wanted to make a big issue of it and said for a price he would help me get the money back. We went over to the man who had changed the money; there was a lot of shouting. While they fought I laughed to myself and walked quietly away. It was only money, and certainly they needed that little bit more than I did.

I turned up avenue de la Libération and walked toward the

center of the city. Traffic was heavy and noisy. A man carrying too many packages in his arms stepped off the curb and into the traffic. At that exact instant, a police moped sped around the corner. There were two policemen on the little cycle, one driving, the other sitting on the back and holding on. The cycle was aiming straight at the man who had just stepped off the curb. The police swerved to avoid him, but came very close. There was no time to think. The policeman on the back of the bike instinctively reached up, and in the flash of a second, just after swerving to miss him, the cop swung his arm out and slapped the man. The cycle screeched to a halt. The passenger cop got off the moped and swaggered over. He berated the poor fellow right there in the middle of the street. Traffic stopped. The whole world watched this fellow's humiliation. No one said a word. Nor did the little man protest. He listened with his head bowed and his eyes averted until the cop had finished his abuse. The two cops rode away. The little man carried on. To them it was no big thing.

I got so hot I thought the fever was back. My fists were clenched. I was in a rage and wanted to hit somebody.

I would not have taken such abuse. If that cop, thinking I was Togolese, had slapped me, I would have returned the favor. Even in my weakened state I was stronger, and much bigger. I would have slugged him and broken his jaw. Then he would have pulled his pistol and shot me.

I hurried back to the grand marché and found the man who had changed money for me. I didn't know if he had really cheated me. I didn't care. If he wanted to cheat other people, fine. But he would not get away with cheating me. I grabbed his wrist with one hand. With the other hand I took his elbow and I pushed in opposite directions at once. He screamed and fell to his knees. A crowd gathered around.

"Where's the money you stole?"

He insisted he hadn't. I didn't listen.

"Give it," I shouted, and with his free hand he reached into his pocket and pulled out the huge wad of bills and thumbed off a few.

"Here, take it," he said. His face contorted in agony.

I took the money. But later I went back to the market. I wasn't sure enough that he had cheated me. Maybe he had surrendered the money out of fear, in which case I was no better than any other agent of terror. I went back and gave him half the money he had surrendered. (Only half because I wasn't sure enough he had *not* cheated me either.) He needed it more than I did. It was what I would say in Nigeria too, though I'd resent it more there. Certainly they needed the money more than I.

In Porto-Novo on a weekend night men and women parade the streets in their "up-downs"—colorful suits that look like pajamas. Porto-Novo is the capital of Benin, but it is no different from any other dusty African town, sunbaked and falling down from decay and neglect, crumbling back into dust. But on a Friday night the men and women put on beautiful print suits that sparkle in the streets. They cruise the streets in old cars, on bicycles, on foot. They might only be going to a movie or to a dance, or only going to the end of the street and back, but they want to be seen. They want to see what others are wearing. They move about until darkness falls. Then they huddle on street corners and talk. Or they sit somewhere having a cold drink. Or they just wander back home. It is what young people do when there isn't much else to do. It is the light that gets them through the dark tunnel of another week. Sometimes that is all there is.

Surviving. Coping. You forget—easily—that all is not bitter.

Sunday morning I bribed my way into Nigeria.

Money was taped to my chest, my stomach, and my thighs. If it were found, it would be confiscated.

In a move to keep people from smuggling naira across the frontier and operating black markets for currency, Nigeria had printed new money and closed its land borders. Old naira had been recalled and exchanged for new bank notes. It was now considered a very serious crime to move naira across the border.

I moved nervously into the no-man's-land between Benin and Nigeria. It was a particularly hot day. I started sweating. The cellophane tape began to lose its adhesion. Money dangled loosely beneath my clothes.

A fourteen-year-old boy came to me out of a crowd of men shouting at travelers. Here on the doorstep of the Nigerian border, the black market was flagrantly thriving. The boy said to me, "Do you have any naira?"

I, of course, lied.

"Then you will need some," he said. "It will make crossing into Nigeria easier."

So that I wouldn't have to disturb the money taped to my body, I changed CFA into naira and followed the boy to the border. He carried my bag.

"Give me the money," he said.

Naive or stupid or trusting, I gave him the money. He peeled off a few bank notes and gave me the rest.

"Hide this," he said. "If they ask you, tell them you don't have any."

I thought the money he kept was going to be payment for his help. It wasn't. He took that money and divided it up, slipping part of it into my passport. At the border station he said something to the soldier in the window. The soldier looked casually at the passport, took out the money, and kept it. He passed the passport back.

The boy did the same again at the next window. The immigration man took the money and handed back the passport.

The boy said to me, "They will ask you how much money you have. Lie to them or they will try to steal it."

This was as far as the boy could go. I paid him for his help.

"Tell many lies," he said. "Don't let them find money or they will keep it."

He was right.

The next official wanted to know how much in CFA I carried.

"Why do you want to know?"

"It's illegal to bring CFA into Nigeria," he said.

"It is not."

"It is if I say it is. How much do you have?"

"Ten thousand."

"Give me half."

"Forget it," I said.

"Then you cannot enter."

"Why not?"

"Do you have any naira?"

"No," I said.

"That is good, because it is illegal to import naira. But if you have no naira, how will you live?"

"I'll change money."

"It is illegal to change money on the streets, and today the banks are closed. You will have to wait here until tomorrow. We cannot let you in."

"I'll give you two thousand CFA," I said, but he wouldn't negotiate. It was five thousand or nothing. I gave it to him.

I passed then to customs, where I was told to enter a little booth. A soldier went into the booth with me and patted me down.

"You have nothing illegal?" he asked. "No drugs? No Nigerian money?"

"No," I said. "Nothing."

I was sweating heavily. I could hear the tape giving way. The soldier patted under my arms and along my ribs. Luckily he didn't touch my chest. The tape was slipping loose. The money slid down my belly. I saw the wad moving beneath my shirt. To my eyes it was as big as a frog wriggling beneath my clothes. The money slid to the waist of my pants.

The soldier felt up and down my legs and between my thighs. My pants were baggy and loose. He didn't feel much. My heart pounded.

"Are you sure you are not smuggling money?" he asked. "Most people try it." He was trying to be friendly—too friendly.

"Not me," I said.

I thought he was going to pat me down one more time, find the wad of notes, and keep them all. But he rose up and smiled.

"Okay," he said. "You are free to go."

He stepped back and started to slide the curtain aside.

"But first," he said. "Don't you have a little gift for me?"

"A what?"

"A gift," he said. "I can keep them from searching you again."

"A gift," I said. "Yeah. Sure." I pulled out a small CFA note and gave it to him. "Happy birthday."

I gave one also to the next man to ask me for a little gift. Baksheesh. A way of life.

▲

The car that drove me from the border to Lagos was stopped almost immediately after pulling out of the lot. Not thirty yards from the start of the journey there was a roadblock, and everyone in the car had to get out. We had just gone through customs and through immigration. But already here was another checkpoint.

"It gives them something to do to keep busy," one of the other passengers said.

It also gave them a chance to earn extra money. They opened the trunk of the car and emptied everything out. They went through bags, checked passports and identity papers. Then they shook the driver down. They took him inside the little shack. As he was coming back to the car, he put his wallet back in his pocket. He was muttering curses under his breath.

Not ten miles farther down the road, we stopped again at another checkpoint.

The soldiers there shook the driver down again, but he complained so vigorously about having just paid off a couple of soldiers that they let him go.

"There won't be any profit for me in this journey," he said. He shrugged and sighed.

"Too bad," I said.

"That's the way it goes here," he said.

Africa? Or Nigeria?

"I had been warned," I said, "that Nigeria is a little like hell."

"Only a little?" he asked.

The streets of Lagos are jam-packed all day with cars in never-ending "go-slows," as Nigerians call them, traffic jams clouding the air with exhaust and heat. On the worst days it can take two hours to go five miles.

When the oil economy was booming, people flocked into Lagos from country villages and farms. But that boom didn't last. Now they are waiting for the next one.

In the late seventies Nigeria's oil wealth rose dramatically. Food production slowed just as drastically and farming was practically abandoned. All of these people, hoping to get even a small slice of good fortune, flooded into Lagos, straining the city's resources and its limited space. Now garbage sits in huge piles at the side of the road. The drainage ditches and trenches at the sidewalks' edges have become open sewers of stagnant water and waste. Water is often rationed. Telephones rarely work. The air is a dusty haze of constant pollution.

People fight for survival. They fight for space, for services, and for money. They fight for themselves, every man for himself. And always there is the shadow of corruption and incompetence.

A taxi driver advised me to take any money I had and hide it in the heating vents of his car. We took a short ride to Victoria, a less crowded section of the city, quieter and greener, with manicured lawns, old colonial homes, and shady tree-lined streets. But it lies right on the edges of the slums. At a checkpoint coming out of Victoria we were stopped at random and searched. The car was practically taken apart, but nothing was found. The driver was let go.

With me, however, it was a different story. There were cops at this checkpoint, not soldiers. Only one of them bothered with me. I was all his.

He searched me. He emptied my pockets. All my stuff was placed on the top of the car and sifted through. He could not find my currency declaration form, but found traveler's checks instead. He didn't know what they were. When he asked, I told him.

"It's like money?" he asked.

"Yeah, it's like money. But they are useless to anyone but me," I said.

"Useless, eh?" He looked defeated. But he counted out the naira I had, and he said, "Since you don't have your declaration, you must come to the station. It is a very serious offense if you cannot produce it."

I knew what he wanted.

"Well," I said. "Let's go to the station."

The driver shook his head at me and whispered. "It might be simpler," he said, "if maybe you offered him a little gift."

"What for?" I said loud enough for the cop to hear. "If he wants to waste his time and drag us down to the station, what do I care? If he hasn't got better things to do, neither have I. His superiors will think he's a fool for this."

So I thought. But everyone is a conspirator.

We climbed into the taxi. The cop sat in the backseat. When we arrived at the station, the sergeant behind the desk repeated what the cop had said.

"What you have done is a very serious thing. You will have to spend the night with us, and that would not be very pleasant. Unless you and the policeman can come to an arrangement."

"What kind of arrangement?"

"Oh, you know."

"No," I said. "Tell me."

He wouldn't tell me anything, but I knew. Of course I knew.

"See what you can do," the sergeant told me. "If not, you can always spend the night here with us."

Stubbornness. Pride. A sense of right and wrong. At times they mean absolutely nothing.

"Okay, you asshole. How much do you want?"

"Get in the car," he said. And as we drove back to where he had picked us up, we negotiated the bribe.

"Give me one hundred naira."

"One hundred naira? You must be crazy."

"Then give me fifty."

"No way, buster. I'll give you ten."

"You'll give me fifty or we go back to the station and you spend a night in the jail."

If he had found the money in the vents, he would have demanded much more. We settled on thirty, about three dollars at black-market exchange rates.

It wasn't the amount, it was the indignity—not only mine but his. My driver told me that soldiers and policemen are so poorly paid that extortion is the only way for them to survive.

And they're so desperate, they'll bargain for bribes.

It wasn't only for me that I wanted to scream.

It is folly to judge this place by standards that are so far foreign to Africa. Quality of life can hardly be of great concern when life itself is so tenuous, when death before age five is too common, and when living to the ripe old age of forty-seven is a major feat.

African standards of right and wrong are not Western standards. There exist in the world other points of view. Right and wrong, good and bad are functions of tradition and history. Too often they are mere luxuries.

Perhaps a traveler ought not judge at all. He should lift his foot from the world he left behind and set it down solidly in the world where he finds himself. He should accept all he sees and all he experiences, take it all in stride. Then perhaps he would never weary, never get fed up, never think about spitting out a bad piece of meat. For is it not judgment also to spit out bad meat, judgment to hate poverty and filth, judgment to crave justice where there seems to be none?

The traveler would then be more like the Africans he visits. Patient and acquiescent, he would not mind the waiting. He would learn ways to endure.

In this, I failed. My heart was bleeding with anger.

I could not get into Cameroon overland. It was the rainy season. The roads were washed out. My visa stipulated that I fly to Douala. I went to Air Cameroon to buy a ticket, but learned that travelers had to pay in foreign currency unless they were residents of Nigeria. For a small fee, however, even that was easily arranged. I bought the ticket with black-market naira and paid only a third of what I normally would have paid. And now I was officially a resident of Nigeria.

But at the airport there was one last checkpoint. The soldier checking my ticket knew the scam.

A cigarette dangled from his lower lip. Smoke curled in front of his face and hid his eyes. He squinted at me.

"Something is improper," he said. "Do you live in Lagos?"

"I am a resident, yes."

"For how long have you been a resident?"

"Since two days ago. Is something wrong?"

"Very wrong. You cannot pay for airline tickets with Nigerian money unless you are Nigerian."

"Then why did they sell me one?"

"I don't know why," he said. "But you cannot use this ticket."

He conferred with a companion, who by the looks of the insignia on his collar was an officer. They whispered. The officer nodded his head. It was as if they were tossing a coin to see which one would profit. I was pulled aside. They asked how much money I had. I just wanted to get out of there.

"How much do you want?"

"Fifty dollars."

"Fifty dollars! Are you crazy? Anyway, I haven't got that much cash."

"How much do you have?"

"I'll give you ten dollars."

"Give me twenty."

"Come on, man. Why do you want to rob me? Do you think I'm rich?"

"This is not robbery and there will be no bargaining."

I handed over twenty dollars.

A third soldier saw what was happening and he pulled me aside.

"How much did you give him?"

"Twenty dollars."

"That is quite improper," he said. "Come with me."

"My flight leaves in a few minutes."

"Come."

He wanted to extort money out of me as well. But his superior caught up with us. He wore no uniform, but from his manner and the way he addressed the soldier, I knew he was either an officer or some official who made the soldier very nervous. He was in a sparkling clean white tunic, brown trousers neatly pressed, and he walked quickly.

"Let this man go," he insisted. "What has he done?"

"He has a ticket paid in naira."

"Let him go."

I was told to wait off to the side.

The superior and the soldier went off together, and a new soldier came to me. He was young. He shrugged in a friendly way and smiled.

"What's going on?"

"Who knows?" I said, exasperated; then I explained the whole scenario.

"Do you have any more money?" he asked.

"Not much."

"How much can you spare?"

"How about ten dollars?" I asked.

"I don't think so," he said. "But give it to me. I'll see if I can help."

He went off after the other two. When he came back, he came back alone.

"Hurry now," he said. "Everything is taken care of."

I hurried.

But of course there was a delay in taking off. Two soldiers came on board and had words with a stewardess. I was certain they were looking for me. One more hassle, one more bribe to pay. I was never going to get out of this hellhole.

They stepped back off the plane and we waited. When they came back on, they were carrying machine guns. They looked fierce, sternly examining the faces of the seated passengers. They weren't, however, looking for me. They were leading a manacled prisoner to a seat in the rear. Following them was the soldier who had helped me in the end. He winked as he passed. Two soldiers got off, the prisoner and his escort stayed on, and finally we left. I slumped in my seat and tried to sleep.

There was only one more panic. The plane flew north. I kept waiting for it to make a wide banking turn and head south, but it never did. We were flying to Benin.

There had not been a flight announcement. I thought I was on the wrong plane. My heart sank, certain that when the error was discovered I would be sent back to Nigeria, a place I never wanted to visit again. And if the error were not discovered, if the plane went all the way to Paris or London, I would stay on it and not come back. I would finish my trip there.

But there was no error. It was the right flight. Planes in Africa rarely fly direct routes. The plane to Douala merely had to go north before it could go south.

River blindness and Guinea worm. Malaria and starvation. Babies dying before they are even babies. Men and women rarely seeing old age. Corruption at every turn. Helpless submission in the face of authority. Mismanagement and waste and idiot leadership. Poverty of purse, poverty of spirit. And yet somehow Africa holds on for one more day. Somehow Africans endure. Something keeps them from total despair and surrender.

From Douala I went by train across the jungle to Yaoundé, a hilly city toward the center of Cameroon, red clay and green forest all around. The city smells of pineapples. Apples are expensive. Oranges are hard and green. But the pineapples are fresh and sweet and fragrant. They are cheap and they are juicy, and when you bite into one, the juice bursts free and flows from the corners of your mouth and over your hand and down your arms. Where once I was a mango man, now I became a pineapple fanatic. It was as if I had never eaten a pineapple before, so sweet and delicious were they, so different from what passes for a pineapple at home. They were the brightest spots near the end of a torturous journey. Until I went to mass. Just an ordinary Sunday mass.

The church was brick and concrete. It sat in the middle of a large dirt field on the crest of a hill and looked down into a valley of forest green and rickety huts. A wooden frame and sheets of corrugated metal made the roof of the church, keeping out the blistering heat of the equatorial sun. Behind heavy wooden doors, the church was ablaze with warmth—not the heat of day but the golden warmth of music and hope. The church rocked with singing. The church resounded with hope.

It seems so simple now, looking back. So simple that I cannot describe it, for there was nothing so extraordinary about it. People prayed, as people in churches do. A priest celebrated the mass. But the mass was celebrated in neither Latin nor French; it was said in the language of one of Cameroon's many ethnic groups, Ewondo. And somehow, in this small church in Yaoundé, in this language I had never heard, whose existence I never suspected, there was a celebration as I had never seen or heard mass celebrated before.

The music spread to every corner and filled the church. Singing lifted the rafters. People rocked and swayed in their pews, dancing to the rhythms. The music came from a balaphon, a kind of marimba made from hollowed-out gourds instead of wooden slats, rapturous, sweet, melodious music, capturing me as it had captured everyone else. I tried to resist but found myself caught in the tempo and the melodies, swaying in my seat and up on my feet dancing. The choir too was boundless. They wore white robes and carried tightly lashed bundles of straw that African women stoop over and use as brooms. Today they were musical instruments, rhythm makers, linking labor and love in song. The women of the choir shook them overhead and swished the air. They beat them on the floor of the church. They danced in the aisles and sang better than the angels sing. They sang with souls on fire. They sang the joyful laments that breathe in the souls of black people and fill their hearts to overflowing, music that runs in their veins and lives in their genes, linking generation to generation to generation.

Here once more the question: *How long, oh Lord, how long?* And here at last the answer, but from the questioner himself. The answer comes back stirring and strong in the music and in the dancing. *As long as it takes, oh Lord. For we will be here, waiting and remembering—and remembering why we are waiting.*

A woman as old as the clay hills sat beside me. She wore a colorful wrap tied around her head. She wore a black and gold pagne tied around her waist. Her face was dark from the sun and lined like old leather. She had no teeth. She could hardly stand. She was frail. Her legs were spindly and brittle. She could not dance in the aisles. But it didn't matter. Her hands, wrinkled and shaky, remembered. Her body rocked only slightly but it moved in rhythm. He feet tapped lightly. Her lips mouthed the words but no sound came from her. But she smiled her toothless smile and her eyes blazed with hope and remembrance and her hands danced for her. Her hands remembered.

And I will never forget.

NINE

THE LONG LAST DAYS ▶▶▶▶▶▶▶

Central African Republic
Zaire
Rwanda
Burundi

      A sound like thunder rumbles low over the land-scape. It roars like a lion. It swooshes like wind. It is the sound of hunger and of hearts beating, the sound of waiting, the sound of time passing, precious days wasted, days that will never come again. It is the sound of remembering.

      These are my last days in Africa. I am waiting, listening to the days grinding away, my last days in Africa and I am losing my voice. Heat and hunger have conspired against me, and the pain of bouncing around in the backs of trucks has left me aching. The constant fatigue of Africa has addled my spirit. But through it all I have seen the miracle in a glass of cold water clean enough to drink.

      Almost a year in Africa and in these my last days the waiting has gotten to me at last. There truly is no waiting in the world like waiting in Africa. Like the heat, it is simply infernal. Like the fires of hell, it hides the way out.

      I am riding a great African river toward the end of my

voyage. The sun is westering, barely above the tops of the trees, and I am headed east along the Zaire River slicing through the jungle. The river is the color of a rusted pipe, following its bent course through the wide cracks in the green wall of forest. The sun has spilled the last of its blood color on the water and now is eaten and swallowed by the jungle. The only color left is the darkening green of trees and brush, a few stripes of orange and gold in the dimming western sky. The river's color turns slowly to puce in the changing light and the river disappears in the darkness, swallowed by the jungle and swallowed by the night. It is a night of tears. Clouds roll together from the east and the night weeps. This has been a trip of tears and broken hearts, a trip too of bizarre laughter and bitter joy.

I am sitting alone, surrounded by dark strangers who call me brother, but I don't feel a part of them anymore. I am isolated, not really one of them. I know it, and so do they, though they like to pretend and say otherwise. We share little more than the color of our skin and the fact of our humanness. The world where I belong is another world far from this one. I have been with them for only this little bit of time. Soon I will be gone. My passage doubtless will go without remark, without much notice. The point where our lives have intersected will surely be as meaningless to them as if it never happened, forgotten in a short while, but scars will mark my soul and my memory for as long as memory lasts. I am exhausted and all alone. I have no one to laugh with. It isn't enough to eat what they eat and go where they go nor to go with them when they go there.

While I waited in Lisala for dysentery to run its course and for this steamer to come, a young woman selling the only cold drinks in town said to me: "You have to be patient. Relax. Sleep a little more than you are used to. The time will pass and the boat will come sooner or later."

I nodded and smiled. I knew she was right, but it had been a week's wait already.

Monique, the woman selling the drinks, said: "You have to be African for a few days."

Hell! I wanted to tell her. *I've been African for nearly a year already.*

I don't suppose I was in any real hurry, but I didn't want

one week to turn into two weeks or a month. What kills you here is the uncertainty. You just never know. Neither does anyone else.

Lisala burns in the afternoon. Steam rises off the river. Heavy heat from the dense forest behind hangs low in air that never stirs until evening. It's like walking cloaked in a thick and weighted shroud of heat and humidity. The effect is enervating.

I was exhausted when I arrived in Lisala and I wanted to eat, but there was little more than dried fish, pineapples, sardines in a can. Afternoon visions of potato salad and fried chicken danced in my daydreams, barbecued ribs and buckets of beer. I knew my days were numbered. I was tired of being African. I was starving to death. I wanted to eat. I wanted a shower. I wanted to soak in a bathtub for an hour and dissolve away the sweat and grime dried on since my last shower I can't remember when. I wanted a glass of cold water to drink. I would have settled for warm water to bathe with, but the man who ran the water treatment plant and pumping station, so they said, was on vacation. The system shut down. *Africa!*

Africa is not easy. I love this place and resent it at the same time, and Africa reciprocates, trapped as we both are in this middle ground somewhere between black and white, past and future.

I am riding this river to the end of my journey, riding on a rickety old steamer that plods upriver. It billows smoke and rattles, fighting sandbars and currents and old age. It seems as ancient as Africa itself, only a camel's straw from collapsing. How it holds together and stays afloat I can only guess: some mysterious combination of voodoo and prayer and spit, some unutterable fatigue that makes this old boat too tired to know how tired it really is, and of course the sad hope that port lies around the next bend, always the next bend.

On the decks, throngs mill about with nowhere to go. They are young men transporting cargo. They are businessmen going upriver to Kisangani. They are villagers who live along these shores and who will get off somewhere during the night. This relic from some ancient time is the main form of transportation along the river, certainly the fastest. There are no real roads in this part of Zaire. The river is the main artery.

There must be a thousand people or more on this boat, a collection of eight rusted barges lashed together and pushed along by this ancient crate. All this movement, all this shouting and music and commotion, everything disorganized, and every man for himself. This is Africa condensed. Music booms loudly from the giant cassette recorders, and there is plenty of beer; the people are contented.

Trussed-up crocodiles lie helpless and brown on the deck of one of the barges. Their hides have already crinkled dry in the hot sun, their eyelids blinking with the languid slowness of thick liquid. They look sinister, as if plotting escape and revenge.

Pigs squeal their loud and horrible fear of slaughter. They can smell disaster in the wind, see it in the way men look hungrily at them. They too plot escape, but they are tied by short ropes, one end tied to the hind leg of each pig, the other end to a rail or a post. The pigs have freedom to move, but only so far. Where they stand, the deck is wet from overflowing toilets and from spilled water drawn up in buckets from the river. The dirt on the deck has turned to mud. The pigs slide about in it. They could almost be happy, but the rope reminds them.

Men walk slow to keep from slipping. They eye the pigs. A short metal stair rises up to the next barge here. The steps are slick. Many parts of the decks are slippery from one thing or another. One wrong move will send you into the river and the boat will go on without you. There are crocodiles in the river.

Farther on, monkeys wait to be sold and slaughtered, the meat dried or cooked in a stew. Many men carry monkeys already dried and stiff, as if they had been stretched on a plank and nailed dead, crucified and baked until rigid. Their arms and legs are outstretched and there is an expression in their faces of horror and pain, but mostly of shock. Their little faces are almost human. They have such sad eyes. Men pick at the dried meat and nibble from the dead monkeys all day.

A baby chimpanzee sits on a rail and clings to a pole as if holding on to its mommy for security. But mommy is made of metal, and the little chimp is tied with a noose around his neck. He wears such a sad face. He sits quietly as if resigned to his fate, but his sadness doesn't end. His watery little eyes seem about to cry. The little baby is for sale. He may soon be someone's pet or someone's dinner. Eating him would be like eating your baby brother.

I have moved away from the fog of marijuana smoke that clouds where I stand, but I cannot escape the noise or the shouting, the music that never ends, night or day. Each giant cassette player booms out its own music, each man's different from that of the next, a mélange of exploding rhythms and repetitious melodies and lyrics that are unintelligible to me.

In the fading light, Africa softens and becomes almost still. Evening becomes this place. Imagination takes hold and runs wild. The rickety steamer sinks. Amid the cries and shrieks of panicky natives, this old boat sinks ever so slowly into the crocodile-infested River Congo (its former name), the survivors eagerly awaited by the pygmy tribes that line these jagged shores and eat human flesh—so the legends say—and I will end up as the meat in a big pot of stew, simmering nicely with carrots and onions and potatoes, coriander and peppers, as in a cartoon.

But the boat does not sink. And the river flows on.

Africa is a serpent that courses on and on endlessly, north to south, east to west, coiling back on itself, exposed in desert, hiding in trees.

I have climbed to the top deck to get above the noise and slightly away from it, more alone and closer to the night. The rain is light and fine but more than mist. The night is cooler here. The rhythms of the cacophony below feel more like a pulse here. The river is a vein and we are cutting across the heart. From this top deck, far away into the black night, I imagine I can see head and tail of this beast, north and south, over the tops of these trees, all the way back to Timbuktu.

Way out there in the middle of nothing and nowhere, Timbuktu rises up from the lower Sahara—the Sahelian desert— hot, dry, and inhospitable, indiscriminately brutal. Misted in legend as lasting as Atlantis's, Timbuktu, this place that every kid knows as the end of the earth, is transformed into a pearl in the mirage of imagination and sits on the Sahara as if on an oyster shell, a sight of welcome and relief for the desert traveler. So it has been for centuries. So it was too for me, holding all the myth and mystique that is Africa. All the disillusioning reality as well.

Timbuktu's former glory is merely a whisper on the constant desert winds. The walls of the city are crumbling down, slowly surrendering to those desert winds and to the drought that has driven the nomads south to Mopti and killed a way of life. Its streets are narrow and dusty. Everything is the color of sand and adobe. Its corridors are wet and reeking with urine. Garbage piles high. People beg continuously. An army of children hold out their tiny hands or little wooden bowls or empty coffee cans, anything they think you might drop a few coins into. They follow the foreigners everywhere.

Up close, the mystery dissolves.

There is something romantic about traveling along a great river. From here the mystery returns. The forest is dense. Walls of darkness close in all around. Color leaves the sky. And in places, the river is miles wide. Beyond those trees is an unknown Africa, mysterious and primitive, hiding behind walls of forest.

There are no cities, no towns, only villages. Naked children come to the river's edge to watch. Sometimes they wave. Sometimes they carry torches—the only light they have. Sometimes there is frenetic activity along the shore as the steamer approaches. People have been waiting all day. Some have been waiting for days. A massive blast from the steamer's horn alerts them.

Pirogues handled carefully paddle out to meet the steamer. They carry loads of cargo to be taken upriver to Kisangani. They carry passengers wanting to go upriver. They ferry away passengers who want to get off at this village or that. The current is swift, but the men paddle standing up. Their strength and agility are remarkable. Their timing is exquisite. They angle out toward the path of the barges and hold in the current. Paddling furiously when the boat draws near, they come alongside the steamer and grab on. Often they tie off among a convey of pirogues being towed in the quiet wake of one of the barges. There they remain until the owner of a pirogue has finished his beer or his visit or has gone far enough upriver. Then he walks over the other pirogues in the covey and reaches his own. Off he goes again.

A pig escapes his bondage, leaps overboard, and swims toward shore. The current carries him far downstream before he can scamper out of the water and up the steep bank into the woods. A man leaps immediately after the pig, which is too valuable to lose. He will find the pig and make his way upstream the best he can. The boat does not slow for him.

The moon rises above the trees. It is a bright sliver of light in the sky; streaks of molten silver shimmer on the water. Africa softens in the moonlight, and I am once more at ease.

Years from now Africa will be muted in my memory and turned into humorous anecdotes. I will remember Africa warmly and with smiles.

I will remember how in Douala, long before I came to the river, I ran out of money.

The advertisements warn travelers not to leave home without an American Express card. With it you can cash personal checks at American Express travel agencies. They will not pay you in cash, but in traveler's checks. And the ads never warn you that the offices, as the one in Douala had done, sometimes run out of traveler's checks. The woman working there had no idea when they might receive more.

"Do you have any suggestions?" I asked her.

She continued to file away papers. She did not smile, did not say anything. She merely shrugged.

I was reminded once again of my friend's story about the old man accusing younger ones of having no grit. The reply: We've got something better. Credit cards.

With no cash, I could only stay in a hotel that accepted plastic, a fancy, comfortable, and expensive hotel, and eat in the hotel restaurant. The spell was being broken. But once I left Douala and Cameroon, credit cards were problematic.

I made my way gingerly across the Central African Republic to Bangui. The American embassy there let me phone home. Money was wired to the State Department in Washington, which then authorized the embassy to release the cash in Bangui.

Foolishly I took the money to a local bank and had the cash converted into traveler's checks. From Bangui until I arrived in Goma on the far eastern end of Zaire, no bank would cash them.

It seems humorous to me now. If it had happened a little sooner, it would have been utter tragedy, one more bitter blow. But after the mass in Yaoundé, I was of a new mind. And the end of my voyage was in sight. I would make my way across the Central African Republic, up the Zaire River, and down to Bujumbura's velvety skies. From there I would continue on to Kenya, where I could be a tourist once more, pampered and comfortable. The wildebeest migration across the Masai Mara would soon be beginning.

Hitchhiking across the Central African Republic was more hiking than hitching. The cars were few, the rides infrequent, but the scenery superb, all jungle and twisting roads dotted with villages. The waiting was fine. The villages were friendly and the people in them invited me to sit and drink millet beer with them. The beer was frothy and sweet and intoxicating.

Not far from Bangui I followed a man down a long dirt road that had crossed the main road. He told me of a place to buy a cold drink not far down the road, but he was in a tremendous hurry. He didn't have time to show me where.

"Keep walking," he said. "You will find it."

He walked quickly and disappeared around a bend.

The road was very long and narrow. It passed through a small village, and there I found a shop selling warm soda and beer. The owner asked if I had come to see the waterfalls.

"What waterfalls?"

"The waterfalls at Boali," he said. "Two Americans passed through here three days ago and they have not come out yet. I thought you knew them."

The falls were a long walk away, but worth the effort. The water rushed over the cliffs and spilled in a great roar into the canyon below. The water was brown and foamy, but I braved it. I hacked through the reeds and the growing corn, took off my clothes, and plunged into the cold water. What relief!

The two Americans turned out to be one American from San Francisco and one Australian. They spoke bad French and could not tell that I was American. I did nothing to let them know. They were traveling overland from Bangui to Cameroon, and we traded information. They had come across from Kenya separately, had met in Kisangani and come down the Zaire River together. They told me about the steamer.

"Oh, you've got to take the steamer," they said. "It alone is worth a trip to Africa."

I left them lying on the warm rocks by the river. I hiked back to the main road and got a lift to Bangui where the road ran out at the Ubangi River.

When I was a small boy, wild and crazy, my mother affectionately called me her little Ubangi. In the atlas in my room I located the Ubangis on a map. I found the river and the people. In the back of the book I found pictures of them. Ubangi women were the ones whose lips were pierced and stretched around wooden plates. They were the ones who fueled my young imaginings of Africa.

In Bangui, at the river's edge, ancient Africa and modern Africa merged.

All that is wrong in the new Africa is typified right here in Bangui and on the other side of the river as well. The Central African Republic and Zaire. Corruption and greed. Two faces of the same bent coin.

An African man stands guard outside the American embassy. We talk. When he has a break, we take a walk. We have lunch in a bar. Manioc leaves, rice, and sauce. Then I follow him to the park and he begins to whisper. He is afraid of being overheard as he quickly tells me the brutal history of the Central African Republic.

In 1957, as the central African Republic approached independence from France, Barthélémy Boganda became head of the first government. His first efforts were to form the United States of Latin Africa, a confederation of neighboring nations. His efforts failed. He was killed two years later when his plane was sabotaged and crashed. His statue is near the center of town on a street that bears his name.

Upon the CAR's independence in 1960, David Dacko became president. Five years later the government was overthrown by Dacko's crazy cousin Jean-Bédel Bokassa, who was also Boganda's nephew. There is an avenue named for David Dacko.

Bokassa mismanaged everything. He took over every facet of government, of course, and got rid of his opposition. As his power increased, so did his abuse of it. One year he ordered the release of all women prisoners. The next year he mandated that thieves lose an ear for each theft committed; after that, a hand.

He converted to Islam to impress Moammar Qaddafi, the dictator in Libya. Qaddafi gave Bokassa a gift of $2 million. Bokassa decided to remain a Christian.

In 1972 Bokassa proclaimed himself president for life. In 1977 he crowned himself emperor of the new Central African Empire. His coronation robe cost $150,000. His crown cost $2 million. The entire gala cost in the neighborhood of $10 million. The per capita income of the Central African Republic is around $200 a year. There aren't more than a thousand miles of paved road.

Apparently France promised to cover any unpaid bills, which was only fitting since France had never relinquished its hold on the republic.

The French presence in the CAR remains solid. French soldiers walk the streets. A jumbo jet stocked with cheese and wine and chocolate flies down from France once a week to keep the French contingent supplied and content. The shops are well stocked, but everything is terribly expensive.

France grew tired of its puppet when Bokassa finally went too far. In 1979 he demanded that schoolchildren wear new uniforms imprinted with his picture. He, of course, owned the factory that made the uniforms. When students protested in the streets of Bangui, Bokassa had them rounded up and put in prison. He and his police clubbed many of them to death. Nearly a hundred people died.

France had had enough. They cut off aid. Bokassa went to Libya for money and support. He didn't come back. French troops had flown to the CAR, and David Dacko was restored to power. He lasted all of two years. General André Kolingba then staged a coup and took control.

Bokassa was exiled first to the Ivory Coast and then to a mansion near Paris. He tried once to return to the CAR but was arrested at the airport. In Bangui there is a street and a university named for him.

The politics of Africa are a mire of vexation.

Not very far from Bangui, on the other side of the Ubangi River, in a town called Gbadolite, Zaire's Mobutu Sese Seko is building another palace. It will be his thirteenth.

Mobutu is one of the wealthiest men in the world. Minerally, Zaire is one of the wealthiest countries in the world. It is rich with uranium, copper, diamonds, cobalt. But Mobutu has squandered the country's mineral wealth on arms and airplanes and private excesses. Zaire has foreign debts of over $5 billion. Mobutu has an estimated $5 billion in Swiss bank accounts.

There was a coup attempt in 1977. Five thousand rebels overran Mobutu's pitiful army. The coup was put down only with the help of France and Belgium, the United States and Germany.

Africa is trying to find its way and desperately needs to, but as long as European powers continue to intervene, as long as colonialism continues, Africa never will.

I crossed the river in a motorized pirogue with a group of missionaries from California. One of them had spent many years in Zaire preaching the Christian gospel, bringing the Bible to the jungle. They were nice people. Their mission had built a small hospital, which I got to see. They treated me with kindness, fed me, arranged rides for me. And yet I resented their presence. They were like Coca-Cola to me. They reminded me of home. They spoke my language. But what the hell were they doing in Zaire? They were eroding the local culture.

With them was a young American family that had hardly been, it seemed, out of Fresno county before, let alone out of the country. The wife was mousy and delicate. The husband was slight. They looked as if the heat and the jungle would swallow them whole. But they had committed themselves and their children to a stay of at least a year and possibly longer. Their intentions, I'm sure, were noble. But like all missionaries, their aims were biased and not entirely selfless.

They rode in the back of a closed truck to shield them from the dust. The rest of us rode together standing in the back of an open truck. We plunged deeper into the forest, a dense cloud of endless trees broken only by an occasional village. The day swelled with the happy noises of village children laughing and shrieking, chasing our caravan and waving. And then there was no noise but the engine and the truck rattling. Between villages there was nothing but trees.

At the top of a hill we stopped to rest, to stretch our legs and clear the road dust from our throats. Down in the valleys below and far into the distance on either side of the road, tall sobi grass covered the rolling hills and waved in the breeze. The road undulated up and down hills like an orange ribbon. Sight went on forever, over the tops of trees and the sea of green.

A noisy truck broke the serenity and came over the hill, a huge old truck packed to completeness with people. Many were hanging off the sides, yelling at us and ineffectually trying to stop any picture taking. The truck had no brakes.

The afternoon heat turned to the cool of evening. A breeze turned to wind. Lightning filled the skies and a storm brewed. The night was heavy with the damp green smells of the jungle, the smell of bat guano, the smell of the tall grass and smoke from the night fires of the villages we passed through. The storm gathered overhead. Clouds erased the stars, but there was twinkling all around, fireflies that lit up the night.

It was a strange comfort I took in being with the missionaries—nothing mysterious or mystical, but simply the comfort of being with fellow countrymen seemingly as out of place as I was, and yet with a twist. For I suddenly felt possessive and protective of this place, even though this place was no more mine than theirs. I felt that if I didn't belong, if I was out of place, certainly they were more so. They were the foreigners. They were the strangers. They were the intruders.

My footprints would be light indentations compared with the gouges they left behind in the landscape.

I stayed with them two nights. I ate what they ate. Oatmeal and vegetables and meat and pie.

I wondered: If an African went to America, would he be afraid to drink the water? Would his system be shocked by the sudden absence of microbes in the food and water? Would he get sick?

Not once had I been intestinally ill since the voyage began. Until now. Eating with Americans, suddenly I was sick. Diarrhea had me in its grip and dysentery was catching up with me.

I left the missionaries and spent a night in Gemena with a truck driver named Yélé. I felt immediately better.

On the way to Yélé's home, we made a delivery to another mission, a huge estate with trees and gardens and nice homes. In back, the long flat field was used as an airstrip.

While the truck was being unloaded, one of the missionaries there invited me to his home for tea and a cheese sandwich. It would have been pleasant if he hadn't asked me if I was going to heaven.

"I don't know," I said. "I hope so, anyway."

"If you're not sure," he said, "then you're not going."

He pulled down his Bible and read to me the four verses that proved I was bound for hell instead. He wanted to convert me the same as he had been converting the Africans. I told him we could discuss it when we both got to hell.

"But I'm going to heaven," he assured me.

"Yeah, well, I'm going to the toilet," I said. My diarrhea had returned.

The next day I hitched a ride in another truck. The road was narrow and a high embankment ran alongside. When another truck came toward us, the truck I was riding in scraped against the embankment and stopped to wait. The other driver did the same, assessed the possibilities, and the two trucks gingerly squeezed past one another.

The road was straight. The hills were high. The road ran up one side of the hill and down the other, up again in the distance, touching the sky, and falling away again, the successive hills getting lower and lower as the land fell into the valley toward the river. It was the simple emotive beauty of Africa, pristine and primitive and untouched.

It rained and then cleared. Mist hung in patches over the trees and over the road, wet orange clay glistening in the sun. The road, though straight, was badly rutted. I was often tossed from my seat, my head bouncing against the top of the cab at every unexpected hump.

We came to Akula and the Mongala River. Dinner was a piece of bread and a bottle of beer. The hotel was a dirt floor and a bed. There was no window and only a kerosene lantern for light. In the morning I waited hours for a boat to carry me across the river. I waited more hours on the other side for a truck to carry me to Mitoko.

The truck had come from Mitoko. A load of people got off. The driver bought a beer and turned the truck around, and the next crowd loaded on. But along the way the driver stopped and got out to participate in some religious ceremony that lasted for hours. A preacher preached. Someone banged a drum. The congregation had been sitting on wooden chairs in the shade of a great tent. Now they rose up and marched around an open field. Forty times around they marched. By the time we arrived in Mitoko, it was nearly night.

The next truck was hauling furniture to Lisala. The back of the truck had been uncovered, but when it started to rain the driver got out and pulled a tarp over us to protect the furniture. We could no longer stand. We knelt, we squatted, we sat on each other. The truck bounced and we bounced with it. To steady myself I put my hand down onto something rough and alive. It was a crocodile loosely trussed and lying next to me. It squirmed and I jumped. But I couldn't jump far. The truck was too full.

It didn't take long for the back of that truck to get warm and musty with sweat and hot breath and the smells of people sleeping. I couldn't breathe. I couldn't see. It was so crowded I couldn't move. I had no idea where we were. All I knew was that I was packed like canned herring in the back of this truck. If it crashed or caught on fire, I would be trapped. I had never been claustrophobic before, but now I was panicky and sweating with fear. My breath came in gasps. I hyperventilated and thought I might faint. But there was a crocodile beside me. Immediately I perked up.

The truck stopped somewhere for a very long time. No one said a word. The front door slammed. It opened a few minutes later and slammed again. Apart from that there was no sound. I couldn't see. I couldn't hear. I couldn't breathe. And I couldn't even sleep. It was like being buried alive. It was like being dead.

In the middle of the night we arrived at Lisala. The town was completely dark. Electricity shut down each night at nine. The town was deserted. The crowd from the back of the truck jumped down quickly and vanished.

Only one passenger remained. He had a very bad limp and I helped him climb down from the truck. We chatted a moment and he explained that, as I would find no place to spend the rest of the night unless I slept on the street, I should come home with him. His wife was not pleased to be awakened in the middle of the night, less pleased about having to search in the dark house to find bedding for a stranger.

I slept on a straw mattress. There was no sheet. I itched and scratched all night. In the morning I found that the mattress was crawling with tiny black bugs.

In the morning I got a room at a hotel. I wanted to bathe, but could not. The water had been shut off. The man in charge of the pumping station was on holiday. Periodically an old man brought to my room a bucket of water that served a double purpose—bathing and flushing the toilet.

There was no water to drink. No food to eat. Nothing to do. I waited for the dysentery to pass. I waited for the boat to come. Down at the harbor, no one had any idea when it might arrive. It apparently had gotten stuck on a sandbar as it left Kinshasa, which was four days away. There was a boat coming downriver from Kisangani headed for Kinshasa, and if I wanted to wait for that it would probably arrive before the boat going upriver. But it too had gotten stuck on a sandbar.

I could have flown. Once a week there was a flight to Kisangani. But it flew first to Kinshasa. From there I might be able to fly to Kisangani or even to Kenya. It was tempting, but the plane never came.

I drank one bar completely out of Cokes. Then I found the only other place in town with a refrigerator. I spent every afternoon there talking to Monique, drinking her *limonade*, eating her pineapples and her bananas and her bread.

"You have to be patient," she said. "Relax. Sleep a little more than you are used to. The time will pass and the boat will come sooner or later."

But the old steamer never did.

Lisala burned. Steam rose off the river. Heat from the dense forest all around hung low in the still air. It was exhausting. There was nothing to eat but sardines in a can, bread, and fruit, unless I wanted to eat what the locals were eating, worms and grubs—thick gray larvae of tree beetles. They were sold and bought in the market, kept in baskets or spread out on wide cloths. They looked like gigantic maggots, slow moving and squirming all in a mass. They made my skin crawl. I wasn't that hungry.

The shops were empty of food. What they did carry—bottled water and bottles of wine—had been imported from South Africa.

And there was nothing to do but read the book I carried. I had already read it twice. I read it twice more.

On the far end of town there was a plaque that proclaimed Mobutu's birth and his greatness. If you read it too long the soldiers in the prison just opposite would call you over and ask you questions.

A little farther on, Mobutu was building another palace. If you strayed too close to it, someone would shoot you.

After a week's wait in Lisala, I took another bouncing ride in the back of a truck to Bumba. At least there would be new scenery. I waited there another week and was only arrested once, but time and sensation seemed to whiz past me. I had gone into a fast forward of the spirit. I do recall that there were pineapples to eat and green oranges that tingled against your lips and burned. There was fish and occasionally a stringy chicken. Finally the boat came, the *Major Mudimbi*.

It was the end of Africa for me. What began next was something else entirely, for aboard the *Major Mudimbi* there were three Englishmen, four Australians, two Dutch, and a New Zealander. Suddenly I didn't know where I belonged. It was so strange to be among so many black people and yet to have so much more in common with the handful of whites.

One Englishman, Justin, and I were hauled off to the bridge for taking pictures. We were warned by the captain that picture taking was forbidden—of course. He didn't hassle us much, but he did preach to me about moving to Zaire to help his country grow.

"The most advanced black man in the world is the American black man," he said. "We need you. This is your home. This is where you belong."

I was shaking my head. I could never live in Africa, I told him. I had been here too long already.

"You prefer to live with the whites?" he said. He pointed

his thumb at Justin. "His ancestors stole your ancestors from this place and took them to America as slaves. How can you live with them?"

Thinking quickly back on all I had seen and all I had felt, I turned to Justin and thanked him. The spell was broken.

We arrived at Kisangani and the place was crawling with white people. From here to the end I would be in the company of the Brits and Aussies who had been on board the *Mudimbi*. There were others I met who were hanging around the open courtyard of the Hotel Olympia. Some were trying to arrange truck rides toward the border with Uganda. Others were readying for a rafting trip down the Zaire River to Kinshasa. Others were resting before hiking three days through the jungle to Bukavu. I could have joined them, but I wanted no more adventures. I just wanted my journey to be over. I was tired of the jungle. I preferred taking a plane to Goma. But even for that there was a three-day wait.

The plane was already at the airport in Kisangani, but it sat on the runway with a flat tire. It couldn't move until a spare was flown in from Kinshasa. When it arrived, I planned to get on that plane, spend a night in Goma, and then make my way down to Bukavu and the nearby game preserve, Kahuzi-Biega, where I would try to find gorillas. I just wanted to be a simple little tourist again.

One of the Brits, a man named Michael who lived in Barcelona, went with me to Goma. Together we went to Bukavu and joined up with a band of Spaniards. They were looking for gorillas too. We hired Zairian guides and hacked through the bamboo forest in search of lowland gorillas. The guides carried rifles in case we found gorillas and the gorillas charged. They also carried dynamite in case we stumbled upon elephants. They would set off the dynamite and scare the elephants away.

We tramped through swamps and jungle, up and down hills, under brush and through tall mazes of bamboo, smooth and cool to the touch. After about four hours we found gorilla spoor. There were soft places in the grass where gorillas had slept the night before. The guides found tracks. We stopped in a quiet place and the chief guide waited until we all had gathered close.

He said, "They are just on the other side of this brush."

He hacked through with his machete and there was the first of the gorillas we found. She was a small female, and we had startled her. She hurried bent on all fours back to the family. Nearby, a huge silver-backed male gorilla prowled angrily in the bushes. He munched bamboo leaves. He was fierce as a warrior, proud and virile. There was a great silver stripe of hairs down his back that sparkled in the dim light of dense forest. He thumped his chest and growled a low rumble.

He kept an eye on us. When we got too close, he charged. It was a mock charge, warning us to keep our distance, telling us who was master of these woods. He must have weighed five hundred pounds. His face was noble and expressive. His fur was shiny, the skin on his chest tight around thick muscles. He was bigger, stronger, handsomer, prouder than anything I had seen in the zoo. And he was indeed fierce.

As if to lead us to the family, he ambled slowly down the hill, stopping now and again to make sure we kept our distance and respected his home and his family. We followed. My heart raced.

In the trees and on the floor of the forest, his family of gorillas lingered and nibbled leaves. The eight females and the horde of baby gorillas were as curious about us as we were about them. They came close and studied us, and then nonchalantly went back to their eating. They were not afraid, not with the big beast nearby. He dominated them, and would continue to do so until a stronger gorilla came and killed him and stole away his harem. Until that time, he would keep his family apart from all other gorilla families, and he would be their protection. Arrogantly, he sat in the shade and crossed his legs.

His features and mannerisms were as human as could be, and we sat there awestricken, quietly watching them until the gorillas grew bored with us and drifted off.

I left Michael in Bukavu and went alone across the mountains and terraced farmland of Rwanda, then down across Burundi to the banks of Lake Tanganyika. I had arrived at last at Bujumbura. It was a magical moment. I was well on the other side of the equator now, in another world far from my home. I slept under a velvet canopy, the nights sprinkled with the stars of the Southern Hemisphere. The Southern Cross hung brightly on the horizon and lit up the sky. The water in the toilet spiraled out clockwise. It was indeed a different world.

But the farther I got from home, the closer I came.

TEN

BEYOND LAND'S END ▶▶▶▶▶▶▶▶

Zambia
Zimbabwe
South Africa

The journey was coming to an end. I had seen the head of this beast. All that remained was the tail that wagged it.

Like a great giant sleeping in the next room, South Africa had been on my mind since the voyage began. Half of me wanted to see it for myself. Half of me, for the same reasons that I will not buy diamonds or gold, hated the thought of going there, spending money there, and even marginally supporting apartheid. And now that I was so close to Kenya, now that I was so tired, I did not relish the thought of much more overland travel.

I wanted to go to Kenya and have an easy time trekking through some game preserve. I had seen gorillas; now I wanted to watch wildebeest in the Masai, elephants and lions in the Ngorongoro Crater. I wanted to be a tourist plain and simple.

But I was at the mercy of gods whose invisible hands were pushing me south. They would not let me go to Kenya. They introduced me instead to two white gentlemen from Johannesburg.

We sat on the veranda of a ritzy hotel in Bujumbura and drank beers. Ian was a pilot in his mid-forties. Peter was almost thirty. They were in the import-export business and had come to Burundi to make deals. They were selling what South Africa exported, things that Burundi needed.

I asked them how they had managed that. In fact, how had they even gotten in?

Peter told me, of course, that they had flown in, but he said it laughing. He knew that wasn't what I meant.

Conventional doctrine in black Africa warns travelers that if they so much as have a valid visa for South Africa or an entry stamp, if they have been anywhere near the place, they will not be allowed into any black African country. South African nationals are prohibited. South African imports too. Black Africa refuses to recognize the white regime in South Africa.

"What they say officially," Ian said, "and what they do are not necessarily the same. In the southern part of Africa, most countries could not survive if they did not do business with us." He was confident, almost smug. He sipped his beer. "Zimbabwe and South Africa," he said, "are the only two African countries that can feed themselves. Look around. You know what I'm saying is true."

Johannesburg, he told me, is as modern a city as Los Angeles.

"You can get anything you want there," he said. "What other African city can make that claim? Joburg is a good place. And South Africa is a good country. Come down and see for yourself."

"What about the way South Africa treats blacks?"

"It's not everything you read about in the papers," he said. "You've been across black Africa. If you come to South Africa you'll see that our blacks are richer and better off than any other black Africans."

"Come see for yourself," Peter said.

"Don't believe us," Ian added. "Come see for yourself."

Was it an invitation, or a challenge?

There I was, sitting with two white men from a country that officially stands for things I hate, that systematically separates blacks from whites, arbitrarily debases the one and elevates the other, and grades people like meat according to color.

And yet they were talking to me, buying me beers, treating me with more civility than some of the blacks I had met. Their offer was tempting, and if there had been space in the plane Peter was flying to Johannesburg the following day, I would have agreed straightaway.

I would have flown straightaway as well to Nairobi, but there were no flights for three days. There was a flight to Kigali in Rwanda, but I might have gotten stranded there. The airline could not guarantee space on the flight from there to Kenya. There were no computers, and the phones were not working. And there was no other flight until the following week.

So I went south instead, thinking I would go down to Kigoma and then across Tanzania to Dar es Salaam and back up to the game parks.

I spent a night at Gombe National Park and hiked with a group into the forest in search of baboons and chimpanzees made famous by Jane Goodall.

From Gombe, I traveled along Lake Tanganyika to Kigoma, where I thought I would catch the train to Dar es Salaam. But there was space only as far as Tabora, and I would have been stranded, waiting around again to squeeze into the back of an old car or truck that would bounce along more horrible roads.

I was tired of discomfort, tired of waiting, tired of the uncertainty. Many of the Brits and the Aussies from the Olympia Hotel in Kisangani had converged on Kigoma and were taking the steamer down the lake to Zambia. There were a few new ones, an American woman and a Canadian. I tagged along.

The gods were indeed pulling me south to Johannesburg. I knew it now and resigned myself to that fact and began even to look forward to it. Maybe there would be trouble.

Two nights after we boarded the steamer, two young Englishmen found themselves in the same predicament I had been in. They had planned to get off the steamer at Kipili or Kasanga and make their way inland to Mbeya, then over to the Tanzanian coast and back toward Nairobi. But it was the middle of the night. It was incredibly dark. Phil and Chris and I sat on the deck of the ship, drinking scotch and looking out into the blackness. Pirogues came to the side of the steamer and took off those who were going. Phil and Chris decided to stay on board.

Their reasons might have been the same as mine: the sudden comfort of new friends, too long a time with discomfort and uncertainty, the quiet ease and safety of being with others like themselves. And it was awfully dark out there. If they weren't scared, I was scared for them and relieved that they were staying.

We drank the rest of the scotch. We played bridge. We stayed up late telling stories.

The steamer was an old World War I vessel. It had been torpedoed and sunk in the lake, so the story went, and raised and refurbished as a passenger ship. There were two bunks per cabin in first class, four bunks in second. The boat was very crowded.

In the day the sun glistened off the wooden decks. The breeze from the lake was mild. It was like being on a luxury cruise to some island—but without the luxury. The days were lazy. We sat on the forward deck near the anchor, which plunged noisily into the water every time we stopped to take on and discharge passengers. The captain gave a blast of the horn to alert the villages along the shore that we were approaching. Pirogues would paddle out to us.

Always the eastern shore stayed in sight. To the west there was nothing but blue and gray. The lake seemed as big as the ocean.

In the night, lines of light stretched eerily across the lake. Nighttime fishermen shone lanterns onto their boats and into the water. There were so many that from a distance the lights seemed strung together. You could not tell what they were until you got closer, and you could not tell how far apart the boats were. They rocked on the waves and danced to music felt but not heard.

We arrived in early morning at Mpulungu in Zambia. There was the usual fear crossing frontiers, and even more as we cut across the country toward Lusaka. At every checkpoint there were thorough searches; the soldiers seemed particularly resentful and vicious.

Two Aussies, the Canadian, and the American left us at Mpulungu. They were trying to make it to Malawi. Word reached me later that they had been arrested for taking photos near a railway station.

From Lusaka we split still further. We hitchhiked in shifts to the Zimbabwe border, riding in the front cabs of semis carrying freight from Malawi.

An amazing thing happened at the Zimbabwe border. I was no longer tired. The roads were paved. People drove as if suddenly there were rules. There was food to eat. They accepted credit cards.

But the most amazing thing was the sudden vanishing of tension.

I had no visa for Zimbabwe. The border guard told me simply that I could not enter. And that was that.

"You need a visa and a return ticket," he explained.

"A return ticket to where?" I asked.

"To Europe, to America, to Kenya," he said. "A ticket to anywhere out of Zimbabwe."

He wore a British summer uniform: crisp white shirt, pressed white shorts, knee socks, and shiny black shoes. There was an air about him of real authority, not a hint that he expected a bribe. He did not try to make me afraid, did not try to throw his weight around. I was almost happy that he was so straightforward, but disappointed that I could not enter. And he realized it.

"What money do you have?" he asked.

I showed him what I had. It wasn't much. Now he was disappointed.

"But I have a credit card," I said. "I can get money in Harare."

"Okay," he said. "I will give you a three-day transit visa. When you get to Harare, you must go right away to buy a plane ticket. Go to the immigration office. Show them your plane ticket and they will give you a visa."

It was a relief. Not just that he had allowed me to enter, but that he acted as an official ought to act.

When I got to Harare I bought a ticket to Paris and got permission to stay for a month.

▲

On Baker Avenue in Harare there is some kind of parliament building. A soldier stands guard there. A chain draped between poles bars the way. I was on my way over to Stanley Avenue. I stepped over the chain and walked through. The soldier yelled at me.

"Where do you think you're going?" he shouted.

"To Stanley Avenue."

"Can't you see this barricade? Don't you know you're not supposed to cross here?"

I yelled back.

"How am I supposed to know? There's no sign."

"Come over here," he yelled. "Don't shout at me."

"Don't you shout at me."

He was as astonished as I was that I was shouting back. He looked at me sideways.

"Where are you from?"

I told him. He tried hard to keep his stern face, but it was impossible. He broke into great laughter. I patted his shoulder. He put his arms around me and for five minutes we held hands in the middle of the day and chatted.

I went to the next corner and howled my pleasure. I could shout at a soldier without the threat or even the fear of getting shot.

Such a relief!

There are of course stories about Prime Minister Robert Mugabe's motorcade screaming through the streets of Harare and shooting at anyone who doesn't get out of the way.

His palace is on a street that closes at night. Mugabe is as afraid of assassination as other African heads of state are, and motorists who have strayed accidentally down the wrong street at the wrong time have been shot by soldiers and killed.

It is still Africa, a mongrel sort of Africa where the black market thrives, but where the black marketeers accept traveler's checks. You can shout back at the police, but you can be shot for being too close to Mugabe's house.

It is still Africa.

▲

The politics of the world never go away. You can never escape them.

From Harare by steam train to Bulawayo and Victoria Falls. Along the banks of the Zambezi River to Mana Pools National Park. Haunted by the musical roar of lions across the river. Awakened in the night by a pack of hyenas scavenging in camp. Buffalo and springbok and zebra. Hippos and crocodiles. Elephants. To be with them is somehow to be in Eden, in a garden all our own. It is a quiet miracle. The elephants are so huge. They seem almost gentle. But they are so strong that when one wraps his trunk around the base of a tree and puts his head against it, the entire tree shakes like a rattle in a baby's hand. All the nuts and berries fall from the branches, and the elephant sniffs them up in his trunk and eats them.

The elephants came so close that if you camped under a tree they would almost step on your tent. But they are surprisingly agile. They know where you lie and step very close but still manage to miss you. Even in the darkness.

They came so close you could touch them. But if you got too close, they would charge—mock charges to keep you away and let you know who's boss.

And all the while you know who really rules this land and this earth. Elephants are disappearing. Their habitat is vanishing and being polluted. Man rules the roost, in the forest as in the city. Men can hardly accommodate other men. How can we be expected to worry for elephants and hippos and giraffes?

Zimbabwe was born out of an accommodation that came only after a bloody war for black liberation.

When Rhodesia became independent from Britain in 1970, it showed no signs of moving toward black majority rule. White farmers produced more than enough food for the country and for the export market. Rhodesian industry could meet nearly all of the country's needs. Even with an international boycott, Rhodesia was sturdy enough to survive. A siege mentality set in. Rhodesian resolve was nearly as staunch as the Boers' in South Africa.

But a guerrilla war ate into the country's tenacity, costing the white government too much money and too many lives. In

1980, Rhodesia became Zimbabwe. Robert Mugabe, one of the guerrilla leaders, became prime minister. The country set out on the road to mending itself.

Whites were guaranteed 20 percent of the seats in parliament. Those who were afraid and chose to leave were paid fair prices for their farms.

Those who stayed worked hard. The country is making do. There is food to eat. Tap water is drinkable. The telephones work.

It was hard to gauge levels of racial tension and equality in the short time I was there. Surely whites have the best jobs. They probably still own the best farms. They make the most money. But there is a sense of accommodation that goes both ways.

I was invited into the homes of wealthy white tobacco farmers and survivors of the guerrilla wars. I slept on the floor of a white woman who knew me only as a traveling companion of one of the Brits. I could just as easily have been at home in America. Or I could have been anywhere else in Africa. The level of hospitality from blacks and whites was almost unsettling. No one called me nigger or kaffir.

Zimbabwe and South Africa were almost an anticlimax.

I went to South Africa expecting trouble, even looking for it, hoping for it. I wanted desperately to hate the place, wanted to be told I couldn't stay in a very nice hotel, wanted to be restricted to black parts of town, wanted to ride the fabled Blue Train to Cape Town and be forced to get off in the middle of nowhere. It supposedly is a train reserved for whites only, but when I arrived at a ticket agent's to book passage, there was no fuss, merely a call to see if there was space available.

On the Wednesday after I arrived in Johannesburg, apartheid in city recreation areas was officially abolished. It was a small, small step, but in the right direction. As Johannesburg goes, so goes the rest of South Africa. Bus integration was coming a few days later. The Group Areas Act was doomed.

In fact the Group Areas Act, though officially on the books, was not entirely enforced. The act limits according to the color of his skin where a person can live. Hillbrow district in Johannesburg is supposedly all white. In practice it is anything but. Progress is being made, however slowly.

I went to Soweto. It is indeed a ghetto, but not the horror I had imagined. I've seen worse neighborhoods in Chicago. And compared to other blacks in Africa, these blacks are doing very well.

But I guess that's not the point. They eat. They work. They drive expensive German cars. Many live in fairly nice homes. But they cannot vote.

I guess I'm not the best judge.

I don't want to be an apologist for apartheid and a racist regime. Certainly my eyes have been clouded by this long voyage. Certainly my vision has been affected by what Africa lacks, by the poverty, by the oppression of blacks by blacks, and by what I as an American have grown used to. Joburg is a modern city. There are steaks to eat, vegetables, milk shakes and cole slaw and ice cream. There are fast-food joints, and the fast food tastes exactly as it tastes at home.

My skin is black. My culture is not. After almost a year in Africa, I have no answers. Only this one question remains: *Who am I?* I have more in common, it sometimes seems, with the Dutch Afrikaner, the Boer.

The British South African has an emotional and even a political attachment to Britain. When the volcano finally erupts, he will have a place to go. He can easily obtain a British passport. Not so the Boer. This is his home, his only home. He is an African and he will vehemently tell you so. He has no place else to go. He will live and fight and die here, make his stand here, make it work or lose it all here. He, ironically, is the example Blackamericans should follow. Africa is not our home. Should the volcano erupt, we will have no place but the United States. If it isn't going to work there, if we can't make it work there, it isn't going to work. As I said during my captivity in Liberia, I could no more return to Africa to live than I could live on the moon. And if someone put a gun to my head and said I must, the only places possible would be Zimbabwe and South Africa.

If you cannot know yourself, how can you expect to know a place like Africa? You can't. You cannot know this place in such a short time, such a short passing through—or should I say, these *places*. Africa is a myriad of people and ways. And Africa is more than that. Africa is change. Africa is contradiction. And Africa brings out the contradictions in the traveler.

There are so many Africas that, like a river, you cannot step into the same Africa twice. There is Africa the cliché, Africa the postcard view. Africa is a Biafran baby with its belly distended from starvation. Africa is flies and illness everywhere, AIDS and malaria and green monkey disease. Africa is a tired old woman selling mangoes by the side of the road, a woman with a baby strapped to her back, a woman walking home with a basket on her head, her feet covered with dust, her back noble and strong but stooped a little from fatigue and from the years of carrying. Africa is music and song and endless patience. Africa is traditions that will not allow it to move forward. Africa is a tired old man waiting for the dirt walls of his ancient house to collapse. Africa is a six-thousand-year-old baby trying to find his legs. Africa is pain. Africa is joy in spite of the pain. Africa is enduring. Africa is the essence of mankind's ability to hunger for something better and the patience to wait for it. The traditions make movement slow, but they make the waiting easier. Africa is incredible generosity, Africa is selfish opportunism, Africa is contradiction. Africa is. . . .

Africa is the birth of mankind. Africa is the land of my ancestors. But Africa is not home. I hardly know this place at all.

But I have drawn my finger in a great S-curve across the icing of the cake that is Africa and I have tasted it, the bitter, chalky-sweet taste and texture of chocolate. The sweetness lingers, leaving me with a desire to return here, to taste still more.

Toward the end of his life, Auguste Renoir was nearly blind from seeing so much, but still he worked, still he painted. By then his colors were muted, his edges soft and gentle, his scenes warm and wonderful, like a grandmother's memories. You cannot get that soft imagery and vision when you're too close and your eyesight is clear and sharp. You have to step back to see what you've got, to see how the colors and shapes blend and blur to create the impressions.

There is also a tendency in man to recollect with kindness, to soften the edges of even the harshest memories, to remember fondly. Otherwise, you get too close and you remember too much, and those memories are full of dullness and pain. So you color them, and you soften them. I hope that with time I do not glorify the horrors and hardships of this place; I hope I do not forget them. When asked how it was, I will say interesting and agony. When asked if it was fun, I will say no.

I do not feel a part of this place, it's true, nor a part of these people simply because of an accident of birth. I am not one them. I do not like their endless patience and their endless waiting, always waiting—for someone else to do, for the will of God to happen. And I do not appreciate how they treat one another, the powerful over the weak, nor this blind respect for authority. Some of this lunacy is tribal and traditional and reaches up out of dark mysteries where I understand nothing. Much is a product of colonial servitude—to the Arab empires and their god Allah, to the Europeans and their gods Jesus and money. The Baptist missionaries and the Arabs teach the same music: Wait for God's time; He'll make everything all right. Just trust.

As much as I would like to trust in God myself, I know that sometimes God is too busy elsewhere and you just have to do things for yourself.

I will go home to my world. I will eat steaks and drink milk shakes and put on the weight I have lost. I will shower when I want and have at the turn of a tap all the clean water I can handle. I will drive the road as far as my eye can see and beyond. There will be no roadblocks to stop me. No one will ask me for my identity papers. And the roads will be good.

When I'm tired of driving, an airplane will be waiting to fly me somewhere else. I am lucky to live where I do.

It is easy to have all the solutions, to say that Africa must reject postcolonial colonialism, that Africa must end its dependence on America and on Europe, on the Peace Corps and Christian churches and missionaries, that we in the West need to stop treating these people as babies and—worse—as statistics, and start treating them as human beings, that we should stop stealing from them and that we should stop throwing money to plug gaps that wouldn't be so big if the interference ended. Perhaps we should let them sink for a while, let them figure out their own way. We did, in our own way and in our own time. But that is very easy—too easy—to say from the comfort of a full belly.

I will eat my steaks and fill my belly the same as always, but now when I do these things there will be second thoughts—I hope—for although I am not one of them, I really am one of them, the Arab and the Berber, the Bassar and the Bantu, and the Boer. There is a connection now, a real one—a racial one, to be sure, but more important, a human one.

Love and hate do not come from the color of your skin, but from what you carry inside.

I went to Cape Town to fish for trout in the nearby mountains. A white farmer invited me onto his land and pointed me toward the stream. It ran through a broad meadow. The hills behind were green. Clouds descended and all the colors changed. A rainbow trout splashed.

It is a beautiful country. It's easy to see why the white South Africans want to keep it for themselves. It is man's nature.

But it could be such a beautiful world, if we could defy the darker sides of our nature.

On the edge of a hill overlooking Victoria Falls, I looked down through the mist of the falls, the smoke that thunders, the roar of the Zambezi plunging into the canyon below. I felt I was sitting on top of the world. My journey came to me all at once in a torrent of sunsets and rivers, people I had met, the ones who had angered me and the ones who had made me laugh. As I watched another African evening come on, the serenity of Eden at twilight fell over me. Evening really does become this place. I felt what God must have felt. Amazement and sadness. But also a touch of hope.

A year from now the roads between Mauritania and Senegal will be closed. There will be tensions along the border between Senegal and Guinea-Bissau. A coup will have taken place in Liberia—the coup they no doubt were expecting when I stumbled across the border. Samuel Doe will suffer a fate similar to the one he dealt to his predecessor: he will be shot and left to die of wounds untreated.

There will be demonstrations in the streets of Abidjan. Presidential elections will be held for the first time in memory.

There will be turmoil too in Zaire. The country's economy will be in shambles and the people finally will begin to clamor for democracy and a voice. And Mobutu will yield—just a little.

In South Africa the Zulus will turn their violence against the Xhosas. Hundreds and hundreds will be killed at the hands of their brothers. But apartheid will be coming apart. Nelson Mandela will have been released from twenty-seven years of imprisonment. Apartheid's end will be a little light at the end of a long, dark tunnel, a tiny light barely visible in the distance—but visible. There is always hope.

On the corner of Mookistraat and the Soweto Highway in Johannesburg, near the Chicken Licken shop, there is a sign: TO SEEK PEACE IS OUR RESPONSIBILITY.

Farther down on the opposite side of the street, another sign: TOGETHER WE WILL BUILD THE FUTURE.

And the evening and the morn were the seventh day. He looked up to the virgin sky, purest azure and brilliant by day, licorice black and velvet soft by night and sprinkled with those stars that sparkle like bubbles in a glass of champagne, and the sun was a flat orange disk setting rayless in the dimming light of the western sky. Here then was Eden at twilight. There were baby elephants learning to galumph and lion cubs hiding in the tall grass. There were mountains and hills, and there were rivers and streams, slow moving or swift, muddy or crystal clear, but always clean. And over it all he put men and women together in dominion. And he saw that his creation was very good. So he stopped right there. His work was done.

Africa's work remains. And ours too.